The Globalization of Environmental Crisis

This collection of essays addresses what is arguably the most pressing and urgent issue of our day—the continuing development of global environmental crises and the need for new and urgent responses to them by the world community.

The contributors include social scientists, environmental historians, anthropologists, and science policy researchers, and together they give an overview of the history of the globalization of environmental crisis over the past several decades, both in terms of the science of measurement and the types of policy and public responses that have emerged to date. The book covers a wide range of topics, including:

- international environmental governance,
- North-South inequalities,
- climate change,
- air pollution,
- economic and paradigm shifts,
- indigenous peoples and eco-conservation,
- EU environmental policy and
- the United States and politicised climate science.

The book will be of particular interest to all those concerned with the on-going debate over the state of the global environment and what to do about it.

This book was previously published as a special issue of *Globalizations*

Jan Oosthoek is Visiting Lecturer in Environmental and World History in the School of Historical Studies, Newcastle University.

Barry K. Gills is Professor of Global Politics at the School of Geography, Politics and Sociology at Newcastle University.

Rethinking Globalizations
Edited by Barry Gills, Newcastle University, UK

This series is designed to break new ground in the literature on globalization and its academic and popular understanding. Rather than perpetuating or simply reacting to the economic understanding of globalization, this series seeks to capture the term and broaden its meaning to encompass a wide range of issues and disciplines and convey a sense of alternative possibilities for the future.

1. Whither Globalization?
The Vortex of Knowledge and Globalization
James H. Mittelman

2. Globalization and Global History
Edited by Barry K Gills, William R. Thompson

3. Rethinking Civilization
Communication and terror in the global village
Majid Tehranian

4. Globalisation and Contestation
The New Great Counter-Movement
Ronaldo Munck

5. Global Activism
Ruth Reitan

6. Globalization, the City and Civil Society in Pacific Asia
Edited by Mike Douglass, K.C. Ho and Giok Ling Ooi

7. Challenging Euro-America's Politics of Identity
The Return of the Native
Jorge Luis Andrade Fernandes

8. The Global Politics of Globalization
"Empire" vs "Cosmopolis"
Edited by Barry K Gills

9. The Globalization of Environmental Crisis
Edited by Jan Oosthoek and Barry K Gills

The Globalization of Environmental Crisis

Edited by Jan Oosthoek and Barry K. Gills

To George for all the support and advice you have given throughout the years.

Jan

Routledge
Taylor & Francis Group
LONDON AND NEW YORK

First published 2008 by Routledge
2 Park Square, Milton Park, Abingdon, Oxon, OX14 4RN

Simultaneously published in the USA and Canada
by Routledge
270 Madison Avenue, New York, NY 10016

Routledge is an imprint of the Taylor & Francis Group, an informa business

Transferred to Digital Printing 2008

© 2008 edited by Jan Oosthoek and Barry K. Gills

Typeset in Times Roman by Techset Composition, Salisbury, UK

All rights reserved. No part of this book may be reprinted or reproduced or utilised in any form or by any electronic, mechanical, or other means, now known or hereafter invented, including photocopying and recording, or in any information storage or retrieval system, without permission in writing from the publishers.

British Library Cataloguing in Publication Data
A catalogue record for this book is available from the British Library

Library of Congress Cataloging in Publication Data

ISBN 10: 0-415-44827-1 (hbk)
ISBN 10: 0-415-46431-5 (pbk)

ISBN 13: 978-0-415-44827-7 (hbk)
ISBN 13: 978-0-415-46431-4 (pbk)

Contents

Foreword: The Eye of the Needle vii
J. R. McNeill

1 Humanity at the Crossroads: The Globalization of
  Environmental Crisis
  Jan Oosthoek and Barry K. Gills 1

2 Global Environmental History: The Long View
  J. Donald Hughes 11

3 Seeking Justice: International Environmental Governance
  and Climate Change
  Jouni Paavola 27

4 The Globalizations of the Environment
  Dimitris Stevis 41

5 Environmental Globalization and Tropical Forests
  Alan Grainger 53

6 The Sustainability Debate: Idealism versus Conformism—the
  Controversy over Economic Growth
  S. W. Verstegen and J. C. Hanekamp 67

7 The European Union as an Environmental Leader in a
  Global Environment
  Anthony R. Zito 81

8 Global Indigenism and Spaceship Earth: Convergence, Space,
  and Re-entry Friction

Jim Igoe   95

9   The Lingering Environmental Impact of Repressive
Governance: The Environmental Legacy of the Apartheid
Era for the New South Africa
Phia Steyn   109

10   From Stockholm to Kyoto and Beyond: A Review of the
Globalization of Global Warming Policy and North–South Relations
Björn-Ola Linnér and Merle Jacob   121

11   State of Denial: The United States and the Politics of Global Warming
Kevin C. Armitage   135

12   The Globalization of Local Air Pollution
Peter Brimblecombe   147

13   The Gleneagles G8 Summit and Climate Change: A Lack of Leadership
Jan Oosthoek   161

14   Views of Kyoto and Beyond: Interviews with Herman Daly
and Jonathan Lash
Nancy Bazilchuk   165

15   Fueling Injustice: Globalization, Ecologically-Unequal Exchange
and Climate Change
J. Timmons Roberts and Bradley C. Parks   169

Index   187

Foreword: The Eye of the Needle

J. R. McNEILL

Acknowledgments: Georgetown University School of Foreign Service colleagues Tim Beach and Nate Hultman offered useful suggestions on short notice.

We have it on good authority that it is easier for a camel to pass through the eye of a needle than for a rich man to enter the kingdom of heaven. The next two or three human generations must perform the equivalent of wedging a camel through a historical needle's eye if we hope to enter an era of relaxed ecological threats and pressures. That future, perhaps 50–70 years hence, will fall somewhat short of heaven no doubt, and getting the camel there will not be easy. But it is possible, with enough foresight, leadership, and luck.

In the pages that follow, I will explain how I think that might happen. As an historian, I am not accustomed to imagining the future, and no better equipped for it than anyone else. The arguments that I offer emphasize the significance of population and energy regimes, which I see as crucial variables in shaping the recent environmental history of the globe. But they also recognize the role of the unforeseeable, of randomness, of luck. It is a glance toward the future anchored in my vision of the past.

The subsequent chapters of this book give a sense of that past and how it has formed the present. Donald Hughes offers a sweeping historical perspective, while the other chapters focus on the last century or in some cases the last decade or so. Some chapters are global in scope, others local. They all recognize the potential transformative power of the social, political, and economic trends we call globalization. Collectively they provide a strong sense of the contemporary quandary and its origins.

I. Population

The human population took hundreds of thousands of years to reach the one billion mark, attained about 1820. It took 110 years (c. 1930) to add the next billion. Since 1960 it has required only 12–13 years to add each subsequent billion. We now number about 6.5 billion. While an extraordinary biological success matched by no other mammal in the history of life on earth, this spectacular growth raised considerable anxieties as early as the 1940s, at least in North America and Europe. Professional demographers did nothing to soothe the worried when they predicted global populations of 12 or 15 billion and vast throngs of malnourished. But lately they have scaled back their forecasts in light of rapidly falling fertility in our species. Demographers now predict we will reach about 8–9 billion by 2050 or 2060. (Just what might follow is most unclear: demographic forecasts carry error terms that grow with time and are worthless more than 50 years out).

The rate of population increase reached its apogee, a little over 2% per annum, about 1962–71.[1] It is now 1.1% or 1.2%, a sharp decline attained despite lengthening life expectancies. The deceleration of demographic growth is a result of rapidly falling fertility among most of the human population. While there are many reasons behind the remarkable reduction in fertility, probably the most basic factor is urbanization. Today more than half our species lives in urban habitats. Cities have proven a powerful contraceptive in our history. Urban living quarters are cramped, children require costly educations before they cease to be a drain on family finances, so most parents choose to have fewer babies. Today they also know the odds of their children surviving to adulthood are good, whereas 50 or 100 years ago those odds in many parts of the world were little better than 50–50, so parents wanting to ensure their posterity normally chose to have several babies. City conditions always and everywhere changed incentives and culture, and thereby reduced fertility. They likely will continue to do so. Where communications and transport allow rural populations to share in urban culture and values, and allow access to health care, country folk often have imitated their city cousins and reduced their fertility sharply too.

Urbanization has not yet run its course, especially in Africa and South Asia, where rural populations outnumber city ones. So the global fertility decline is almost certain to continue, making the eye of the needle a little larger.

But even less than 8–9 billion may be too much for comfort. Much depends not only on how many are alive, but on how the many live. We cannot know with certainty in advance how many of us the most crucial components of the planet's ecosystems can withstand. Thus it is prudent to take measures to hasten fertility decline.[2] On the evidence of recent experience, the best ways to do that are to permit further urbanization, to maximize formal education for females, and to raise health care standards so that parents acquire higher confidence that their babies will survive. These are feasible goals of public policy, especially in those societies where child and infant mortality is high and female education levels low. In Finland lowering child and infant mortality would be very difficult, because it is already so low; but in Mali even small interventions could bring substantial results.

II. Energy

If there is anything more important than population for modern environmental history and for the environmental future, it is energy systems. Six or eight billion people on earth is one thing; six or eight billion each of whom is on average emitting several tons of carbon dioxide into the atmosphere annually is quite another. It is not so much economic activity *per se* that menaces the global environment, but energy-intensive economic activity within a pollution-intensive energy regime.

The last 200 years produced a 'perfect storm' of environmental stress in that it witnessed fabulous and unprecedented economic growth, the emergence of more energy-intensive economic activities (e.g. manufacturing, motorized transport) and a pollution-intensive fossil fuel energy regime. When energy use involved muscles buttressed by a little wind and water power, increases in the use of energy carried minor environmental consequences. But since the invention of the steam engine, fossil fuels, with their carbon and sulfur, have accounted for growing proportions of the world's energy mix. By the 1890s fossil fuels (overwhelmingly coal) made up half of the energy used. Today they (oil, coal, and natural gas) account for about three-quarters. This resulted in air pollutants that killed tens of millions and still kills millions through lung and other diseases; sulfur deposition that sterilized lakes and rivers and damaged forests; and the accumulation of carbon dioxide in the atmosphere which has brought us the most rapid climate change in the past 10,000 years and, before it stabilizes, possibly the past few million years.

Happily, in the next 50 years or so we will likely see a new energy regime take shape. For the purpose of calming the turbulence of the global environment, the new regime can hardly be worse than the current one. Indeed, because of serious and appropriate anxieties about the impacts of carbon emissions, it seems politically inconceivable that the next energy regime could be as ecologically risky as the last one, unless its risks were unknown (as was the case with fossil fuels and climate change) at the time of adoption.

It is impossible (at least for me) to predict the character of the coming energy regime. It will involve technologies as yet undeveloped and perhaps unimagined. But it will surely rest much less thoroughly on fossil fuels and be far less pollution-intensive. When it might arrive is also impossible to foretell, and a decade or two either way might matter a great deal.

As with the (disappearing) regime of high fertility, it is prudent to take measures to hasten the passing of the fossil fuel energy regime. We are grappling to understand how urgent this might be, because the world's climate system is so intriguingly complex we cannot understand and model it in adequate detail. This complexity also means uncertainty, which allows some to argue that no actions are required because the risks might be small. While the logic of that position is not impressive (would one cheerfully play Russian roulette if one's gun had many chambers and only one bullet?) it requires that those who favor genuine action on the energy and climate front offer compelling and politically appealing policy recommendations. The best I have encountered is simple and calibrated to an age of great corporate power: replace all corporate taxes with carbon taxes sufficient to generate equal revenue. Add to that a carbon emissions market (already organized in the EU).

Such a policy would politically isolate the fossil fuel firms from all others. Coal, oil, and gas producers would correctly see this as the death knell for their industries, and would resist it. So would those corporations whose businesses use vast amounts of fossil fuels. But all other corporations would see this, correctly, as an enormous windfall for them, and would support it with all the formidable tools at their disposal. To soften the resistance of the fossil fuel firms it would help to do this in stages and to create a series of national, supranational, or even global carbon markets, so that those businesses that can easily reduce their emissions can help out, at a price, those that cannot. This worked extremely well in reducing sulfur emissions over the past 20 years.

III. Conclusion

Policies that successfully bring a new energy regime, and an earlier cessation of population growth, while probably necessary steps, are likely not sufficient by themselves to get our camel through the eye of the needle. We need a new "technological cluster" that puts less stress on the pressure points of the environment, we might need a more benign era in international politics, and we surely need some luck.

Historians of technology speak of technology clusters, meaning groups of related technologies that somehow fit together and mesh with existing (or emerging) economic, social, and political conditions. They see in the past 250 years a series of such clusters, one succeeding another, so that an age of coal, iron, steam engines, and factories evolved into one of steel, railroads, and electric dynamos. In the first half of the 20th century another cluster took shape, based on oil, chemicals, assembly lines, automobiles, and electrification.

Today the pace of technological change is as great as at any time in the past. A new cluster is likely taking shape, based on information technology and the brave new worlds of biotechnology. We cannot now predict the shape of things to come, but we must hope that whatever it may be, its implications for the environment are gentler than those of the last few technological clusters. This is not a forlorn hope. For the same reason that the next energy regime (energy and technology are firmly linked) is likely to be more ecologically benign than the last, new technologies are too. They are and will be vetted for their environmental impacts, and if those impacts are likely to be harmful, then the chance of such technologies succeeding will shrink. As long as anxieties about the environment persist, a modest 'green bias' will endure affecting the process by which new technologies are adopted and new clusters form. Of course, as with energy regimes, this leaves open the possibility of unforeseen regrettable effects. There are no certain paths through the eye of the needle.

One of the most volatile uncertainties is and will remain international politics. Any and all policies that emphasize priorities other than immediate survival are easily trumped. A single event can relegate them to the margins for years. And a climate of sustained risk and anxiety about war or terrorism can easily dominate all other concerns in any society and polity. In the years between 1914 and 1945 most of the world's big states and economies felt obliged to put geopolitical concerns front and center, at the expense of everything else. This was the case for the biggest powers in the early years of the Cold War too, but those tensions relaxed gradually as the status quo, initially appearing so rickety, lasted for decade after decade. Other priorities, including environmental ones, found an opening. The end of the Cold War initially offered a great liberation from geopolitical worry, at least for the world's big societies and economies (the same cannot be said for Yugoslavia or Somalia). The recent spate of terrorism, and the militarist responses favored by, for example, Russia and the United States, appear to have ended that moment of liberation. That may change of course. There is no point in forecasting political evolution: that's much harder to get right than demography or even technology. But the awkward truth is that any and all favorable trends foreseen in the future of demography, energy, or technology, remain hostage to what Thucydides once called the 'imperious necessities' of war, and indeed to fear of war.

Even if all the trends, political ones included, evolve in favorable directions, we may still need a little luck to squeeze the camel through the eye of the needle. In the first place, if we are unlucky it may already be too late to avoid the worst. Nobody knows for sure whether we stand at the edge of a metaphorical precipice or some safe ways off. We might even be over the edge and not know it. It could be that the carbon already pumped into the atmosphere over the past century is enough to heat the earth's oceans enough that the currents that have lasted for millennia will quickly switch course, shutting down the oceanic circulation system (including the Gulf Stream). This apparently happened once before, triggering a sudden return to Ice Age conditions in Europe. It could be that we have already committed the earth to sea-level rise enough to swamp low-lying countries and warmed both atmosphere and oceans to such an extent that lethally violent weather will become routine.

The history of climate, of great spasms of species extinctions, and much else indicates that earth and ecological systems, like social systems, have 'tipping points,' or thresholds. Below these thresholds, incremental changes sometimes have no notable consequences. Above them, major consequences follow upon an additional increment of change and there is no going back. To put it another way, ecological systems often have switches that, once thrown, cannot easily (or cannot at any price) be put back to their previous state. Camels' backs may be broken by one straw too many—and cramming a broken-backed camel through the eye of a needle, well, that is a real long shot.

So we need some luck too. We must hope that we have not unknowingly already applied the last straw, and that we are not so close to doing so that we do not have time to wiggle our camel through the eye of the needle.

Notes

1 US Census Bureau. http://www.census.gov/ipc/www/worldpop.html [1 August 2006]
2 Contrary arguments exist. Some take the view that further economic growth is likeliest with further population growth, which is undoubtedly true. If one discounts the notion of ecological costs to further growth, then it may make sense to seek to raise rather than check human population. Others have argued that the probability of further Mozarts and Einsteins (substitute Bob Marleys and Nelson Mandelas if you wish) is improved if more babies are born. This is undeniable; but so is the counter-argument (which I have yet to see acknowledged) that the same is true of future Hitlers and Pol Pots.

   Moreover, within those countries that at present have sub-replacement fertility, the argument is routinely made that more people would be better, e.g. by Vladimir Putin in Russia.

Humanity at the Crossroads: The Globalization of Environmental Crisis

JAN OOSTHOEK AND BARRY K. GILLS

> The whole planet is now one economic community, and the proper exploitation of its natural resources demands one comprehensive direction.
> (Wells, 1946, p. 232)

> The present-day global set of local sovereign states is . . . not capable of saving the biosphere from man-made pollution or of conserving the biosphere's non-replaceable natural resources . . . Will mankind murder Mother Earth or will he redeem her? This is the enigmatic question which now confronts (sic) Man.
> (Toynbee, 1976, pp. 593, 596)

> The facts are plain and uncontestable: the biosphere is finite, nongrowing, closed (except for the constant input of solar energy), and constrained by the laws of thermodynamics. Any subsystem, such as the economy, must at some point cease growing and adapt itself to a dynamic equilibrium, something like a steady state.
> (Daly, 2005, p. 80)

As described in this book, the world is facing a series of environmental crises that reach into every corner of the globe. This is primarily due to the unprecedented growth of the human population and the world economy over the past 60 years. In the 50 years between 1950 and 2000 the world economy grew 2.5 times in terms of GDP. This was mostly driven by the exceptional population growth pushing humanity's number from 2.5 billion in 1950 to over 6 billion in 2000 (McNeill, 2000, pp. 6–8). The environmental, social and economic challenges that this poses are all interconnected and can not be treated separately. To help to understand the profound changes that are affecting the global environment, the authors in this book provide a rich palette of topics addressing the variety of environmental crises now facing humanity.

Humanity at a Crossroads

Humanity, and with it all life on earth, stands at a crossroads. That was the message of a recent special issue of the Scientific American (2005) devoted to the global state of the environment and the future prospect of avoiding environmental catastrophe. These authors, discussing population pressure, poverty, species diversity and environmental economics, among other issues, warn that if we continue to ignore the signs of serious environmental degradation then humanity will find itself facing a momentous global environmental crisis.

The Scientific American is only one among several major scientific journals that have recently devoted space to the grave environmental threats that are facing us today. A recent article in the New Scientist warns that we must urgently address global warming before it is too late. By changing the climate system of the planet we are conducting an experiment that cannot be controlled. When the forces of climate change are truly unleashed it will be hard to reverse their effects. The melting of the polar icecaps, once commenced, may have a logic of its own. A host of similar publications has appeared in recent years.[1]

Are these leading scientific journals merely scaremongering? If you believe the United States Government and some vocal sceptics, the situation is not so serious, and the best policy they offer seems to be taking some lukewarm technological action, just as a precaution.[2] But that position is untenable in the light of a statement by the joint science academies of the G8 countries just before the start of the G8 meeting in July 2005 in Gleneagles, Scotland.[3] This statement stresses that 'the scientific understanding of climate change is now sufficiently clear to justify... prompt action' (Joint Science Academies). Among the scientific community there is now a surprising sense of consensus about human-induced global warming and environmental deterioration in general (see Oreskes, 2004).[4] Moreover, and more hopefully, there is also a strong sense that we can in fact control or even reverse these negative trends, but we must act decisively and immediately.

This might seem a bit of dejavu to some people, given that during the 1970s some writers were predicting environmental and economic catastrophe caused by unlimited pollution and resource shortages. Now, some 30 years later, it may seem that we are still waiting for this big crisis to materialize. Well, our waiting may be over. Environmental degradation is unfolding around us in ways we could not even have imagined in the 1970s.

The Phases of Environmental Concern

Over the past 40 years modern concerns about the environment have gone through a series of phases. One of the important features of the phases is that they tend to become increasingly globalized and are directly linked to the massive economic expansion since World War II. The initial first phase started in the 1950s when the early concerns were raised about the use of chemicals in agriculture and the first comprehensive legislation to combat air pollution in Britain and the US were introduced. The first phase saw the publication of Rachel Carson's Silent Spring in 1962 and led to the ban on DDT in Britain and other countries during the 1960s. The second phase started in the late 1960s, when a flurry of publications voiced concern about the degradation of the planet's environment caused by unbridled population growth and economic development. Paul Ehrlich's *The Population Bomb* warned that the rapid increase of the world's population over the course of the 20th century would soon hit a ceiling. By doing so, Malthus' thesis of population growth and collapse caused by reaching environmental limits was reintroduced into contemporary political thinking in economics as well as environmentalism. A second seminal text published in 1968 in *Science* was Garrett Hardin's 'The Tragedy of the Commons', arguing that if there is no regulation of the use of resources no one will take responsibility to use them sustainably. The new environmental concern culminated in 1972 in the report for the Club of Rome, *Limits to Growth*, which warned of inevitable resource depletion, increasing environmental degradation, and the possible collapse of global civilisation.[5]

Newcastle, 21 February 2008

Dear George,

Enclosed you find a copy of the book that I co-edited and which was published last autumn. I had meant to send it earlier but a mix up of addresses with the publisher led to a delay in receiving my copies. It is very likely that there will be a follow-up book on this volume and the provisional title is: The end of globalization. The book will explore how the environmental problems we are facing could lead to a collapse of the present globalised civilisation. This will be put in a historical framework. It is early days but we are confident that this is going to work.

What my own book is concerned, the rewriting and editing process has slowed down due to the new job in Edinburgh, which asks more of my time than expected. It all results in pushing the publication date back to early summer, which is extremely unfortunate. The work in Edinburgh is quite challenging, in particular the writing of teaching material for people who are studying on-line without the convenience of having face to face meetings and lectures. That means that everything needs to be as clear as possible and the assignments must be diverse and challenging. One of the skills modules I am working on at the moment is centred on the "landscape and environment of the whisky industry". This topic provides us with an industrial activity which is closely linked to landscape and environmental factors such as the availability of clean water and other resources (peat, barley etc.), impacts such as water pollution and social history related to the construction of workers villages. We use all these aspects to introduce students to the different sources available for studying landscape and environmental aspects of history. It is coming together but it is a slow process It is good that this is only a part-time position, three days per week, something I must stick to in order to get the most important task ahead done: the book.

On the domestic front there is some very happy news that will change many things: if all goes well I will become a father in August. I am working hard to get the baby room ready and the grandparents to be are of course delighted. It puts life in a new perspective.

I hope that the treatment of your vascular and heart problems is going well and that you will completely recover soon.

Very best wishes,

These warnings, that humanity was heading toward an ecological disaster, had a profound impact on politics and society in the 1970s. Many countries introduced measures and legislation to combat local or regional air and water pollution as well as the contamination of soils. Furthermore, measures were taken to make economies more energy efficient, something that became even more urgent after the energy crises of 1973 and 1979. The second phase of environmental concern came to an abrupt end when, by the early 1980s, scientists started to observe disturbing signs that human activity was significantly affecting the environment on a global scale. The third phase of environmental concern had begun.

The first of these signs came in the form of a thinning of the stratospheric ozone layer over the polar regions of the globe. This was caused by CFC aerosols used in spray cans and refrigerating systems which, when released into the atmosphere, led to a depletion of stratospheric ozone. Since stratospheric ozone protects us from deadly cosmic radiation it was an urgent problem that had to be tackled since we could not afford to let this get out of control. If that happened, life on earth was facing a very uncertain future. Swift action was taken and by 1987 the Montreal Protocol outlawed the production of all CFCs. By that time the major producers of this gas, the US, Canada and Scandinavian countries had already ceased production. Soon the rest of the world followed (McNeill, 2000, pp. 113–114). It must be stressed that a combination of luck and foresight neutralised the threat caused by CFCs. If bromine instead of chlorine had been used the ozone hole would have been global by 1970. More by luck than wisdom the catastrophe did not develop. Next time we might not be so lucky (Flannery, 2005, pp. 216–219).[6]

The second global environmental threat observed by scientists was global warming, caused by the massive use of fossil fuels releasing large amounts of greenhouse gases into the atmosphere. Scientific evidence indicated that this would alter climatic patterns in a dramatic way for both humanity and many other species on the planet. The discovery of these global environmental threats was driven by scientific research and discourse and led to the emergence of a new environmental awareness that is truly global. But in contrast to the decisive and immediate action taken to counter the negative effects of CFCs, global warming has been largely ignored by politicians over the past two decades.[7] The reasons for this are complex but in essence boil down to two important issues: the primacy of economics and competition, and the shifting balance of power in an ever more destabilized world. The collapse of the Soviet Union, the internal weakening of the US and the rise of new industrial powers like China, India and Brazil have further complicated the issues of responsibility and adjustment. But there are more fundamental causes underpinning our present global environmental crises.

Science and the Primacy of the Economy

Some critics have argued that the development of modern science and technology is ultimately to blame for the environmental problems we are presently facing (Ozdemir, 1996). That is only a partial analysis, however, since science itself is not the driver of environmental degradation, species extinctions or climate change. It is society, responsible for using technology and science in harmful ways, that is directly culpable, and there are social, economic and political pressures that lay behind this. In other words, technology or science in general are perhaps morally or socially neutral. Rather, it is the human use and misuse of science and technology that is morally and politically charged. Humans are the fundamental problem, not necessarily the technologies through which the problems are created.[8] If we want to turn our ship around and avoid the coming global environmental catastrophes, it is we who must change our ways. What is most urgently needed for doing so is not mere short-term technological fixes but a different paradigm of political economy. This new political economy must take our impact on the planet's environment fully and realistically into account. The status quo of economic growth through globally distorted and harmful over-production and over-consumption for some and under-production and under-consumption for others is no longer acceptable.[9]

The reigning, globally orthodox economic growth model was an outcome of the misery caused by the economic depression and World War II and was meant to lift the masses out of poverty indefinitely. To do so, the remedy was thought to be unlimited economic growth, that is unlimited increase of production and consumption. This only works up to a certain point, as has recently been pointed out by economist Herman Daly,[10] who argues that if everyone in a society has reached a high standard of living it becomes futile to try to increase the size of the economy by doing harm to the environment and the social wellbeing of members of society (Daly, 2005).

However, the problem is that global capitalism presently puts much more power in the hands of corporations than it does ordinary concerned citizens. Corporations are, on the whole, not very sensitive to environmental arguments. The main aim of large corporations is to make a profit for a limited number of people, normally the shareholders. In principle, corporations have no necessary regard for the environment if that interferes with the business of profit making. If making profit for the shareholders can be assured by excluding increasing numbers of people or by exploiting the environment, then that may be desirable from the point of view of corporations. This leads to the accumulation of wealth and power in the hands of small groups of elites. If these elites grab political power they can entrench themselves even more. This is essentially what happened during the 1980s and 1990s when neo-liberalism rose to ideological, economic and political hegemony across the globe (see Gills, 2001). Hyperliberal think tanks were created around the world, advocating an extreme individualism in liberalism which is anti-state, anti-social and in favour of limitless corporate power. However, there is a fundamental contradiction within this hyper-liberalism: it is against state power but at the same time it is stimulating corporate power. Some corporations are so large and powerful that they can act like states. Yet hyper-liberals regard corporations as individuals which should enjoy the same rights as individual persons. This is now being enshrined in domestic and international law, leaving citizens increasingly excluded since they can not compete with the economic, legal and political resources that can be used against them by corporations. As a result of this legal privatization and commodification of the world, corporations now have virtually free reign and can use and deplete natural resources at will, as well as pollute the planetary environment. What is needed to prevent this tendency is comprehensive worldwide resource management on a rational and democratic basis that does not lead to depletion or environmental destruction.

Global Fate

The environment is the most global system of all, but humanity has only recently become aware of this. Although we have barely started to understand the complexities of the global system, for thousands of years we have been acting on the global environment. For example, it is now thought that the introduction of agriculture between 3,000 and 8,000 years ago led to the first anthropogenic global warming, altering the climate systems of the globe and delaying the next Ice Age (Ruddiman, 2005). By interfering in the earth's environmental systems, humanity has unwittingly 'taken charge' of the ecosystems of planet earth. To put it into a metaphor: humanity has taken its seat in the cockpit of planet earth, and is tinkering with the controls. However, there is only one problem. We don't have a flight manual or even a flight plan! The problem is that we can't get off spaceship earth. Destroying the life support systems by pushing the wrong buttons equates to species suicide. For this reason it is also paramount that humanity takes concerted action to understand better how the earth's ecosystems really work, a task that goes far beyond normal political, economic and social planning.

At present we have only a rudimentary understanding of the earth's global environmental systems and we are barely capable of making any truly accurate predictions within the systems. What is therefore needed is a comprehensive model of all systems that make up the earth's biosphere. In effect we need a flight manual of planet earth, and only science can provide us with that. This model could be used to take the rational action needed to avoid the possibly catastrophic consequences of our actions. However, at the moment we are still largely flying in the dark without a clue of what might be happening next. What is needed is to pool our knowledge in large worldwide projects, a sort of global Manhattan or Apollo project for the environment.[11] There are developments that point in this direction, and academies of science around the world as well as some space agencies are already pooling their knowledge to create a worldwide network of sensors, earth observation satellites and simulation capacity that will make it possible to make increasingly accurate models of the earth's systems. National interests should not be involved in this kind of undertaking since it is an effort that touches not only all humans on the planet but all living things.[12] Humanity not only has the capability to influence and create but also destroy life on the planet, and with this kind of power comes great responsibility. Humanity has indeed taken a seat in the cockpit of planet earth and by doing so has become responsible for all its passengers, something argued by Julian Huxley several generations ago (Huxley, 1957).

Global Alternative Routes

What needs to be done to avoid environmental catastrophe? As discussed before we need a rethink of our economic and social policies. Second, an investment in environmental technologies is urgently needed. But this requires political leadership and imagination: instead of conducting unwinnable and expensive oil wars, we need to invest vast sums of money in renewable forms of energy, creating economic environments that stimulate green technologies. Moreover, we need to change our ways of living in terms of transport habits, attitudes to consumption, work ethic and nature. The free market will not do this. Oil companies and multinationals will only go so far voluntarily without government action, since their first objective is to make a profit, not to save the planet. Ignoring the environment, however, could turn out to be the most ill-fated business decision of all time. To put it in the words of environmental journalist Mark Hertsgaard: 'In fact, if humans are smart, repairing the environment could become one of the biggest businesses of the coming century, a huge source of profits, jobs, and general economic wellbeing' (Hertsgaart, 1998).

Whether we continue to follow the route of unbridled quantitative growth, or create a radically new type of 'qualitative growth', there is only one alternative: invest in environmentally friendly technology. In the 1980s the US was the world leader in renewable energy. Now, 20 years later, it lags far behind the leading countries such as Germany, Denmark and Sweden. In Germany over 130,000 people are now employed in the renewable energy sector and the outlook is bright. This is indicated by the enormous growth of the renewable energy sector in Germany which soared in 2000–2001 by 20 per cent to around 8.2 billion Euro. In 2003 over 900,000 people were directly employed in the environment sector in Germany, and this figure continues to rise (Hornbach, 2003). In Denmark the story is much the same.[13]

Countries, companies and communities that invest now in these technologies will reap the benefits in the future. The potential global market of technologies based on clean renewable energies and lower resource consumption is certainly no less than hundreds of billions of dollars or euros. Some industries already realize this and press the political authorities to change environmental policies. Some would like to see clear targets set and incentives put in place so that they can adapt technologically and organizationally to meet them. Moreover, there is a case for compensatory mechanisms that operate between richer and poorer nations, whereby global resources are redirected to address the needs of the most needy. In this case this could mean introducing global taxation on pollution and resource extraction at source and redistributing the revenue to help finance clean and renewable energy technologies for the poorest societies.

Some corporations have now overtaken governments in investment in clean technologies. General Electric, for example, recently launched an initiative that aims to invest $1.5 billion annually in research in cleaner technologies by 2010, up from $700 million in 2004.[14] This is more than the US government is at present directly investing in clean technologies. Oil company BP has also recently started an investment programme in research in alternative energy sources and cleaner technologies.[15] This is of course in their own interest since sooner or later we will run out of oil. The only sensible strategy, if they want to stay in business, is to invest in alternative energy technologies and sources.

Some of the newly industrialized countries are, despite bad press to the contrary, beginning to understand that the future lies in environmentally friendly technology. Recently China announced that it will introduce strict EU standards on air pollution and subsidize its car industry to produce cleaner cars.[16] Perhaps this is also inspired by the realization that without these measures billions of Chinese will likely choke on the air of an ever increasingly industrialized economy.

Green technologies and economies are not, however, the whole story of making more secure our survival on the planet. The market cannot do it all. A behavioural change is also needed in virtually every aspect of our way of life, including transport and energy use as well as in the preferences of what we eat and where it comes from. In order to make these changes possible we need greater social stability and social justice, which will allow governments to work with their citizens to change society and the economy, making them more environmentally friendly. That may sound utopian but in fact it is not, it is eminently practical. Governments do have the power to change environmentally harmful practices, and positive examples of this do exist, even in some of the poorest communities in the world, as the policies pursued in Porto Alegre and Curitiba, Brazil, illustrate (Menegat, 2002; Rabinovitch, 1996; Gret and Sintomer, 2005).[17]

The primacy of the economy and the idea of limitless expansion of production and consumption regardless of the real environmental costs and consequences is the root cause of our present global environmental crisis. This central idea has led to short termism, as long as the wealth of shareholders is more important than the health of the planet. This attitude must change once and for all.

Conclusions: Redefining 'Progress'

The greatest challenge of the global environmental crisis is to overturn our historically deeply embedded assumption that 'progress' via unlimited exploitation of natural resources is both inevitable and desirable. Present evidence strongly suggests that humanity must now abandon the idea that such 'progress' is 'natural' and accept that, on the contrary, our present global civilization is on course for what could be, if urgent decisive action is not taken, a terminal crisis. If we examine historically 'the progress of the idea of progress', we can see how the rise of this idea has been inextricable from that of western and then global capitalism and the harnessing of the discoveries of modern science to these ends, so much so that 'progress' itself has been naturalized in our mentality and motivates and mediates almost everything we do. Yet today we are living through a profound crisis of the idea of progress. This crisis has come about due to the manifest failures of our reigning economic paradigm, not only in relation to the global environment but in many other ways, including the elusiveness of real peace and human security and the persistence and massive extent of grinding poverty and global inequality. Therefore, and by necessity of history, we are experiencing a deep ideological and material malaise that history itself teaches us will culminate in the demise of the old social order and will require the emergence of a new set of guiding principles and practices in order to reach a lasting resolution of the crisis.

It is our view that the key move in this process of change will occur at the level of ideas, of individual and collective mentality, and in which a new environmental awareness will play a necessarily central and positive role. We must finally abandon the old political economy, and its rather crude material goals and inherent falsehoods concerning the uses and abuses of natural resources and systems, and adopt a new paradigm based on respecting the objective laws and limitations of natural environmental systems and resources that support all life, including our own. Furthermore, we must finally give up the idea of limitless quantitative growth and consumption, Daly's (2005) 'uneconomic growth', and concentrate our energies on achieving qualitative improvement in the standard of living for all people (correcting the distortions of both overconsumption by the rich and under-consumption by the poor) and sustainability and stability. What may seem individually or even nationally 'rational' (e.g. the pursuit of bigger cars and more flight holidays) may well be irrational on a global scale.

Among the leading philosophes of the European Enlightenment during the 18th century were those who could already foresee that unlimited expansion of wealth and the pursuit of crude scientism would not automatically produce 'progressive' historical outcomes. True progress, argued Helvetius (1758) and Mercier (1770) would require qualitative improvements in life, through better education, public health, social organization, legal and political institutions, and moral and mental development. Greater human happiness would not come through unlimited accumulation of wealth, but rather by learning to live within reasonable means, trading only for necessities and redistributing wealth from the rich to the poor. Happiness would be realized not through ever greater production and consumption, but actually by consuming less rather than producing more.

It is perhaps time to seriously revisit, as Herman Daly does, John Stuart Mill's classic idea of the 'stationary' or 'steady-state' economy, which recognizes the limits of brute quantitative growth, due to such historical factors as population growth, energy supplies, the laws of 'diminishing returns' and related ideas on utility and futility, and the chronic tendency to 'over-accumulate' in the financial sphere, to name some of the more prominent aspects. Nevertheless, this does not at all imply abandoning the idea of genuine human improvement or progress, if by those terms we mean a steady bettering of the human condition and the greater happiness of all humanity. On the contrary, it re-invokes this idea of human progress and with even greater historical urgency than was the case several centuries ago when the original idea of progress first captured the imagination of the West (Daly, 1973; Mill, 1848). Now the difference is that the new idea of progress must apply to the globe in a way that is in conformity to the laws of nature understood in the modern ecological sense of that phrase. In conclusion, the present globalization of environmental crises could become a great opportunity for all humanity to rise to its challenge and create a renewed global civilization. Otherwise, 'Overshoot – and subsequent decline – in societal welfare will result when society does not prepare sufficiently well for the future' (Meadows et al., 2005, p. xxi).

Notes

1 See, amongst others, *New Scientist*, 185, 12 February 2005, pp. 8–11; *American Scientist*, 90(1), pp. 35–39; *Science*, 316, 13 April 2007, pp. 188–190.
2 In May 2007 the US Administration tabled a plan for tackling climate change under which the world's 15 greatest polluters would set their own, loose goals for reducing CO_2 emissions. Business leaders have for some time accepted that some sort of global agreement to reduce carbon emissions is inevitable and desirable and have been asking for hard targets, something the Bush Administration has refused so far. See Paul Maidment, *G8 Makes Business Climate Clearer*, Forbes.com, 8 June 2007, www.forbes.com/business/energy/2007/06/07/notes-news-climate-oped-cx_pm_0608notn.html, accessed 23 June 2007.
3 See commentary by Jan Oosthoek in this volume, pp. 161–164.
4 The fourth report published by the IPPC in February 2007 reveals a strong consensus among the world's scientific community that climate change is largely caused by humans.
5 For detailed discussion see de Steiguer (1997).
6 Bromine and chlorine can be used interchangeably for many purposes. Bromine is 45 times more potent than chlorine to destroy ozone.
7 For a discussion of global warming, see the contributions in this volume by Björn-Ola Linnér and Merle Jacob (pp. 121–134) and Kevin C. Armitage (pp. 135–146).
8 In the case of nuclear weapons, which we deplore for their capabilities to destroy all life, the science is not morally neutral at all. Einstein recognized this but never considered not publishing his early theories although he could foresee that one day someone could develop nuclear weapons based on his discoveries. (see Nathan and Norden, 1981, p. 350).
9 See for a discussion of growth and sustainability Verstegen and Hanekamp in this volume, pp. 67–80.
10 See Nancy Bazilchuk's interview with Daly and Lash in this issue, pp. 447–450.
11 The Apollo Alliance proposes a project on the scale of the Apollo moon project to develop clean and environmentally friendly technologies and to make the US independent of fossil fuels. See www.apolloalliance.org. In February 2005 the Global Earth Observation System of Systems (GEOSS) was launched. Its objective is to create a global earth observation network and pool expertise from around the world. See Clery (2005).
12 The International Polar Year is an example of a large global scientific programme focused on the Arctic and the Antarctic from March 2007 to March 2009. The IPCC has declared the environments of the Arctic and Antarctic as indicators of global environmental change. See http://www.ipy.org/, accessed 24 June 2007.
13 Between 1998 and 2002 of the total energy export of US$ 3.1, wind turbine exports amounted to just over US$ 1.5 bn., corresponding to slightly less than 50 per cent. Source: Danish Trade Council, http://www.um.dk/Publikationer/Eksportraadgivning/FocusDenmark/0202/0202/html/chapter01.htm, accessed 24 June 2007.
14 GE Ecomagination, http://ge.ecomagination.com, accessed 20 October 2005.
15 BP Environment and Society, http://www.bp.com/genericsection.do, accessed 23 October 2005.
16 China has adopted the Euro III vehicle emission standards developed by the EU and is planning to adopt the Euro IV standards only a couple of years after the EU itself (see EC, 2005).
17 Porto Alegre is one of the greenest cities in the world. This was achieved by introducing participatory democracy, the integration of public environmental management policies and the regeneration of public spaces. The city of Curitiba provides the world with a model of how to integrate sustainable transport considerations with the development of business, road infrastructure, and local communities. This has been actively and successfully pursued by the local authorities.

References

Carson, R. (1962) *Silent Spring* (Boston: Houghton Mifflin).
Clery, D. (2005) Forging a global network to watch the planet, *Science*, 307(5713), p. 1182.
Daly, H. E. (1973) The steady-state economy: toward a political economy of biophysical equilibrium and moral growth, in Daly, H. E. (ed.) *Towards a Steady-state Economy* (San Francisco: W.H. Freeman).
Daly, H. E. (2005) Economics in a full world, *Scientific American*, 293(3), pp. 78–85.
de Steiguer, J. L. (1997) *The Age of Environmentalism* (New York: McGraw-Hill).
EC (European Commission) (2005) *Questions and answers on the thematic strategy on air pollution*, EC Memo 05/334, 21 September, available at http://europa.eu.int/rapid/searchAction.do, accessed 23 October 2005.
Ehrlich, P. (1968) *The Population Bomb* (Ballantine Books: New York).
Flannery, Tim (2005) *The weather makers. The history and future impact of climate change* (Melbourne: The Text Publishing Company).
Garrett, H. (1968) The tragedy of the commons, *Science*, 162(1968), pp. 1243–1248.
Gills, B. (ed.) (2001) *Globalization and the Politics of Resistance* (London: Routledge).
Gret, M. & Yves, S. (2005) *The Porto Alegre Experiment: Learning Lessons for Better Democracy* (London: Zed Press).
Helvetius, Claude-Adrien (1758) *De l'esprit* (On the Mind) (Paris: Durand).
Hertsgaart, M. (1998) *Earth Odyssey: Around the World in Search of Our Environmental Future* (New York: Broadway Books).
Hornbach, Jens (2003) *Employment and Innovations in the Environmental Sector: Determinants and Econometrical Results for Germany* (Milan: Fondazione Eni Enrico Mattei), available at http://www.feem.it/Feem/Pub/Publications/WPapers/default.html, accessed 23 October 2005.
Huxley, J. (1957) Transhumanism, pp. 13–17 in *New Bottles for New Wine* (London: Chatto & Windus).
Joint Science Academies' Statement (2005) *Joint Science Academies' Statement: Global Response to Climate Change*, 7 June, http://www.royalsoc.ac.uk/displaypagedoc.asp?id1/413618, accessed 22 October 2005.
McNeill, J. R. (2000.) *Something New Under the Sun. An Environmental History of the Twentieth Century* (London: Penguin).
Meadows, D., Randers, J. & Meadows, D. (2005) *Limits to Growth: The 30-year Update* (London: Earthscan).
Meadows, D. H., Meadows, D. L., Randers, J. & Behrens, W. W. (1972) *The Limits to Growth* (New York: University Books).
Menegat, R. (2002) Participatory democracy and sustainable development: integrated urban environmental management in Porto Alegre, Brazil, *Environment & Urbanization*, 14(2), pp. 181–206.
Mercier, Louis-Sébastien (1758[1977]) *L'an 2440: reı̀,ve s'il en fut jamais* (Paris: F. Adel).
Mill, J. S. (1848[1965]) Principles of Political Economy with Some of Their Applications to Social Philosophy (Reprints of Economic Classics; New York: Augustus M. Kelley).
Nathan, Otto and Heinz Norden, Einstein on Peace (New York: Avenel Books, 1981).
Oreskes, N. (2004) Beyond the ivory tower: the scientific consensus on climate change, *Science*, 306(5702), p. 1686.
Ozdemir, Ibrahim (1996) Science and the Environment: Is Science Responsible for Environmental Crisis? *The Journal of the Environment and Social Sciences*, 1(1-2), pp. 35–46.
Rabinovitch, J. (1996) Innovative land use and public transport policy: the case of Curitiba, Brazil, *Land Use Policy*, 13(1), pp. 51–67.
Ruddiman, W. F. (2005) How did humans first alter global climate? *Scientific American*, 292(3), pp. 34–41.
Scientific American (2005) Special issue: 'Crossroads for Planet Earth', 293(3).
Toynbee, A. (1976) *Mankind and Mother Earth* (Oxford: Oxford University Press).
Wells, H. G. (1946) *A Short History of the World* (London: Penguin).

Global Environmental History: The Long View

J. DONALD HUGHES

Introduction

Someone once asked the American composer Aaron Copland whether music has a meaning. 'Yes', he replied. Then the questioner asked him if he could say what that meaning is, in words. 'No', concluded Copland (Copland, 1957, p. 9). Today I feel as if I am in Copland's position. Whenever someone asks me what my profession—environmental history—actually does, that is, of what use it is, I tend to reply that it provides perspective on what is happening to the environment, and to the environmental movement, in the present. We cannot understand the present, after all, without firm grounding in the past. So far, so good, but what about the future? Should not this perspective also enable me to make predictions, or at least forecast some general trends in the new century? With the hubris of an academic who has presumed to write a book with the title *An Environmental History of the World* (Hughes, 2001), I am tempted to answer, 'indeed it does'. Then the voice of caution whispers, 'emulate Copland'.

Just such a cautionary mood seized me a few months ago when I looked at two or three books that purported to examine American foreign policy in the twenty-first century. One even bore the date September 2001, but it had obviously been written before the eleventh (Lieber, 2001). I scanned the chapter headings and perused the indices. None of the books had any more than a minor, passing reference to terrorism. How could the authors, one of whom is Henry Kissinger (Kissinger, 2001), have lacked the foresight to see the importance of that theme, which has assumed a formative role in the foreign policy of the first new administration of the century, and seems certain to continue? Will my own projections suffer the fate of theirs? Possibly so, I admit. I can hear some colleagues' voices correcting me: *probably* so. They are probably right.

They tell me, not 'Shoemaker, stick to your last', but 'Historian, stick to your past'. But even there daunting questions resound. Let me ask one. Are there common themes in global environmental history? I think I can identify some. And if I can, it seems likely that these themes will play themselves onward past the opening bars of this century. So I will throw caution to the winds and anticipate the next movement in what I hope will someday prove to have been the symphony of nature and culture, but fear will be a cacophony.

I do not mean that I will simply take present tendencies and extrapolate them into the remaining 95 years or so of the century. As an environmental historian, I realize that trends often reverse when new events and forces intervene. They will do so, but it is difficult to anticipate when or why. In music, when one hears a crescendo, one knows it will end, and one develops a feeling for when that might happen. In history, one may not be so fortunate. A historian at the beginning of the twentieth century might reasonably have predicted the continued exponential growth of the railroad system in the US, for example, since foreseeing the success of the automobile and the airplane would have taken imagination worthy of Jules Verne. Science fiction, in fact, may not be entirely irrelevant to this line of inquiry. But let me proceed, and select four themes out of those I regard as most important for the environment and environmentalism in the coming decades. They are growth of population, the declining power of local communities over their own environments, the history of energy and energy resources, and loss of biodiversity.

Population Growth

The first theme is population growth and the heights it may reach before a possible crash. The historical trend is clear. Ten thousand years ago, there were only five to ten million humans on Earth. With the invention of agriculture, a modest increase began, and by Roman times there were perhaps 200 million. That doubled by 1492. At the beginning of the twentieth century world population was 1.6 billion. The United Nations observed the day of birth of the 6 billionth living human on 12 October 1999. The UN conservatively predicted that we shall reach 8.9 billion by 2050, and that more than 90% of that increase will be in the developing nations. China, with the world's most effective population control program, will nonetheless reach 1.4 billion (Elvin, 2004; Elvin & Liu, 1998), and India will add 400 million to pass China as the most populous nation on Earth.

I visited China a few years ago, and discovered that to walk through a Chinese city helps to appreciate how overcrowded the world can become. On a bridge over the Grand Canal in Suzhou, when we could barely move in the press of bodies, my Chinese guide turned to me and said, 'Could America please take 500 million? After all, it's only half.' She was only half in jest; it gives me pause to realize that if China sent just one-quarter of its inhabitants to the US, it would double our population. I do not advocate an end to movement of people from one country to another; it is a way of encouraging cultural exchange and diversity. After the Tienanmen Square incident my wife and I helped a Chinese student come to the US, and we treat him like a son. He is presently a Ph.D. candidate at the University of California. Population problems take on a different appearance when viewed one by one.

Nevertheless, population growth is the most potent engine driving environmental destruction. No value that environmentalists prize can survive the uncontrolled multiplication of our species. For some of those values, we have already passed a critical point. Burgeoning population adds to the scale of environmental effects caused by humans, and makes changes happen faster. One village near a forest might use so little firewood that it could continue to do so forever, but ten villages would exceed sustainable yield and destroy the forest in ten years. This is not theoretical; it is happening in much of the tropical world.

People in poorer countries do less damage per capita, but even a small amount of resource use becomes major when multiplied by millions or billions, and they can afford fewer restorative measures. In the industrial countries, the environmental footprint of each inhabitant is bigger, so that even a small population increase causes correspondingly greater impact. The US has the largest rate of annual population growth of any developed country, almost all of it due to immigration. Environmentalist groups like the Sierra Club have been pressed by some of their own members to speak softly on the latter point. An excellent review of the population debate is given by Joel Cohen in *How Many People Can the Earth Support?* (Cohen, 1995). Also see J. R. McNeill's article on human population (McNeill, 2004).

Looking toward the twenty-first century, the UN has predicted that population growth will slow and stop at some maximum figure between 10 and 12 billion. Such an expectation is based partly on declining birth rates that have been observed in most nations over the past 5 to 15 years. These are believed to result from improving health and education, availability of birth control, higher standards of living, and the increasing participation of women in reproductive decisions. I hope these are the reasons, and that they continue to operate in the coming decades. Recent discussions at the UN were optimistic that they will. But I am suspicious of this model of the future. Population expansion in developing countries itself undercuts some of the positive factors just cited.

I suspect that genetic technology, combined with breakthroughs in immunology, will have an effect equal to or greater than any other factor. Designer crops will continue to improve yields for several decades, although not indefinitely. Biotechnology has its built-in evolutionary paradoxes. Monoculture is risky; pest evolution will eventually catch up. Even so, food supplies will stay adequate beyond mid-century, so famine will not constrain population. The Malthusian crunch will be postponed again. But when it does occur, it will be difficult to counter. The 'terminator genes' that make it necessary for farmers to buy their seeds from industrial-agricultural suppliers may transfer into the native crops that preserve the source genotypes of crops. Additionally, many benefits of biotech will remain affordable only in the affluent nations. Cloning as a reproductive device will not catch on, but gene therapy in reproduction, should it become widely available, will enable elites, especially in affluent nations, to assure that their children will be intelligent, athletic, free of genetic disease, and few in number. This improved generation will demand jobs in highly skilled and highly paid professions. They will live longer and remain productive later in life. The slack in unskilled jobs in those places will, therefore, have to be made up by immigration from the Third World. This will assure crowding in the north without relieving it in the south.

If this occurs the UN predictions will prove conservative indeed. When such an upward swing of population pushing the limits of resources has occurred in history, as happened in the southern Maya lowlands between 650 and 850 CE, and in Europe during the two centuries or so before 1300, it was followed by a crash and the abandonment of many settlements. The Club of Rome in 1972 and again in 1992 projected a similar crash in population during the twenty-first century. The major causes would be resource shortages, pollution, and depreciation of resource capital due to failure of new investment (Meadows et al., 1972; Meadows et al., 1992). Some of the deadlines set by the first report have already passed without the debacles it predicted (Schoijet, 1999), but it is hard to argue with the Club's conclusions that without measures to curb population growth, along with controls on pollution and resource use, a demographic crash later in the century or shortly beyond seems inevitable. One of the most ominous trends making that likely is our treatment of renewable resources. For example, fisheries are conducted as a form of mining, and due to the depletion of the resource, the most efficient forms of mechanization in fishing fleets now produce about the same return as traditional technologies once did. Wars over resources, such as the Gulf Wars, have occurred and threaten to become more prevalent.

Local versus Global Determination of Policy

The second theme is the local versus the global. The course of the relationship between culture and nature is determined to a major extent by the scale on which decisions about environmental policy are made. Does a local community make its own choices about what will happen to its environment? Or are the operative decisions made on national, regional, or even global levels? Also, which mode is most environmentally friendly?

The direction of the trend through history seems clear. Hunter-gatherers followed local tribal customs, often including taboos that, whatever their motives, operated to control the scale of killing species of economic importance. Early farming villages allotted the land, decided what to plant, and often reserved a tract of forest for communal use, including an inviolable sacred grove. People with both ways of life made impacts on the environment, but they witnessed these impacts and limited them to some extent.

City-states established hierarchies of priests, kings, and assemblies that made decisions on land use. The areas under their control were larger than those of villages, but the scale was still local. This is important because it meant that the authorities could see some of the results of their decisions. They received feedback from nature within a comprehensible sphere and within a time frame that extended over human life spans aided by collective memory and record keeping. Even so, some long term and accumulative environmental problems such as deposition of waterborne sediments, salinization of agricultural soil, and exhaustion of timber defied their efforts.

Ancient empires enabled trade over longer distances and in greater volume than before. The overall effects of the use of resources were less apparent to local people. Imperial authorities sought to establish economic policy. Roman leaders, for example, subsidized grain trade with Egypt in order to feed citizens in the capital city. But they did not have a sophisticated grasp of the principles of supply and demand. When the autocratic emperor Diocletian proclaimed his Edict of Prices, it resulted in shortages of the goods designated in the law and a flourishing black market. Other efforts for reform met opposition from large landholders and failed. Among environmental results were the exhaustion of resources, especially of forests in some areas, and agricultural decline.

The European nation states of the early modern period were able to exercise increased supervision over local communities. Seeking a positive trade balance, they encouraged the growth and manufacture of products for trade and established measures to protect home industries from competition. Colonialism enabled metropolitan countries to profit from environmental damage in other parts of the world, and in doing so to limit self-determination of communities in the colonies.

An example is provided by forest policy in India. The British colonial power's interests lay in controlling exploitation of the country's sylvan resources, and they created the Forest Department in 1864 to do this. The Forest Department made working plans for timber production, with lip-service to principles of sustainable harvest (Buchy, 1993). It deprived communities of power to regulate harvests by their own members, or to keep others out of local forests, including the numerous sacred groves, which had been protected by villagers since time immemorial. Thus formerly communal property became open-access resources liable to unrestrained usage, an example of 'the tragedy of the commons' (Hardin, 1968). Meanwhile, the best trees fell to the demands of railroad construction for ties. When India won independence in 1947, the Forest Department continued the policies begun in the British Raj. Thus local communities initially found that independence brought them no rights in this respect. The area of forest in local control diminished to a remnant (Gadgil and Chandran, 1988). Today a new plan, Joint Forest Management, is returning control of forests to villages, sharing the revenue with communities and offering hope for harmonization of local and national in some parts of India.

The principle of exporting environmental damage by importing resources at low cost from far away became a keynote of the policy of industrial nations in the twentieth century, who found they could implement colonial policy without direct rule. Demand in one region could be met by impacting the environment in a distant part of the world. For example, North Americans who want fruits in winter can buy them from Chile, where seasons are reversed. Japan prefers to import timber from the tropics rather than increase pressure on domestic forests.

Local determination, already weakened in respect to national and colonial power, passed into the shadow of global power in the twentieth century, when a number of international institutions transformed the world market economy. The financial experts of capitalist nations erected a structure to encourage free trade and open resources of the world, renewable and non-renewable, to exploitation. These include the International Monetary Fund (IMF) and World Bank, which emerged from the Bretton Woods Conference of 1944 (Kenwood & Lougheed, 1971), and the General Agreement on Tariffs and Trade (GATT). GATT's supervising body, the World Trade Organization (WTO) (Reisman, 1996), with a membership of over 150 nations including the largest ones, can make a claim to oversight of the world economy. WTO is committed to ceaseless growth. It provides limited support to measures for environmental improvement by permitting its member nations to enforce laws necessary to protect the life and health of humans and to conserve natural resources, but has not stressed the broader area of environmental protection.

Some economic theorists regard environmental regulations as an unnecessary restraint of trade, including laws intended to protect endangered species in international trade. Many oppose on principle such measures as the ban on trade in ivory, although the market seems designed to assure by inflating prices on rare commodities that the trade would continue until the last tusker is harvested.

Institutions of the world economy have, in their own sphere, achieved ascendancy even over nation-states. WTO decisions have nullified national bans on products considered environmentally damaging. A landmark case was brought by Mexico in 1991 before a GATT panel. The US, under its Marine Mammal Protection Act, had decided that Mexican-caught tuna would be excluded unless Mexican fishermen used methods that would spare thousands of dolphins that were being destroyed in their nets. GATT decided that this was an improper attempt by the US to impose its environmental regulations on Mexico, and ordered the US to accept tuna that was not 'dolphin-safe'. The ruling became a precedent.

As global institutions and multinational corporations become more powerful, nations, especially in the Third World, become smaller as colonial empires split apart and separatist movements succeed. Many tropical countries are not only small but also poor, and their economic sectors sometimes have to depend on inadequately educated management. They face powerful supranational organizations that can summon up huge amounts of money and numbers of employees greater than those of the governments concerned, and sometimes even weaponry. Violence is seldom necessary, however; large national and multinational corporations can promise jobs and other rewards that are hard to refuse. But local people are seldom skilled in the jobs demanded by the corporations, which bring in workers from outside who do not share local attitudes and customs. Virtually all these factors operated in the case of the island of Nauru, where exploitation of phosphates for fertilizer resulted not only in the destruction of forests and other biota, but also in the transformation of most of the island into uninhabitable and virtually inaccessible wasteland (McDaniel & Gowdy, 2000). Elsewhere, government programs to encourage exports, rising prices of timber and other wood products, and the depletion of accessible forests to exploit, drove multinational logging concerns to seek out new resources. The effect on local peoples who depend on forests has been catastrophic.

Environmental organizations that operate on the global level often do not trust local communities to care for their own environments. They encourage the establishment of national parks and other central government programs, which sometimes are paper measures, when the best way of protecting natural pieces in the mosaic landscape might be to gain the active support of the people who live in and near them.

But the biggest demand for resources and the greatest influx of population are seen in urban and industrialized areas. In the twenty-first century, more than half of all humans will live in large urban concentrations. Photographs taken in the early 1990s showed workers in polluted industrial centers of Romania covered with soot. It is cities in less industrialized countries, however, that grow most rapidly, and slums make up most of this growth. In Cairo, to give one instance, people actually live in cemeteries and garbage dumps. The vision of a third-world megalopolis with a rapidly growing population straining an already inadequate infrastructure threatens to make the concept of a local community meaningless.

What about local and global forces in the twenty-first century? If I were to extrapolate present trends, I would predict that global entities will continue to increase control over local environments everywhere. The power of small nations will decrease even as their number increases, and some will disappear under rising sea levels. Traditional communities will lose people to swelling formless conurbations.

Most of the major technological advances that I can conjure up with my limited imagination, such as bioengineering with its designer children and species on demand, miniaturized computers of incredible speed and memory, robotic spy insects, and brain-scanners capable of viewing mental images directly, all seem likely to strengthen the anti-local powers. They also make terrorism scarier, if that is possible.

Is there, as Jane Goodall's recent book asks, *Reason for Hope*? (Goodall, 1999). I think there is, and I would look in two directions for it. The local–global dichotomy can be resolved if local projects play their parts in preserving the global environment, and at the same time global institutions compose viable environmental law and policy and are given the ability to conduct them. For decades we have heard the motto, 'Think globally, act locally.' This must be balanced by its converse, 'Think locally, act globally.'

Finding local models for this century is difficult, but some exist. Some communities in North America and Europe have enacted antipollution measures and preserve their own parks and forests. Cities such as Denver and Tucson years ago acquired mountain parks outside their limits as amenities for citizens and others. It is encouraging to see a Third World city such as

Curitiba, Brazil, planning parks, pedestrian malls, public transport, garbage and recycling systems that make it an ecological success and a great place to live. Smaller communities have turned from hunting bush meat and burning forests to ecotourism. Others resist destruction of their local forests by movements like Chipko, in which women in the Himalayas actively opposed the cutting of trees on the watersheds above their villages by talking to the laborers and hugging the trees, and finally won a moratorium (Shiva, 1989). Grassroots efforts in environmental education offer some of the best hope. For example, the Amazon Center for Environmental Education and Research in Peru (http://www.aceer.org) supports teachers and provides materials in local schools.

Turning to the global side, I wonder if UN programs offer signs of hope. While there was hardly any recognition of the importance of environmental problems when the UN was founded in 1945, a number of initiatives have appeared since. Several agencies have worked on environmental health. Others have limited maritime pollution and the killing of whales. UNESCO, through its 'Man and the Biosphere Program', has established biosphere reserves that are planned to encourage local peoples to engage in traditional economic activities in buffer zones. The UN Environment Program (UNEP) fostered the erection of a framework of international environmental law through such agreements as the 1987 Montreal Protocol on Substances That Deplete the Ozone Layer. UNEP is the only UN agency with headquarters in a developing country. Nevertheless, a worrisome trend in UN environmental affairs may be symbolized by the progression of titles of its three great world environmental conferences. In 1972, the Stockholm meeting was called the UN Conference on the Human Environment. In 1992 came Rio and the UN Conference on Environment and Development, which signaled that economic growth was as important as the environment. The 2002 Johannesburg meeting, however, was called the UN World Summit on Sustainable Development, dropping any reference to the environment. The agenda was summarized under three headings, only one of which is 'conserving natural resources and the environment', the other two were 'economic growth and equity' (listed first) and 'social development'. The achievements of Johannesburg were fewer than those of Rio, as Rio's were less visionary than those of Stockholm. I predict, however, that as the century moves onward, the importance of environmental conservation will loom larger due to exhaustion of resources and widespread environmental damage, and will involve a larger segment of UN and other international agendas.

Global financial institutions could exercise positive direction in the new century if they fund programs for environmental conservation and economic viability of traditional communities. The World Bank is the largest source of development assistance, but projects it has supported have often been environmentally damaging, and have resulted in the displacement of more than two million people from their home communities. In India, for example, it loaned $850 million for the Singrauli complex of pit mines and coal-burning power plants that annually emits 10 million tons of carbon and has destroyed forests and ousted tribal people (Soroos, 1999). In recent years, the World Bank has admitted some of its failings and has created an environment department, but it is uncertain whether its overall efforts have been diverted in an environmental direction. I am afraid that I foresee a momentum of economic growth only marginally checked by environmental considerations in the coming decades, at least initially.

Threats to Biodiversity

A third theme that will be played out in the environment and environmentalism in the coming decades is the preservation or destruction of the great orchestra of species that makes up the biodiversity of life on Earth. From the beginning of culture, humans have found their lives intertwined with those of other species. The Greek philosopher Democritus thought that people learned how to weave from spiders, and how to sing from songbirds, swans, and nightingales. They got the inspiration to build houses of clay from watching swallows at work on their nests. 'In the most important concerns', he wrote, 'We are pupils of the animals' (Wheelwright, 1966, p. 184). In a perceptive book, Steven Lonsdale adduced examples from every part of the world to show that dance owes its origin and development to human imitation of the varied movements of mammals, reptiles, amphibians, fish, birds, and even invertebrates (Lonsdale, 1981). Interaction with countless kinds of animals and plants helped to form our bodies and minds, and in many important respects made us what we are. If we lose that interaction, it will affect us more deeply than we may think.

Humans were formed by interaction with countless other forms of life, probably within a great Pleistocene flourishing of large mammals and contrasting plant communities in East and South Africa. Danger and complexity stimulated early humans as they hunted, gathered, dwelt, and served as prey in that nexus of constant interaction between species. It seems that human intelligence is a response to the challenges offered by living among many other species. To quote Edward O. Wilson, 'We stay alert and alive in the vanished forests of the world' (Wilson, 1984, p. 101).

Over time, human actions have reduced the number of species, and the number of individual organisms within most species, diminishing biodiversity and the complexity of ecosystems. This process began in the ancient world; the Indian epic, *Mahabharata*, records the burning of a great forest, with every creature in it, as an offering to the fire god. The ecological historians Madhav Gadgil and Ramachandra Guha suggest that this text preserves the memory of a fire set by farmers to displace hunters and gatherers (Gadgil & Guha, 1993).

The Romans depleted the wildlife of the Mediterranean area for shows in their amphitheaters. Mosaics at a villa in Sicily show hunters rounding up every large creature including tigers and ostriches. In exhibitions honoring Trajan's conquests, armed men killed 11,000 wild animals. There was opposition even then; Cicero pitied the elephants he saw being killed in Pompey's show, and as governor refused to make the citizens of his province collect leopards for the games. Juba II of Mauretania objected to the destruction of African wildlife by the Romans, and his son Ptolemy, grandson of Antony and Cleopatra, closed the arenas, shut down the animal-port, and enacted a conservation law. These measures were ineffective; elephant, rhinoceros, and zebra became extinct in North Africa, and others declined (Hughes, 1994).

The reduction of biodiversity continued in the medieval period. Hunters killed Britain's last native brown bear in the tenth century. Kings reserved forests for hunting, but killed thousands of animals. By 1526 the last British beaver perished (Verney, 1979). Elk, aurochs and European bison diminished in number, as much because the expansion of agriculture restricted their habitats as from hunting. The woodland in much of Europe was cleared during the twelfth and thirteenth centuries, and although trees recaptured some territory after the Black Death, by the sixteenth century vast tracts had again been denuded (Bowlus, 1980).

In the early modern age, European ships brought shocks almost everywhere not only of military and economic power, but also of ecological disruption. From the moment they dropped anchor beside a new land, their passengers began to change it. They modified landscapes by introducing animals, plants, and microorganisms, extracting resources, deforesting, establishing plantations, and decimating indigenous human populations that had formed their own ways of interrelating with local environments. European enterprise caused a great homogenization of the Earth's ecosystems, unparalleled in geological time (Crosby, 1972, 1986). In the Americas, Australia, and almost all islands, along with the slaughter of wildlife by the human invaders, immigrant species increased aggressively, crowded out indigenous species, and upset ecosystems. The dominant attitude toward animals and plants by Europeans was economic materialism: other species were viewed as commodities. As Francis Bacon expostulated, 'The world is made for man, not man for the world' (Worster, 1993, p. 212).

In the last two centuries, destruction of other forms of life by humans escalated as the result of powerful technology, exploitation of natural resources, and increasing human population. In 1800, large sections of the continents were still wilderness teeming with wildlife. There seemed no end to the bounty of the sea. By the end of the twentieth century, extinctions had occurred on a scale only matched by catastrophes of the geological record (Wilson, 1992; Ehrlich & Ehrlich, 1981). Species of fish that had been staples of trade vanished from the Atlantic market, and the great whales were endangered. Varieties of frogs and other amphibians disappeared mysteriously in ecosystems around the world (Phillips, 1994). India had 4 million blackbuck antelope in 1800; only 25,000 remain, and the blackbuck's major predator, the cheetah, has vanished. Similar declines have been recorded for other animals around the world.

At present, humans are making an unprecedented impact on the environment. This has given many people a sense of unease. Some have a feeling that nature will have the last impact, and it is unclear just what it will be. In recent years, scientists, writers, and others have recognized a crisis of biodiversity. But the tenor of international discussions of the question is not encouraging for the survival of natural ecosystems.

When environmental questions first appeared on the agenda of international bodies the welfare of other species was prominent. The constitution of the first environmental organization under UN auspices, the International Union for the Protection of Nature, in 1949 defined its purpose as 'the preservation of the entire world biotic community' (McCormick, 1989). Changing its name to the International Union for the Conservation of Nature and Natural Resources (IUCN), it undertook a survey of threatened animals that became the Red Data Book, the standard international list of endangered species. Realistically but ominously, this was a loose-leaf book, allowing the insertion of additional pages. Many have been added.

In the years since, UNEP has cooperated with other agencies in negotiating international agreements such as the Convention on International Trade in Endangered Species of Wild Fauna and Flora (CITES), the Bonn Convention on Migratory Species, and a whaling moratorium.

Concern often appeared over the danger to single species: the spotted owl in the US northwest, the panda in China, the tiger in India and Siberia, and the elephant in Africa. These are highly visible indicator species, but the real problem in each case is the diminution of the ecosystem to which each of them belongs. It is a process called 'habitat destruction', but is really the fragmentation of communities of life.

One argument used for preservation of ancient forests was that they are storehouses of species producing substances that might prove of use as foods or medicines. This is certainly true; researchers derived many healing drugs from tropical rainforests, and in the US taxol, a derivative of the yew tree, a species that loggers once destroyed as a useless 'weed', proved valuable in treating ovarian cancer. Biodiversity, the world realized, had economic value, and the discussion changed its tenor. Multinationals started patenting species, such as the neem tree, whose multiple uses had long been known in traditional South Asia. Farmers in India and Pakistan have worked together to try to save their plants from this form of exploitation.

Biodiversity was on the agenda at Rio in 1992, and the Convention on Biological Diversity was one of five primary documents approved. Most of the discussion, however, was not on the need to preserve species and ecosystems, but the desirability of assuring sustainable economic development and to distribute equitably the gains realized from biological resources.

The goals expressed in the final draft were the conservation and sustainable use of biodiversity and fair trade and compensation involving products made from genetic resources. It charged each country to make plans to protect habitats and species, and requested aid to developing countries to help them do this. The treaty was signed by 153 nations of 178 attending; only the United States voiced a refusal to sign, on grounds that the financial obligations were insufficiently supervised. India has embarked on a National Biodiversity Strategy Action Plan that will inventory species and ecosystems. A number of pilot projects have been started. A similar project for the US has been frustrated in Congress by opposition from businesses and landowners who fear that it would discover a host of endangered species—which it probably would.

One of the most important areas of biodiversity conservation is the world's oceans and seas, which actually constitute the largest segment of the biosphere (Van Sittert, 2005). Human use of the great bodies of saltwater includes transportation, trade, fisheries and other use of marine life including the great whales, and extraction of resources. Some human communities actually live on the seas. Looking back through history, the seas were the place of origin of life, avenues for the peopling of islands, and the open ways for discovery, colonization, and slavery. They have tested and killed seafarers, and are the spawning grounds for storms by whatever names they are called: cyclones, typhoons, hurricanes. The project, History of Marine Animal Populations (http://www.hmapcoml.org), is surveying the variations and decline of species in the sea during past periods. Nations have claimed territories for economic use of the seas, and international negotiation has created laws of the sea. Dangers of pollution, over-fishing, extinctions and the destruction of coral reefs have raised concern around the world.

The international consensus on biodiversity raises several questions. It assumes that the other forms of life on earth are the property and under control of nation-states. It forbids interference in the way any nation chooses to protect or exploit the species within its borders. Yet national frontiers rarely coincide with ecosystems, and the welfare of life on the whole planet concerns everyone.

It is worth asking what effect living in a world of declining and disappearing species and diminishing ecosystems will be in the twenty-first century. Human beings coevolved along with other species within communities of life, but now those communities are losing their complexity as they shrink in area and relinquish many of the species that were members of them. It can be inferred that changes in relationships to other species are exerting evolutionary forces on the human species, and altering not only the quality of life, but human nature as well.

It is interesting to speculate what the response of the human species might be to this challenge. The challenge is serious because *Homo sapiens* is not immune to the threat of extinction through degradation of supporting ecosystems. A danger derives from the tendency to treat the natural world not as a series of ecosystems that include human beings, but as a set of resources and commodities separate from humankind. The subsidy the economy has been taking from wild nature may be near an end (Anderson et al., 1991) as the last wild places yield to the advance of tree farms, industrial agriculture, strip mines, power plants, and urban encroachment. Pollution carried by air and water to distant regions affects even protected wilderness. When most wild species are extinct or survive only in captivity, not a few people will feel lonely and less free.

Energy and Materials

The use of energy by human societies has been increasing substantially since the onset of the Industrial Revolution, but in the twentieth century an unprecedented exponential growth began and continues. The environmental history of energy use has been the story of the exploitation of a series of resources as technology granted access to them, one after another. The first industrial fuel was wood, including charcoal, a use that placed great demands on the forest resource. European governments, perceiving an incipient timber crisis due to fuel demands in the early modern period, enacted a series of laws intended to ensure the supply of timber for essential purposes such as naval construction. An example is the French Forest Ordinance of 1669, which turned forestry into a branch of the state-managed economy and restricted the production of charcoal (Williams, 2003).

The shift from wood, which is at least theoretically a renewable resource, to the non-renewable fossil fuels occurred in the industrialized nations during the second half of the nineteenth century. Perhaps that development provided the forests of Europe with a reprieve. Although pollution certainly worsened, it was ameliorated to some extent by use of coke, a form of coal processed to remove most of the volatile components. Coal became the dominant fuel for industry and transportation first in Europe and North America and then through much of the world, but with the invention of the internal combustion engine and its spread in the twentieth century, coal's primacy was challenged by petroleum and an associated resource, natural gas. These latter fossil fuels matched or exceeded the energy production of coal by the middle of the century. Historically, therefore, the modern world has seen a series of epochs each marked by the predominance of a different energy resource, first wood, then coal, and then petroleum and natural gas (McNeill, 2000). Musically, it might be described as a theme and variations. The last-named of these epochs continues today, but there are strong indications that it will not survive the twenty-first century, and that is a salient reason for its importance as a theme in environmental history as we consider the future.

The movement from one natural energy resource to another generally was dictated by considerations of technology, energy density, ease of use, and price, rather than supply of the resources or their possible exhaustion. There was, as we have noted, concern about the supply of wood and a potential timber famine in the early Industrial Revolution, but the switch to coal came before the forests reached a critical point of depletion. Forests are a renewable resource, and sustained yield is a theoretical possibility, but it would not have been possible to fuel the industries of the late nineteenth and twentieth centuries using only the wood produced by the natural rate of forest growth. That is, the use of wood as fuel was unsustainable, and the resource would have been exhausted without the shift to coal. Today we face the loss of forests, particularly in the tropics, for reasons other than fuel needs.

Coal presents another picture of supply. Most estimates of coal reserves indicate that they could be used at present rates, allowing for foreseeable increase, for centuries into the future. The probable effects on the composition of the atmosphere and the thermal regime are relevant considerations, but at least total supply is not a pressing issue. Petroleum and natural gas replaced coal for other reasons such as the internal combustion engine and its economic advantages.

Almost all economists who study the subject recognize limits to recoverable petroleum resources. Just what these limits are is unclear because the extent of undiscovered oil deposits can only be estimated, and technological improvements in the ability to recover oil from existing fields may occur. However, the looming danger is not exhaustion of the resource, but inability of production to satisfy demand to the extent that a sharp upward spiral of prices will result. Disagreement exists as to the time frame within which this will happen, with estimates varying between the idea that the present rise in oil prices is the beginning of just such a crisis, and the assumption that ways will be found to increase production until alternate sources of energy can help meet demand. Probably the present consensus is that a peak of conventional oil extraction, with a rise in prices to unacceptable levels, will take place between 2020 and 2050. Vaclav Smil perceptively notes, however, that resource costs exist not just in monetary terms:

> Resource exhaustion is not a matter of actual physical depletion but rather one of eventually unacceptable costs, and the latter designation may now mean not just in an economic sense (too expensive to recover or to deliver to a distant market) but also in environmental (causing excessive pollution or unacceptable ecosystemic destruction or degradation) and social terms (where their recovery would necessitate displacement of a large number of people, or bring serious health problems). (Smil, 2003, p. 181)

It would be the worst sort of irresponsibility to fail to plan for a shift away from petroleum as the primary energy resource within the next few decades.

Another source of energy that expanded in the twentieth century was hydroelectric. Water power in a kinetic sense had been used since ancient times, but the construction of large dams using water to turn electric power generators came into its own only after 1900. Hydroelectric power is in one sense renewable, since it can be used as long as river flow continues, but it is limited in that there exist a finite number of practical dam-sites. It has the advantage of producing relatively little pollution. The United States created a Bureau of Reclamation in 1902, and began an aggressive program of large dam building marked by megaprojects such as Hoover Dam (1936) and Grand Coulee Dam (1941). Much of the rest of the world followed suit, and during the 1960s and 1970s about 5,000 new dams were built per decade worldwide. In that period Egypt constructed the Aswan High Dam, which has been a mixed blessing environmentally, and strategically hangs like a sword of Damocles over the whole nation. Since then the rate has decreased, but countries such as China and India continue to regard monumental dams as a source of national pride in spite of the fact that they have effects that are harmful to the environment, involve moving many thousands of people from their homes and farms, and are often dubious from a properly considered economic standpoint. Hydropower generates about 20% of the world's electricity today, but its future expansion is limited, especially in regions like North America, where most appropriate sites have been occupied, along with some inappropriate ones. It will not be the resource that replaces oil.

Nuclear power generation was thought to be the energy source of the future after its use to generate electricity was experimentally demonstrated in 1951, and the first nuclear power plants began operating soon afterwards. Growth in generating capacity and number of plants was extremely rapid during the next three decades. By 1987, 417 plants were in operation in 27 nations, generating 17% of the world's electricity, with 120 additional units planned (Nisbet, 1991). This was achieved not because of any economic efficiency of the new power source, but due to massive government subsidies. The United States had the largest number of operating reactors and the largest generating capacity, but France could be described as the nation most enthusiastic about nuclear power, which provided 77% of the electricity in that nation by 1996. Others with extensive development included Russia, Japan, Germany, Canada, and the UK. Although the actual production of electricity by a nuclear plant is almost free of chemical pollution, it does produce large amounts of thermal pollution. But the inescapable problem of nuclear power generation is radioactivity. Spent nuclear fuel continues to be radioactive at various levels, and some radioisotopes have exceptionally long half-lives that will keep them dangerous for thousands of years. What can be done with the wastes? They have been stored on-site, injected through wells into deep rock formations, dumped in containers onto the sea floor, and placed in salt mines or other underground chambers. All of these methods are in some ways unsatisfactory. But the most threatening factor is release of radioactive materials into the atmosphere by explosions. This had, of course, occurred through use of nuclear weapons and weapons tests, and weapons-related nuclear accidents such as those at Windscale in the UK (1957) and Kyshtym in the USSR (1958), along with many other catastrophes including fires at the Rocky Flats nuclear weapons facility in Colorado, US. But an accidental meltdown at the Three Mile Island plant in the US (1979), which released a relatively small amount of radioactivity, alerted the world to the possibility of disaster connected with nuclear power. Then on 26 April 1986 a reactor core at the Chernobyl plant in the Soviet Union exploded, injecting 50 tons of nuclear fuel into the atmosphere as dispersed particles, in addition to 70 tons of other fuel and 700 tons of radioactive graphite that settled nearer the site of the accident. Thirty-one rescue workers died, along with unknown numbers of those exposed to fallout, which continues to claim victims to the present day. Fallout was detected in Europe, and throughout the Northern Hemisphere in lesser amounts. Chernobyl changed the public perception of nuclear power throughout the world, and in North America and most of Europe plans for more plants were cancelled. The growth of this form of energy stopped abruptly, except in France and Belgium. Nuclear power did not replace fossil fuels in the way that fossil fuels had replaced wood. But barring another horrendous accident, it is likely that a new expansion of nuclear energy will be advocated, and may well occur, in the face of a likely oil crisis.

A number of alternative sources of energy have been developed and may have potential in easing the coming transition away from oil, although none of them as yet provides more than a minuscule percentage of the world's energy needs. These include wind energy, solar energy through photovoltaic cells, geothermal energy, tidal turbines, and hydrogen fuel cells. All of them should be investigated for technological improvement and economic viability. Some are limited in geographic availability, of course. Geothermal development can only take place along tectonic boundaries, and solar energy is not available in the near-polar winters. Another perspective that will need renewed attention is that of energy conservation and efficiency. All these will help, but none as yet offers the promise of a new energy regime that will fulfill the demands of an increasing population without imposing unacceptable costs on the Earth's living systems.

Concluding Thoughts

The human species is at a turning point. If the cultural attitudes of the modern industrial age remain the determiners of actions in regard to ecosystems, while the population continues to increase, an unprecedented crisis of survival is certain in this new century. Recently Lester Brown urged a paradigm shift as radical as the Copernican Revolution, which was the acceptance of the idea that it is the Earth that revolves around the sun, rather than the sun around the Earth. 'Today we're faced with a somewhat similar situation', he writes, 'The question is whether the economy ... is part of the environment or whether the environment is part of the economy ... Most economists, and I think business leaders, would think of the environment as being a subsector of the economy' (Brown, 2001, p. 224). But Brown argues that the reverse is true: those who conduct the economy must recognize limits set by the ecosystem or face the consequences. Students of history know that such major paradigm shifts have occurred before. Humankind is subject to change as a result of the impact of a rapidly diminishing biosphere. Our culture is malleable, and will alter in unpredictable ways. Our thoughts and words shift from day to day. Even our genome is changing.

It is interesting to speculate what kinds of changes might reflect an adaptation of humankind to the threatened loss of species and communities. One would be a fall in the birth rate to or below the replacement level. The worldwide trend is moving in that direction, but not rapidly enough to avert a crisis. Ecologically sustainable agriculture and a forestry that assures the survival of the forest community are absolutely necessary, or we will lose these essential renewable systems. A widespread encouragement of a revival of local communities that take responsibility for protecting their own ecosystems would be one of the most positive efforts the environmental movement could make. More pressure on governments by movements opposing the destruction of nature, like India's Chipko, would be a positive sign. Preservation of examples of undisturbed ecosystems in biosphere reserves would provide some refugia for biodiversity and aid in the restoration of other areas. The Bruntland Report of 1987 advocated that 12% of the Earth's land surface should be set aside in this way. One of the most effective trends would be wider education of children and adults in the facts of ecological and reproductive responsibility. Without this element, it is difficult to predict any major positive trends on the social level. We must learn to think of ourselves not only as humans, but also as forms of Life, since that is what we are. As Edward Wilson put it, 'We are in the fullest sense a biological species and will find little ultimate meaning apart from the remainder of life' (Wilson, 1984, p. 81). It is the community of life itself, in its many forms, and not humankind alone, on which we depend, that made us what we are, and that we must in turn foster and protect.

As an observer of human behavior within the natural setting in the past, which is what an environmental historian must be, I cannot expect all these positive trends to appear at once. I cannot even expect all of them to succeed once they do appear. What I do expect is that environmental movements will gain strength as problems manifest themselves ever more urgently. In his newest book, *The Future of Life*, E. O. Wilson sees humankind in the twenty-first century passing through a bottleneck of population and resource use, and believes that we will not get through without great losses, including the extinction of hundreds of species (Wilson, 2002). I agree with him, and fear a threatening diminuendo. But I am also aware, as he is, that humanity when challenged is capable of consciousness and creativity. I expect dissonance in the new century, but I also expect that contemporary composers will find a way to use it as the base of a new music.

References

Anderson, A. B., May, P. H. & Balick, M. J. (1991) *The Subsidy from Nature: Palm Forests, Peasantry, and Development on an Amazon Frontier* (New York: Columbia University Press).

Bowlus, C. R. (1980) Ecological crises in fourteenth century Europe, in Bilsky, L. J. (ed.) *Historical Ecology: Essays on Environment and Social Change* (Port Washington, NY: Kennikat Press, National University Publications).

Brown, L. (2001) *Eco-Economy: Building a New Economy for the Environmental Age* (New York: W. W. Norton).

Buchy, M. (1993) Quest for a sustainable forest management: a study of the working plans of North Canara District (1890–1945), pp. 141–162 in Rawat, A. S. (ed.) *Indian Forestry: A Perspective* (New Delhi: Indus Publishing Company).

Cohen, J. E. (1995) *How Many People Can the Earth Support?* (New York: W. W. Norton & Co.).

Copland, A. (1957) *What to Listen for in Music* (New York: Signet Classic).

Crosby, A. W., Jr. (1972) *The Columbian Exchange: Biological and Cultural Consequences of 1492* (Westport, CT: Greenwood Press).
Crosby, A. W., Jr. (1986) *Ecological Imperialism: The Biological Expansion of Europe, 900–1900* (Cambridge: Cambridge University Press).
Ehrlich, P. & Ehrlich, A. (1981) *Extinction: The Causes and Consequences of the Disappearance of Species* (New York: Random House).
Elvin, M. (2004) *The Retreat of the Elephants: An Environmental History of China* (New Haven: Yale University Press).
Elvin, M. & Liu Tsui-jung (eds) (1998) *Sediments of Time: Environment and Society in Chinese History* (Cambridge: Cambridge University Press).
Gadgil, M. & Chandran, M. D. S. (1988) On the history of Uttara Kannada forests, pp. 47–58 in Dargavel, J., Dixon, K. & Semple, N. (eds) *Changing Tropical Forests: Historical Perspectives on Today's Challenges in Asia, Australasia and Oceania* (Canberra: Centre for Resource and Environmental Studies).
Gadgil, M. & Guha, R. (1993) *This Fissured Land: An Ecological History of India* (Berkeley & Los Angeles: University of California Press).
Goodall, J. (1999) *Reason for Hope: A Spiritual Journey* (New York: Warner Books).
Hardin, G. (1968) The tragedy of the commons, *Science*, 162 (13 December), pp. 1243–1248.
Hughes, J. D. (1994) *Pan's Travail: Environmental Problems of the Ancient Greeks and Romans* (Baltimore, MD: Johns Hopkins University Press).
Hughes, J. D. (2001) *An Environmental History of the World: Humankind's Changing Role in the Community of Life* (London: Routledge).
Kenwood, A. G. & Lougheed, A. L. (1971) *The Growth of the International Economy, 1820–1960* (London: George Allen & Unwin).
Kissinger, H. (2001) *Does America Need a Foreign Policy?* (New York: Simon & Schuster).
Lieber, R. J. (2001) *Eagle Rules? Foreign Policy and American Primacy in the Twenty-First Century* (New York: Prentice-Hall).
Lonsdale, S. (1981) *Animals and the Origin of Dance* (London: Thames & Hudson).
McCormick, J. (1989) *Reclaiming Paradise: The Global Environmental Movement* (Bloomington, IN: Indiana University Press).
McDaniel, C. N. & Gowdy, J. M. (2000) *Paradise for Sale: A Parable of Nature* (Berkeley & Los Angeles: University of California Press).
McNeill, J. R. (2000) *Something New Under the Sun: An Environmental History of the Twentieth-Century World.* (New York: W. W. Norton).
McNeill, J. R. (2004) Population, human, in Krech, S., III, McNeill, J. R. & Merchant, C. (eds) *Encyclopedia of World Environmental History* (New York & London: Routledge).
Meadows, D. H., Meadows, D. L., Randers, J. & Behrens, W. W., III (1972) *The Limits to Growth* (New York: Universe Books).
Meadows, D. H., Meadows, D. L. & Randers, J. (1992) *Beyond the Limits: Confronting Global Collapse and Envisioning a Sustainable Future* (Post Mills, VT: Chelsea Green Publishing).
Phillips, K. (1994) *Tracking the Vanishing Frogs: An Ecological Mystery* (New York: St. Martin's Press).
Reisman, S. (1996) The birth of a world trading system: ITO and GATT, pp. 82–89 in Kirshner, O. (ed.) *The Bretton Woods–GATT System: Retrospect and Prospect After Fifty Years* (Armonk, NY: M. E. Sharpe).
Schoijet, M. (1999) Limits to growth and the rise of catastrophism, *Environmental History*, 4(4), pp. 515–530.
Shiva, V. (1989) *Staying Alive: Women, Ecology and Development* (London: Zed Books).
Smil, V. (2003) *Energy at the Crossroads: Global Perspectives and Uncertainties* (Cambridge, MA: MIT Press).
Soroos, M. S. (1999) Global institutions and the environment: an evolutionary perspective, pp. 27–51 in Vig, N. J. & Axelrod, R. S. (eds) *The Global Environment: Institutions, Law, and Policy* (Washington, DC: Congressional Quarterly Press).
Van Sittert, L. (2005) The other seven tenths, *Environmental History*, 10(1), pp. 106–109.
Verney, P. (1979) *Animals in Peril* (Provo, UT: Brigham Young University Press).
Wheelwright, P. (1966) *The Presocratics* (New York: Odyssey Press).
Williams, M. (2003) *Deforesting the Earth: From Prehistory to Global Crisis* (Chicago, IL: University of Chicago Press).
Wilson, E. O. (1984) *Biophilia* (Cambridge, MA: Harvard University Press).
Wilson, E. O. (1992) *The Diversity of Life* (Cambridge, MA: Harvard University Press).
Wilson, E. O. (2002) *The Future of Life* (New York: Alfred A. Knopf).
Worster, D. (1993) *The Wealth of Nature* (Oxford: Oxford University Press).

J. Donald Hughes is John Evans Distinguished Professor in the Department of History at the University of Denver. A founding member of the American Society for Environmental History and of the European Society for Environmental History, he is a past editor of the journal *Environmental History* (then titled *Environmental Review*). His published works include *Pan's Travail: Environmental Problems of the Ancient Greeks and Romans* (Johns Hopkins, 1994), *An Environmental History of the World: Humankind's Changing Role in the Community of Life* (Routledge, 2001) and *The Mediterranean: An Environmental History* (ABC-CLIO, 2005).

Seeking Justice: International Environmental Governance and Climate Change

JOUNI PAAVOLA

Introduction

International environmental conferences, international governmental organizations, multilateral environmental agreements, and international environmental non-governmental organizations are all aspects of political globalization in environmental matters. They form a system of international environmental governance for environmental resources of global importance from the high seas to the Antarctic and to the key environmental resources providing life support services such as the atmospheric ozone layer, global atmospheric sinks and biodiversity. Some also call these international structures and organizations 'the world environmental regime' (Meyer et al., 1997).

There are many interpretations of political globalization in environmental matters. Realist scholars consider it a recent phenomenon, set in motion by increasing environmental degradation and depletion of natural resources. For this line of reasoning, nation-states greened first and then started acting collectively to resolve shared environmental problems. Institutional scholars have pointed out that international cooperation has long roots although the thickening of international environmental regimes quickened after the Second World War. World systems scholars have argued that political globalization has preceded and been the driver of national environmental management (Frank, 1997; Frank et al., 2000). They and constructivists have also suggested that environmental science has fostered international environmental governance by generating shared rationalizations of environmental problems (Meyer et al., 1997). Analyses of outcomes of political globalization are similarly diverse. For realists, international environmental regimes are temporary and mostly ineffective alliances of convenience. On the other side of the spectrum, political globalization—which is often accompanied by localization as the term 'glocalization' indicates—is seen as an indication of the decreasing role or the 'hollowing out' of the state (Rhodes, 1994) in environmental matters. Institutionalists in turn see that multi-level solutions of international environmental governance preserve an important role for the states.

This article acknowledges that political globalization has complex causation *and* varied outcomes, which may differ from one area of environmental governance to another. The article asks how political globalization and the emergence of international environmental governance solutions relate to social justice in environmental matters. Social justice aspects of international environmental governance have not received due attention because the dominant traditions in international relations are not well equipped to shed light on them. The article indicates how this results from the way in which they define and understand international environmental governance. The article argues that international environmental governance is best understood as the resolution of environmental conflicts through the establishment, change or reaffirmation of environmental governance institutions (Adger et al., 2003). This definition highlights the role of social justice in environmental governance. The article suggests that social justice in international environmental governance should be understood broadly, so as to encompass distributive and procedural justice in the society of states and in cross-level interactions between the states and non-state actors.

The article examines social justice in the governance of adaptation to climate change in greater detail, arguing that the climate change regime does not address the key issue of distributive justice—the responsibility of developed countries for the impacts of their greenhouse gas emissions. These emissions cause climate change impacts that burden vulnerable people in developing countries who have not contributed to climate change and have little capacity to deal with it. The climate change regime makes a commitment to assisting developing countries but it is not a substitute for responsibility. The climate change regime also addresses issues of procedural justice among the states and in cross-level linkages. Still, it does not enable equal participation of all countries or fair participation of affected parties across levels of governance. The article suggests that responsibility could be operationalized by adopting a carbon tax replenishing a compensation and assistance fund and that a cross-level grievance procedure would address procedural justice deficiencies.

Emerging International Environmental Governance

The emergence of international environmental governance is often attributed to the late 1960s and the early 1970s, particularly to the UNESCO's Biosphere Conference in 1968 and the

United Nations Conference on the Human Environment held in Stockholm in 1972 (Caldwell, 1996). The aftermath of these two conferences did indeed witness a flurry of activity related to international environmental governance, such as the negotiation of multilateral environmental agreements and the establishment of the Man and Biosphere Program and the United Nations Environment Programme (UNEP). But international environmental governance has longer roots that extend to the early twentieth century. Over a quarter of multilateral environmental agreements that were negotiated by 2004 date from before 1970 (Mitchell, 2003).[1] Pre-Stockholm MEAs include agreements on whaling, the Antarctic, high seas, fisheries, water pollution, nuclear safety, water power and transboundary bodies of water, and control of pests and weeds.[2]

A common explanation for the emergence of international environmental governance is that it reflects growing environmental degradation and resource depletion (Mitchell, 2002) or post-materialist concerns for the environment (Inglehart, 1995). For this line of reasoning, environmental change or a change in values first results in the adoption of domestic environmental measures. The greening of nation-states can then be followed by collective action between the states when they consider this to be in their interests (Sprinz & Vaahtoranta, 1994). From this viewpoint, international environmental governance reflects changing state interests in a particular time and context.

Institutionalists recognize that interdependent states cannot realize their environmental interests on their own (Mitchell, 2002). This is why international environmental regimes are needed: they are 'the rules of the game' that complement national environmental policies and facilitate the management of trans-boundary environmental resources (Roberts et al., 2004; Vogler, 2003). Institutionalists also acknowledge that states act collectively in the context of significant transaction costs which prevent the attainment of 'optimal institutional solutions'.

Constructivists and world systems scholars hold that shared worldviews or discourses underpin international collective action on the environment. They (Haas, 1992; Meyer et al., 1997) highlight that shared scientific lenses have facilitated research on, and policy responses to, many environmental problems. For example, global environmental change scholarship constructs many environmental problems as pertaining to large-scale if not global environmental systems (Schellnhuber & Held, 2002; Steffen et al., 2004; Vitousek et al., 1997). The global scale of environmental problems is seen to warrant global environmental solutions, which results in 'globalism' in environmental matters.

All of the approaches discussed above shed light on aspects of international environmental governance. States *are* the main players in international relations as realists argue and can often override concerns other than their own. For institutionalists, this is an institutionally generated outcome, not an ontological necessity: the current international institutional framework structures collective environmental decision-making so as to give a central role to the states, a situation which is slowly changing (Raustiala, 1997; Wapner, 2002). But rational choice institutionalism has narrow cognitive, motivational and behavioural assumptions which fail to capture many challenges of international collective action (Roberts et al., 2004). Constructivism and world systems scholarship highlight how social constructions of environmental problems vary from one problem context (or period) to another and matter to the capacity to act collectively (Meyer et al., 1997; Roberts et al., 2004).

Ways to understand international environmental governance are important because they influence how its social justice dimensions are perceived. The realist tradition understands international environmental governance solutions as outcomes of voluntary collective action in the 'society of states'. This conception gives limited scope for justice in international environmental governance: rationally acting sovereign states would not consent to agreements that are not in their interest. Moreover, if agreed-upon governance solutions have justice implications, they are limited to justice between the states (Kapstein, 2004). While the institutional tradition focuses 'on the overlapping networks of inter-state regimes on environmental issues' (Paterson et al., 2003, p. 4), it need not be state-centred like realism: it can acknowledge the role of non-state players (Vogler, 2003). Moreover, it can (but does not often) treat institutional choice as an issue of social justice because institutional solutions distribute benefits and costs among participants in different ways. Constructivism can award an even more important role for non-state actors, while the world systems scholars remind us that the agency of state and non-state actors has important structural and other constraints.

I suggest that defining environmental governance as the resolution of environmental conflicts best highlights its social justice aspects (Adger et al., 2003; Paavola & Adger, 2005a; O. R. Young, 1994: 15). Environmental conflicts have their origin in the attributes of environmental resources and the attributes of actors interested in and affected by their use. Environmental conflicts are resolved by the establishment, reaffirmation or change of governance institutions, which include for example informal local arrangements such as common property, formal national environmental and natural resource use policies, and international environmental regimes. This conception highlights that international environmental governance solutions perform the same governance functions, albeit at a larger scale, as other solutions (Paavola, forthcoming). Governance functions include the sharing of beneficial and adverse consequences and the organization of collective choices which are both intimately intertwined with social justice (ibid.). In what follows, I will look in greater detail at the social justice aspects of environmental governance.

Global Environmental Governance and Social Justice

Although some consider international justice a moot question (Armstrong, 1999; Welch, 2000, p. 3), in reality a number of justice issues are involved in international environmental governance (Dower, 1998; Kapstein, 2004). Even conventional scholarship in international affairs recognizes that there are matters of justice in the 'society of states'. For example, game theoretic reasoning suggests that in heterogeneous groups those that most depend on the attainment of new institutional solutions may have to forgo benefits to make side payments or concessions to states which would not cooperate otherwise. Choosing a point along the contract curve is a matter of distributive justice rather than of efficiency.

But, more importantly, states do not represent the interests of their citizens equally. Therefore, state consent to international agreements does not guarantee the absence of negative impacts (of either environmental change or response measures) on some of its citizens. In the same vein, states may not consent to agreements that would be in the best interests of their citizens. To put it differently, the realist tradition affirms a particular notion of communitarianism: that of nationalism (Attfield, 2005). The opposing cosmopolitan argument is that individuals do have rights—for example human rights—which are not limited by the borders of the state where they reside (Cochran, 1999, p. 21). This means that international environmental governance has another justice dimension: justice in cross-level interactions between states and non-state actors such as individuals and their communities and organizations (Figure 1).

From another viewpoint, social justice should be understood broadly so as to encompass both distributive and procedural justice (Paavola, 2005; Paavola & Adger, 2005b, Figure 1). Distributive justice relates to the incidence of beneficial and adverse consequences of a decision or an action (Kolm, 1996; H. P. Young, 1994). Procedural justice relates to the way in which

	Distributive justice	**Procedural justice**
Society of States	• Incidence of beneficial and adverse consequences between the states • Arrangements to (re)distribute burdens and benefits between states	• De jure and de facto capacity of the states to participate in environmental planning and decision-making
Cross-Level Interactions	• Incidence of beneficial and adverse consequences between states and non-state actors • Arrangements to (re)distribute burdens and benefits between states and non-state actors	• De jure and de facto capacity of non-state actors such as individuals, communities, and organisations to participate in environmental planning and decision-making

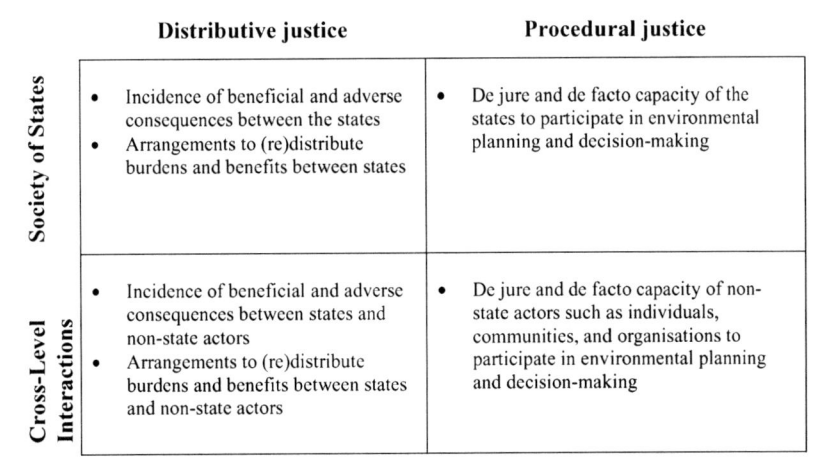

Figure 1. Social justice in international environmental governance

parties are positioned vis-à-vis the processes of planning or decision-making (Fraser, 2001; Tyler et al., 1997). Distributive and procedural justice considerations are relevant both within a generation and between generations. However, I will limit my discussion here to intra-generational justice.

In the area of distributive justice, decisions on governance institutions resolve whose interests in environmental resources are realized and what is the incidence of beneficial and adverse consequences. These decisions are often informed by traditional equity rules such as Aristotle's contributory principle of 'just deserts', Bentham's rule of greatest happiness for the greatest numbers, Rawls' maximin rule, 'no envy', or equality of opportunity, resources or welfare (Sen, 1992, pp. 12–30; H. P. Young, 1994, pp. 9–13). These rules are frequently applied as if the distribution of some overarching good such as 'utility' or 'welfare' could resolve all distributive dilemmas. This would require commensuration of goods and bads and allow compensating one bad with another kind of good. For example, some consider adequate compensation to resolve unequal incidence of environmental degradation and hazards.

However, it is not at all obvious that this line of reasoning should be accepted. For example, cosmopolitan theories can extend human rights to several non-commensurated aspects of the environment, such as absence of environmental hazards, healthy environment, and access to environmental amenities. Other social justice theorists have argued that justice is specific to particular communities or that rules of justice are tentative and likely to vary across issues and contexts (Bell, 1993; Radin, 1996). Walzer's (1983) notion of complex equality in turn requires the absence of domination by one group across 'spheres of justice'. For example, it could be argued that vital interests in health and safety should be considered distinct from those related to levels of income, and to occupy their own sphere. Justice would demand the protection of these interests to avoid repeating the injustice of income and wealth distribution. But even if the existence of spheres of justice is acknowledged, it remains difficult to agree on distributive justice when the values, goals, resources, interests and positions of actors are heterogeneous—a commonplace in global environmental politics. The difficulty of reaching agreement on distributive justice in the context of heterogeneity means that the legitimacy of environmental decisions must rest at least in part on procedural justice (Paavola, 2005).

Procedural justice is important for legitimacy because fair procedures can assure those whose interests are not endorsed by a particular environmental plan or decision that their interests can count in other plans and decisions. It also enables affected parties to express their dissent or consent and to maintain their dignity (Schlosberg, 1999, pp. 12–13, 90; Soyinka, 2004). Procedural justice encompasses issues such as recognition, participation and distribution of power in environmental planning, decision-making and governance (Lind & Tyler, 1988; Fraser, 2001; Schlosberg, 1999; Shrader-Frechette, 2002).

Recognition is the foundation of procedural justice (Fraser, 2001) but it can take forms which do not involve participation. For example, President Clinton's Executive Order 12898 required federal agencies to identify and address the consequences of their programmes, policies and actions to minority and low-income populations (Paavola, in press). The climate change regime has in turn established guidelines for the preparation of National Adaptation Plans of Action (NAPAs) which require public consultation in the setting of national adaptation priorities. Guidelines like these can recognize and make the consideration of certain groups' interests an integral part of planning and decision-making processes.

Participation requires recognition but can again take many forms from simply hearing affected parties to giving them power in decision-making. Public participation should be understood to encompass: 1) participation in environmental policy and law making; 2) rights to information and to be heard in environmental policy and law making; 3) access to environmental justice, including access to remedies to environmental harms and to breaches of environmental regulations, and; 4) right of individuals to a general review of a government's performance in enforcing environmental laws (Fitzmaurice, 2003, p. 339). In international environmental governance, each of these aspects of public participation presents issues related to rights at the national level of environmental decision-making within one's own country, rights at the national level of environmental decision-making in another country, and rights at the international level (ibid.).

The solutions for recognition and participation, together with political-economic factors of a distributive nature, generate a particular *distribution of power*. The relative power of involved parties determines to what extent they can make their interests count in environmental planning, decision-making and governance. This highlights that distributive and procedural justice are tied together in practice despite being separate fields of scholarship. Distributive outcomes influence recognition, participation and power in different spheres of action. Recognition, participation and distribution of power in turn influence plans and decisions, including their distributive implications.

To summarize, legitimate environmental decisions have to reflect both distributive and procedural justice concerns. In the context of the pluralism that prevails in the global community, distributive justice matters in the broad sense of whose interests and values will be realized by the establishment, change or affirmation of environmental governance institutions. Often there are multiple governance goals and this may require different governance solutions for the achievement of different goals. Yet dilemmas of distributive justice will remain difficult to resolve to everybody's satisfaction. Therefore, procedural justice plays an important role in justifying decisions to those whose interests and values are sacrificed to realize some other interests and values.

Thus all international environmental regimes address social justice issues related to their area of jurisdiction. Distributive justice is often at the heart of international environmental regimes as the intense debates on how to share the burden of mitigating emissions of greenhouse gases under the UN Framework Convention on Climate Change indicate. But procedural justice is also important. This is underlined by the gradual evolution of international institutional solutions that address issues of procedural justice. These include the Vienna Convention on the

Law of Treaties (1969) and the more recent Aarhus Convention on Access to Information, Public Participation in Decision-Making and Access to Justice in Environmental Matters (1998). Comparable international institutional solutions have not emerged for distributive justice. In what follows, I will examine social justice issues related to the governance of adaptation to climate change, with an emphasis on procedural justice.

Climate Change and Adaptation

Adaptation to climate change forms the less debated half of the climate change problem. There will be a need to adapt to changing climate because there is no foreseeable way to prevent climate from changing for the generations to come. Even the most optimistic mitigation scenarios accept the nearly doubling of atmospheric CO_2 concentration from its pre-industrial level in the coming decades. Despite not being considered to cause 'dangerous interference with the climate system', these CO_2 concentrations are high enough to cause changed weather patterns and more frequent and severe floods, droughts, heat waves and storms which will be particularly problematic for the small island states and the least developed countries but which will also be felt across the globe (Adger et al., 2006).

Different impacts of current climate variability indicate that climate change will particularly affect vulnerable populations. Recent heat waves in the US and Europe have caused excess deaths mainly among the elderly and those with pre-existing health problems (Klinenberg, 2002; Schär & Jendritzky, 2004). In developing countries, weather-related disasters can cost up to a quarter of GDP (Guranko, 2003) and cause thousands of premature deaths. Hurricane Mitch in Honduras in 1998, the hurricanes of 2004 in Haiti and the Caribbean, and severe flooding in Mozambique in 2000 and Bangladesh in 2004 are examples of events of this kind. Uninsured economic losses of extreme weather events fall on poor and vulnerable households who are dependent on risky agriculture and other natural resource based livelihoods. Across the world, vulnerable groups have no other option but to adapt to climate changes to which they have not contributed.

Adaptation will consist of uncoordinated actions of households, firms and organizations; collective action at the local, national and international levels; and interactions between these levels. It will encompass public policies, public and private burden sharing arrangements, provision of public goods, public and private investments and behavioural changes. *Proactive responses* involve anticipation and planning so as to best deal with climate change impacts. *Reactive responses*, such as the rebuilding of infrastructure after flood damage, are taken after climate change impacts are realized. Proactive and reactive responses frequently complement each other. For example, the building of additional water storage capacity complements and facilitates rationing of water. Yet proactive and reactive measures will not result in perfect adaptation: some *residual impacts* are inevitable.

Institutional framework for the governance of adaptation is still largely in the making. It will partly consist of international environmental law, including the UN Framework Convention for Climate Change (UNFCCC), the Kyoto Protocol (KP), and the decisions of the Conferences of the Parties (COPs) (Melkas, 2002; Verheyen, 2002). Other international law, including the Vienna Convention on the Law of Treaties (1969) and international custom is also relevant for the governance of adaptation. However, adaptation will be governed by a multi-level solution where key decisions and guidelines are established at the international level while many governance functions such as adaptation planning and implementation of adaptation measures will be undertaken at national or sub-national levels. Thus the governance of adaptation will rest to a significant degree on national legislation, on both already existing and new legislation responding to international initiatives.

All decisions and actions related to adaptation to climate change, including omissions to act, have social justice implications. Adaptation decisions and measures have distributive justice implications because they generate a particular incidence of benefits and costs (broadly conceived so as to include both monetary and non-monetary impacts) and because they determine the magnitude and distribution of residual climate change impacts. Similarly, the decision-making procedures for choosing adaptation measures have procedural justice implications. I have argued elsewhere (Paavola & Adger, 2005b) that the four main social justice issues involved in adaptation to climate change include:

- What is the responsibility of developed countries for climate change impacts caused by their greenhouse gas emissions?
- How much assistance developed countries should make available for developing countries and how should developed countries share the burden of assistance?[3]
- How should assistance be distributed between recipient countries and adaptive measures?
- How should planning and decisions regarding adaptation be made at different levels?

These four dilemmas encompass the four fields of justice in international environmental governance that were discussed in section three. The responsibility for climate change impacts is primarily a cross-level distributive justice issue prevailing between developed countries and households, communities and organizations that are harmed by climate change impacts, although it also involves distributive justice between the states (see Figure 2). Assistance for adaptation is an issue of distributive justice both among the states and between states and non-state actors. Finally, adaptation planning and decisions present procedural justice issues both among the states and between states and non-state actors. To date, the climate change regime has addressed these issues unevenly.

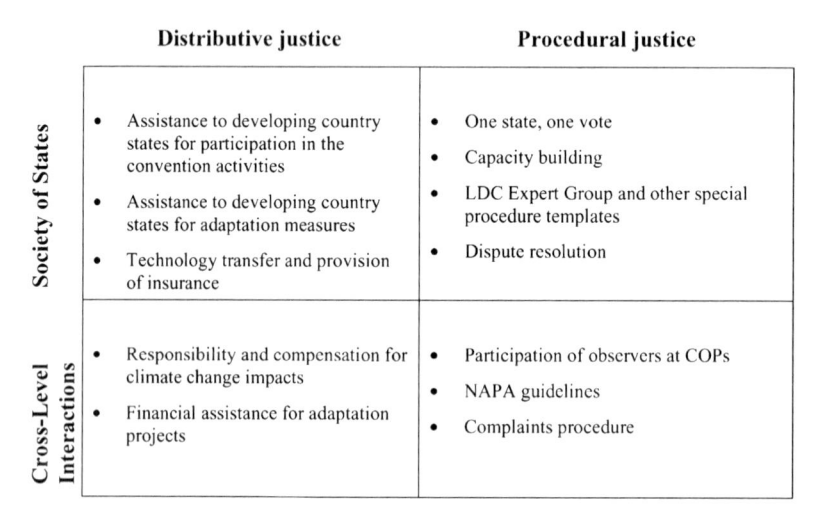

	Distributive justice	Procedural justice
Society of States	- Assistance to developing country states for participation in the convention activities - Assistance to developing country states for adaptation measures - Technology transfer and provision of insurance	- One state, one vote - Capacity building - LDC Expert Group and other special procedure templates - Dispute resolution
Cross-Level Interactions	- Responsibility and compensation for climate change impacts - Financial assistance for adaptation projects	- Participation of observers at COPs - NAPA guidelines - Complaints procedure

Figure 2. Justice in adaptation to climate change

Distributive Justice between the States

Paragraph 3, Article 4 of the Convention commits developed countries to cover the costs of developing countries in meeting their obligations under the Convention. These obligations include the preparation of national inventories of sources and sinks of greenhouse gases; technology needs assessments; national vulnerability, impacts and adaptations assessments; and the preparation of national communications. Financial assistance for these activities has been provided through the Global Environmental Facility (FCCC/CP/2001/8; FCCC/CP/1998/12/Add.1). Paragraph 4 of Article 4 also commits developed countries to assist particularly vulnerable developing countries in adaptation. The Convention process has established the Adaptation Fund, the Special Climate Change Fund and the Least Developed Countries Fund (Dessai & Schipper, 2003) to assist developing countries. However, raising and distribution of assistance funds have not been operationalized. The Convention also calls for transfer of technology and provision of insurance, the latter of which has been neglected. To summarize, the Convention makes commitments regarding distributive justice between the states which have not been fulfilled. This could prove an obstacle in future international negotiations on the participation of developing country parties in mitigation of climate change.

Cross-Level Distributive Justice

Assistance for adaptation has a cross-level dimension—individuals, organizations and communities can have legitimate claims to assistance for adaptation independently of their governments' claims. Pilot projects of this kind have received GEF funding and are likely to form one strand of assistance in the future. However, rules regarding the availability and distribution of this assistance do not yet exist. But the most significant issue of cross-level distributive justice is the responsibility of developed countries for the impacts of their greenhouse gas emissions. Responsibility should be considered primarily a cross-level issue because climate change impacts will be experienced by households, communities, firms and other organizations, although it is also an issue of distributive justice between the states. The Convention has not addressed responsibility satisfactorily. In fact, the only provision that relates to responsibility is the goal of the Convention contained in Article 2: it suggests that greenhouse gas concentrations in the atmosphere should be limited to a level which does not pose danger to the ability of natural systems, food production systems and economic systems to adapt.

I have argued elsewhere (Paavola & Adger, 2005b) that responsibility for greenhouse gas emissions could be institutionalized by agreeing a uniform carbon tax under the Convention process and by implementing it through national legislation. Further social justice concerns could be included by setting a tax-free per capita quota, for example a half of the global per capita carbon consumption. This would place the tax burden largely on the now already developed countries but also extend it to other countries when they become significant per capita greenhouse gas emitters. Carbon tax revenue should be used for compensating the impacts of climate change and for assisting adaptation to climate change. This tax system would, besides addressing social justice in adaptation to climate change, provide incentives for efficient choices in both mitigation and adaptation. The tax would encourage the adoption of all efficient abatement solutions, thereby decreasing greenhouse gas emissions, climate change impacts, and tax burden. A combined compensation and assistance fund would also give incentives for proactive adaptation, reducing the need to compensate for residual impacts yet maintaining the availability of funds for it.

Procedural Justice between the States

The Vienna Convention of the Law of Treaties (1969) and international custom treat parties to international agreements such as the UNFCCC as formally equal sovereign nations. However, developing countries do not have the same possibilities to participate in international negotiations and actions on climate change as developed countries have. Developing countries have less capacity to support their delegations, the small size of their delegations makes participation in simultaneous meetings impossible, and the use of English as the working language in less formal meetings is an impediment to many negotiators (Gupta, 2002; Mwandosya, 1999). Assistance to developing countries for participation in the Convention activities aims to address these issues. The Convention also contains provisions for capacity building and for institutional solutions such as the Least Developed Countries Expert Group to address procedural justice issues. Yet these measures are modest in the face of the difficulties the heterogeneous group of developing countries face in international climate change negotiations and actions.

Cross-Level Procedural Justice

While the Convention has sought to address procedural justice issues among the states, it has paid less attention to cross-level procedural justice. This is partly an indication that the governance framework of adaptation is not yet complete. Yet cross-level procedural justice merits attention because the effectiveness and legitimacy of adaptation measures will depend on it. The Convention has granted limited participation to non-state actors as observers in the Conferences of the Parties. The Convention process has also established guidelines for the preparation of National Adaptation Plans of Action (NAPAs) which require multidisciplinarity and public consultation in the preparation of the NAPAs (Decision 29/CP.7). The guidelines seek to ensure that non-transparent and unaccountable governments cannot dictate the content of NAPAs: vulnerable groups exposed to climate change impacts should be heard and their interests made to count. But these provisions are not sufficient to ensure that local interests have a fair hearing and a chance to exert influence over decisions that impact on them.[4]

One way to address cross-level procedural justice in the climate change regime would be to create a body to investigate public complaints (Paavola & Adger, 2005b). The North American Agreement on Environmental Cooperation (NAAEC) could provide a template. The NAEEC formed the Commission for Environmental Cooperation (CEC) to implement the Agreement. The CEC consists of a Council, a Secretariat and a Joint Public Advisory Committee. The Secretariat plays a key role in public participation under the NAEEC. Articles 14 and 15 of the NAAEC establish the Citizens' Submission Procedure whereby the public can draw the Secretariat's attention to an alleged failure of a government to enforce its environmental laws effectively. If the submissions meet the criteria set for them, the Secretariat will request a response from the party in question. If the submission has merit, the Secretariat can decide to develop a full factual record on the basis of the submission. The Secretariat has to submit the draft record to the Council which may adopt it with a two-thirds majority. The decision will also make the factual record public. CEC has received over 50 submissions since 1995 and it has published ten full records to date (CEC, 2005).[5]

The Citizen Submission Procedure of the NAAEC is not an effective measure for enforcing environmental laws because factual records do not constitute binding factual determinations or legal findings (Fitzmaurice, 2003). At best, they cast light, and public attention, on omissions and inaction in the enforcement of existing environmental policies. Nevertheless, the template of the Citizen's Submission Procedure could be revised for use in the governance of adaptation to climate change to bring controversies regarding national adaptation planning and measures undertaken on the basis of international agreements to international scrutiny. The process would be an instrument for non-state actors to have more voice at the international level. If the investigating body was authorized to make non-binding judgements on the basis of the gathered record, it could set the standard for international best practice. Teeth could be added to these judgements by making them count in decisions to fund adaptation measures and to provide other benefits (Paavola & Adger, 2005b).

Conclusions

In this article I have discussed views on the emergence and significance of international environmental governance, including why its social justice implications have not received adequate attention. I suggested that defining international environmental governance as resolution of environmental conflicts would highlight its social justice dimensions. I have also argued that social justice in international environmental governance must be understood broadly, so as to include both distributive and procedural justice within the society of states and across the levels of governance between state and non-state actors.

Examination of governance of adaptation indicates that justice among the states has clearly received more attention than cross-level justice. There are also more procedural responses than distributive ones. This reflects the emerging nature of governance of adaptation: the governance framework is still not operative. But it also indicates that difficult distributive issues are not addressed before there are compelling reasons to do so, and that relationships between the states are still reified in the practice of international relations. The greatest problem in the current institutional framework is its failure to address responsibility for climate change impacts. Procedural justice in cross-level interactions will also need new solutions that can address local grievances related to the implementation of the climate change regime. Moreover, current commitments have to be operationalized.

Responsibility for climate change impacts has to be addressed to create a functioning system for compensating for climate change impacts and assisting adaptation. This could be done by adopting a uniform carbon tax, replenishing a joint compensation and assistance fund. While this solution requires equitable distribution of funds between recipient countries, it can also reach non-state actors within impacted states. The best way to address cross-level procedural justice issues would be to establish a body and a procedure to investigate and adjudicate complaints on the implementation of the climate change regime and related national legislation. It could draw international attention and scrutiny to local injustices, whether they originate from national or international levels of governance.

Acknowledgements

This paper forms a part of programme on environmental decision-making (PEDM) of the Centre for Social and Economic Research on the Global Environment (CSERGE) at the University of East Anglia. I gratefully acknowledge the support of the UK Economic and Social Research Council (ESRC). I thank Jan Oosthoek and Barry Gills for helpful comments and suggestions. As usual, any shortcomings remain entirely my own responsibility.

Notes

1 Data derived from Ronald B. Mitchell. 2003–2005. *International Environmental Agreements Website*. Available at http://iea.uoregon.edu/and described and interpreted in greater detail in Mitchell (2003).
2 See the Convention for the Regulation of Whaling (1931); Constitution of the Food and Agriculture Organization of the United Nations (1945); the United Nations Convention on the Law of the Seas (1958); Antarctic Treaty (1959); Agreement Concerning the International Commission for the Protection of the Rhine Against Pollution (1963); and the Treaty Banning Nuclear Weapon Tests in the Atmosphere, in Outer Space and Under Water (1963).
3 Developed countries can be considered to have a duty to assist developing countries irrespective of being responsible for climate change impacts. Duty to assist is based on the capacity to assist while responsibility arises from the harm caused to others.
4 Guidelines for the preparation of NAPAs only relate to national planning of adaptation measures. Implementation of these plans and decisions and actions of international governmental organizations such as the GEF are not covered by the guidelines.
5 Nearly a half of the submissions have concerned Mexico while less than 20% of the submissions have related to the US.

References

Adger, W. N., Brown, K., Fairbrass, J., Jordan, A., Paavola, J., Rosendo, S. & Seyfang, G. (2003) Governance for sustainability: towards a thick analysis of environmental decisions, *Environment and Planning A*, 35, pp. 1095–1110.
Adger, W. N., Paavola, J., Huq, S. & Mace, M. J. (eds) (2006) *Fairness in Adaptation to Climate Change* (Cambridge, MA: The MIT Press, in press).
Armstrong, D. (1999) Law, justice and the idea of world society, *International Affairs*, 75, pp. 547–561.
Attfield, R. (2005) Environmental values, nationalism, global citizenship and the common heritage of humanity, pp. 38–50, in Paavola, J. & Lowe, I. (eds) *Environmental Values in a Globalising World: Nature, Justice and Governance* (London: Routledge).
Bell, D. A. (1993) *Communitarianism and its Critics* (Oxford: Clarendon Press).
Caldwell, L. C. (1996) *International Environmental Policy: From the Twentieth to Twenty-First Century*, 3rd edn (Durham, NC: Duke University Press).
Cochran, M. (1999) *Normative Theory in International Relations: A Pragmatic Approach* (Cambridge: Cambridge University Press).
Commission for Environmental Cooperation (CEC) (2005) *Citizen Submissions on Enforcement Matters: Current Status of Filed Submissions*. Available online at http://www.cec.org/citizen/status/index.cfm?varlan=english (accessed 20 April 2005).
Dessai, S. & Schipper, E. L. (2003) The Marrakech Accords to the Kyoto Protocol: analysis and future prospects, *Global Environmental Change*, 13, pp. 149–153.
Dower, N. (1998) *World Ethics: The New Agenda* (Edinburgh: Edinburgh University Press).
Fitzmaurice, M. (2003) Public participation in the North American Agreement on Environmental Cooperation, *International and Comparative Law Quarterly*, 52, pp. 333–368.
Frank, D.J. (1997) Science, nature and the globalization of the environment, 1870–1990, *Social Forces*, 76, 409–425.
Frank, D. J., Hironaka, A. & Schofer, A. (2000) The nation-state and the natural environment over the twentieth century, *American Sociological Review*, 65, pp. 96–116.
Fraser, N. (2001) Recognition without ethics? *Theory, Culture and Society*, 18(2–3), pp. 21–42.
Gupta, J. (2002) The climate change regime: can a divided world unite?, pp. 129–155 in Briden, J. C. & Downing, T. E. (eds) *Managing the Earth: The Linacre Lectures* (Oxford: Oxford University Press).
Guranko, E. N. (2003) *Introduction to the World Bank Insurance Practice: Key Lessons Learned and the Road Ahead*. A presentation at Financing the Risks of Natural Disasters conference, Washington DC, 2–3 June, 2003. Available online at http://www.worldbank.org/wbi/banking/insurance/natdisaster/pdf/Gurenko.ppt (accessed 9 November 2004).
Haas, P. M. (1992) Introduction: epistemic communities and international policy coordination, *International Organization*, 46(1), pp. 1–35.
Inglehart, R. (1995) Public support for environmental protection: the impact of objective problems and subjective values in 43 societies, *Political Science and Politics*, 28, pp. 57–71.
Kapstein, E. B. (2004) Models of international economic justice, *Ethics and International Affairs*, 8(2), pp. 79–92.

Klinenberg, E. (2002) *Heat Wave: A Social Autopsy of Disaster in Chicago* (Chicago, IL: University of Chicago Press).
Kolm, S.-C. (1996) *Modern Theories of Justice* (Cambridge, MA: The MIT Press).
Lind, E. A. & Tyler, T. R. (1988) *The Social Psychology of Procedural Justice* (New York & London: Plenum Press).
Melkas, E. (2002) Sovereignty and equity within the framework of the climate regime, *Review of European Community and International Environmental Law*, 11, pp. 115–128.
Meyer, J. W., Frank, D. J., Hironaka, A., Schofer, E. & Tuma, N. B. (1997) The structuring of a world environmental regime, 1870–1990, *International Organization*, 51, pp. 623–651.
Mitchell, R. B. (2002) International environment, pp. 500–516 in Risse, T., Simmons, B. & Carlsnaes, W. (eds) *Handbook of International Relations* (London: Sage Publications).
Mitchell, R. B. (2003) International environmental agreements: a survey of their features, formation, and effects, *Annual Review of Environment and Resources*, 28, pp. 429–461.
Mwandosya, M. J. (1999) *Survival Emissions: A Perspective from the South on Global Climate Change Negotiations* (Dar es Salaam: Dar es Salaam University Press).
Paavola, J. (2005) Interdependence, pluralism and globalisation: implications for environmental governance, pp. 143–158 in Paavola, J. & Lowe, I. (eds) *Environmental Values in a Globalising World: Nature, Justice and Governance* (London: Routledge).
Paavola, J. (in press) Environmental justice and equity, in O'Hara, P. (ed.), *International Encyclopedia of Public Policy: Governance in a Global Age* (London: Routledge).
Paavola, J. (forthcoming). Environmental conflicts, institutions and environmental governance. *Ecological Economics*.
Paavola, J. & Adger, W. N. (2005a) Institutional ecological economics, *Ecological Economics*, 53, pp. 353–368.
Paavola, J. & Adger, W. N. (2005b) Fair adaptation to climate change, *Ecological Economics*, in press.
Paterson, M., Humphreys, D. & Pettiford, L. (2003) Conceptualizing environmental governance: from interstate regimes to counter-hegemonic struggles, *Global Environmental Politics*, 3(2), pp. 1–10.
Radin, M. J. (1996) *Contested Commodities* (Cambridge, MA: Harvard University Press).
Raustiala, K. (1997) States, NGOs, and international environmental institutions, *International Studies Quarterly*, 41, pp. 719–740.
Rhodes, R. A. W. (1994). The hollowing out of the state: the changing nature of the public service in Britain, *Political Quarterly*, 65, pp. 138–151.
Roberts, J. T., Parks, B. C. & Vásquez, A. A. (2004) Who ratifies environmental treaties and why: institutionalism, structuralism and participation by 192 nations in 22 treaties, *Global Environmental Politics*, 4(3), pp. 22–64.
Schär, C. & Jendritzky, G. (2004) Climate change: hot news from summer 2003, *Nature*, 432, pp. 559–560.
Schellnhuber, H.-J. & Held, H. (2002) How fragile is the earth system?, pp. 5–34 in Briden, J. C. & Downing, T. E. (eds) *Managing the Earth: The Linacre Lectures* (Oxford: Oxford University Press).
Schlosberg, D. (1999) *Environmental Justice and the New Pluralism: The Challenge of Difference for Environmentalism* (Oxford & New York: Oxford University Press).
Sen, A. (1992) *Inequality Reexamined* (New York: Russell Sage Foundation & Oxford: Clarendon Press).
Shrader-Frechette, K. (2002) *Environmental Justice: Creating Equality, Reclaiming Democracy* (Oxford: Oxford University Press).
Soyinka, W. (2004) *A Quest for Dignity. Fourth Reith Lecture on Climate of Fear*, University of Leeds, broadcast on BBC4 24 April 2004, 8 pm. Available online at http://www.bbc.co.uk/radio4/reith2004/schedule.shtml (accessed 29 April 2004).
Sprinz, D. & Vaahtoranta, T. (1994) The interest-based explanation of international environmental policy, *International Organization*, 48, pp. 77–105.
Steffen, W., Sanderson, A., Jäger, J., Tyson, P. D., Moore, B., III, Matson, P. A., Richardson, K., Oldfield, F., Schellnhuber, H.-J., Turner, B. L., II & Wasson, R. J. (2004) *Global Change and the Earth System: A Planet Under Pressure* (Heidelberg: Springer Verlag).
Tyler, T. R, Boeckmann R. J., Smith, H. J. & Huo, Y. J. (1997) *Social Justice in a Diverse Society* (Boulder, CO: Westview Press).
Verheyen, R. (2002) Adaptation to the impacts of anthropogenic climate change: the international legal framework, *Review of European Community and International Environmental Law*, 11, pp. 129–143.
Vitousek, P. M., Mooney, H. A., Lubchenko, J. & Melillo, J. M. (1997) Human domination of earth's ecosystems, *Science*, 277, pp. 494–499.
Vogler, J. (2003) Taking institutions seriously: how regime analysis can be relevant to multilevel environmental governance, *Global Environmental Politics*, 3(2), pp. 25–39.
Walzer, M. (1983) *Spheres of Justice: A Defence of Pluralism and Equality* (Oxford: Blackwell).

Wapner, P. (2002) Horizontal politics: transnational environmental activism and global cultural change, *Global Environmental Politics*, 2(2), pp. 37–62.
Welch, D. A. (2000) Morality and 'the national interest', pp. 3–12 in Walls, A. & Held, V. (eds) *Ethics in International Affairs* (Lanham, MD: Rowman & Littlefield).
Young, H. P. (1994) *Equity: In Theory and Practice* (Princeton, NJ: Princeton University Press).
Young, O. R. (1994) *International Governance: Protecting the Environment in Stateless Society* (Ithaca, NY: Cornell University Press).

Jouni Paavola is a Senior Research Associate in the Centre for Social and Economic Research on the Global Environment (CSERGE) at the University of East Angalia. His research examines the role of institutions and justice in environmental decision-making and governance and develops broad-based institutional analysis for examining the links between plural governance goals, institutional designs and governance outcomes. He has published several dozen book chapters and journal articles in journals such as *Science, Ecological Economics* and *Environment and Planning A*. His books include *Fairness in Adaptation to Climate Change*, co-edited with W. Neil Adger, Saleemul Huq and MJ Mace and to be published by the MIT Press in 2006; *Environmental Values in a Globalising World: Nature, Justice and Governance*, co-edited with Ian Lowe (Routledge, 2005); and *Economics, Ethics, and Environmental Policy: Contested Choices*, co-edited with Daniel W. Bromley (Blackwell, 2002). He is also a member of the Board of European Society of Ecological Economics (ESEE)

The Globalizations of the Environment

DIMITRIS STEVIS

Introduction

Along with communications and finance, the environment has been considered as a paradigmatic example of globalization. Environmental processes routinely cross territorial boundaries and some of them are already global in a real rather than potential sense. Moreover, what adds to the globalizing dynamics of environmental processes is the central role of nature, presumably impervious to human volition.

What is worth noting, however, is that the environment—and the economy—was cast in global terms at least since the 1940s. Ever since, the meanings of the global environment have changed to reflect broader developments in the world political economy and the ability of the various social forces to frame environmental politics. As a result, the global environment is a significant case. More specifically, it is worth investigating the various rationales/dynamics that have led to framing the environment as global—keeping in mind that most environmental problems are local or regional in scope. More broadly, by examining the contested and shifting nature of global/ization in such a paradigmatic case we can cast a critical glance upon globalization.

In the first part of this article I discuss my understanding of globalization in order to undermine the facile framing of the environment in globalized terms. This is followed by the main part of the essay which traces some of the key framings of the global environment since World War II in order to highlight the shifting conceptions of the environment as well as the politics behind them. I do not pretend to be comprehensive as this would require a whole volume. Rather, my goal is to provide enough information to illuminate the main argument. I close by very briefly outlining some of the implications of the globalization discourse for our understanding of the environment.

The Global and the Globalized

The concept of globalization sprang upon social analysis during the last 15 years, obscuring in its ascent the many previous attempts at capturing the world as a whole (on the environment as a global issue see Yearley, 1996; Kütting & Rose, 2005; Stevis, 2005). As we know well, however, there have been many attempts, at least as far back as the nineteenth century, to understand the world political economy in global terms. Moreover, those accounts were based on both social and natural realities. Socially, the expansion of Europe had reshaped the whole globe into empires. Even though communications and other exchanges were slower and smaller scale by comparison to contemporary levels they were no less consequential, while the divisions of labor established continue to shape the present. Naturally, epidemics spread throughout the Old World and then the whole world for centuries if not millennia, carried along by long distance trade.

If the term 'globalization' is to mean something different than the term 'global' there must be some consequential distinguishing quality (on globalization see Steger, 2005; Held & McGrew, 2003; Gills, 2000). The most compelling distinguishing quality is the iterative nature of globalized interactions, with no government able or willing to stop them. If so, then some of the most prominent environmental processes are global, in the same fashion that epidemics have been global, rather than globalized. Ozone depleting and climate changing substances originate in particular parts of the globe and migrate over the planet. Even with the ascent of the industrial semiperiphery, there is a clear geopolitical bias in these ideal types of global problems.

What globalizes the environment, in my view, are social processes that introduce iteration. Global conferences and rules transform global problems into globalized ones, as do economic transactions such as the spread of agricultural technologies or the demands of global economic organizations. As a result, the globalization of the environment is as uneven and unfair as that of any other social process. The real natural dynamics of environmental processes do not obliterate the social inequalities of environmental causes and impacts. Environmental processes do put us in the same boat but in the same way that crises do so for workers and employers.

A second, related, issue worth addressing is that of the hidden charm of the 'subpolitical'—the tendency to consider economic, infrastructural, and environmental processes as separate from the overall political economy. As is well known, the paradigmatic examples of globalization have required political choices and the use of force in order to become a reality. Financial globalization, for instance, was very much based on constitutive decisions by the USA and the UK after World War II. The Internet is the product of military research by the USA. While the market plays such a subpolitical role with respect to the economy, natural dynamics plays a similar role with respect to the environment, tending to cast human-generated environmental processes as separate from the overall political economy. When exaggerated, this obscures more than it reveals. The point of all this is that we should pay closer attention to political choices in our accounts of environmental globalization. Global meetings and rules are central to turning the global into the globalized. As they have done in other areas, they have been very prominent in environmental affairs at least since the 1940s.

As a consequence, whether and in what terms to speak of the world as globalized involves a politics of framing. This is not to say that such politics is not founded on some external or material processes. Rather, that different people accent different aspects. Socialists, for instance, accent the exploitative nature of capitalism while liberals its potential for growth. Liberals highlight globalization as evidence of the hopelessness of national regulation—the primary location of regulation—while environmentalists highlight the globality of environmental problems in order to promote global rules against free riders.

Of course, there are differences amongst environmentalists. Social environmentalists point to the adverse effects of liberal trade and structural adjustment in order to highlight the uneven impacts of various countries and sectors and in order to promote appropriate social regulations. Techno-environmentalists, on the other hand, are likely to highlight aggregate global environmental change while downplaying its distributive implications.

Which process or channel of environmental globalization one chooses to emphasize is a political choice. With that in mind we propose three ideal types of environmental globalization evident since World War II: the *social*, the *ecosystemic* and that of *externalization*. All, of course, are social in their origins but differ in terms of the paths that people choose to emphasize. Moreover, there are important divergences within them since, at particular times, one or the other played a hegemonic discursive role, leading to a wide variety of analysts and practitioners having to use the language of the day in order to be heard. I briefly clarify each process before showing how it has been used historically.

The social path of environmental globalization has received a great deal of attention during the last 20 years as a result of global treaties to protect the ozone layer and forestall climate change and, more importantly, over the impacts of the GATT/WTO on global and national environmental regulation (Niemeyer, 2000; Williams, 2001; Clapp, 2005). In line with the earlier comments over the influence of the 'subpolitical', we must also highlight the environmental impacts of the Cold War, as evident by nuclear testing in the atmosphere and the military abuses of oceans and space. Moreover, it is worth noting that before the WTO there had been a series of global conferences and scientific collaborations that globalized the environment.

Every environmentalist has some sense that things are connected. Not all environmentalists, however, adopt a global ecosystemic view—whether thinking of our world as an ecosphere or a biosphere. Some do not need such holistic views to make their case and others may be suspicious of its implications. As early as the interwar period Vernadsky's ideas received some attention, but it was not until the 1960s that strong ecosystemic claims became common in environmental debates (Caldwell, 1972; di Castri, 1985; Alker & Haas, 1993; Golley, 1993; Mooney, 1999).

Finally, many analysts and practitioners have highlighted the adverse global impacts of certain negative externalities. While some arguments based on externalities draw upon ecosystemic rationales, that is not always the case as they can very easily be based on property rights or conceptualizations of fairness (for various views see Hardin & Baden, 1977; Orr & Soroos, 1979; Charney, 1982; Keohane & Ostrom, 1995; Pearce, 2002). Accordingly, the impacts of nuclear tests and dumping in the oceans can be considered as the instances *par excellence* of negative externalities with global implications. As I will note in the narrative, the concept of the commons, used to justify the regulation of the oceans and other spaces outside of state jurisdiction, draws largely on a social rather than an ecosystemic framing.

The Globalizations of the Environment since the 1940s

From the Social to the Ecosystemic: The Late 1940s to the Mid-1960s

The environment was cast in global terms immediately after World War II. Even though the concepts of the biosphere and 'carrying capacity' were known and used, it was social rationales and dynamics that dominated.

At the political level this was manifested by the formation of global environmental organizations and the calling of global conferences to deal with global issues of resource conservation and preservation. Without going into much detail (see Nicholson, 1970; Caldwell, 1972; McCormick, 1989) the politics of the period reflected the efforts of the ascending hegemon, the USA, to promote its version of conservationism and the efforts of the Europeans to promote preservation, which they practiced largely in the colonies. Behind the conservation-preservation schism, of course, lay a struggle among friends over the shape of the world to come. The same struggle was evident in labor affairs, with the USA criticizing colonialism and the role of European unions in the colonies.

The divisions were evident at the level of global organizations and conferences. The Europeans used UNESCO as their vehicle, creating a hybrid organization whose early name—International Union for the Protection of Nature—reflected their views. On the other hand, the USA dominated the 1949 conference on resources (Goodrich, 1951). Its influence was further felt when the International Union was renamed as the International Union for the Conservation of Nature and Natural Resources (for more background see Boardman, 1981; McCormick, 1989).

The analysts of the period, mostly American, also cast the environment in global terms (Osborn, 1948, 1953; Vogt, 1948; Brown, 1954). Osborn (1948), for example, talks about the world as a whole due to economic rather than ecosystemic processes. What happens in India, in his view, would inevitably flow into the rest of the world as a result of global economic interdependence and the existence of a global society. Others pointed to the impacts of population pressures on regional or local carrying capacity in the third world (Vogt, 1948). Influenced by the development efforts of the period, these authors pointed to the global implications of such pressures and the ethical or practical responsibilities of the over-consuming industrial core.

While most analysts adopted a population-resources-scarcity approach, it is worth noting that they did not all agree on the more Malthusian views that became very prominent in years to come. In general, however, we can locate the origins of the global scarcity worldview during those early years and, interestingly enough, in those parts of the North most interested in promoting particular resource policies over the South.

By the late 1950s there appears a second, more ecosystemic view of the environment as large scale, collaborative science starts maturing. Ever since, there has been a continuous string of projects, largely led by the industrial world, that have sought to frame the globe as an ecosystem. The earliest examples were the 1957 International Geophysical Year, the International Biological Program (1964–1975), and UNESCO's Biosphere Conference (1968). The holistic approach to the biosphere, coupled with emerging space exploration, is also reflected in the language of social analysts and political ecologists who started using images such as that of 'spaceship earth' as early as the mid-1960s (e.g., Ward, 1966).

By the mid to late 1960s, therefore, ecosystemic and scarcity views of globalization dominate, sometimes at odds with each other and sometimes in fusion. Generally, however, even the most distributively minded of ecologists and environmentalists assumed the logic of scarcities or employed its language, thus downplaying distributive concerns.

Between Global Scarcity and the South: The Late 1960s to Early 1980s

The aggregate and globalist models associated with the Club of Rome are well known and there is no need to review them in much depth here (for a review see Onuf, 1983; also Meadows et al., 1982). Suffice it to say that they viewed the world as a whole. Their global models placed the interconnected world economy within global ecosystemic limits, reflecting the ascendance of that discourse during the late 1960s and early 1970s. The perceived techno-environmentalism of the scarcity views, some associated with the Club of Rome and others with Malthusians such as Ophuls (1977), Hardin (Hardin & Baden, 1977), Goldsmith (1972) & Ehrlich (1968), came to a head with the emerging semiperiphery and its call for a New International Economic Order. This led to two additional global framings of the environment that were largely social in their assumptions. One of them came directly from the developmentalist elites of the South and the other from reformists in the North.

The South's view was that the costs of environmental measures were too high, making development prohibitive (de Araujo Castro, 1972; for broader views and reviews see Woodhouse, 1972; Farvar, 1974; James, 1978). Moreover, they considered the aggregate scarcity views coming from the North as insincere, given the environmental degradation that had allowed the North to industrialize. What we had, therefore, was a political globalization of the environment that was based on the assumption of the world political economy as interrelated. Not only was the North assumed to be the cause of environmental harm but, also, that any global environmental policies would require significant transfers to the South and strong consideration of the South's special circumstances. This connection of environment and development was very much evident before and at the Stockholm Conference and has colored environmental debates ever since.

In addition to governments, societal forces also picked up the concerns of the South. One explicitly globalist view was that of the World Order Models Project (WOMP), centered in the USA but with connections in various continents. Leaders of the project adopted environmental concerns early on and integrated them into their models (Falk, 1971). Although some may have criticized them for paying lip service to the environment the centrality that they assign to it is self-evident (Falk, 1975). Yet some scarcity environmentalists felt that distributive concerns were more likely to undermine environmental goals. While the developmentalist goals of Southern elites were clearly anti-environmentalist, the efforts of the WOMP and other organizations that took the South seriously cannot be treated in the same fashion.

The debates between ecosystemic, scarcity and distributive environmentalists were joined during this period by debates over the oceans. The impact of nuclear testing had put externalities on the global agenda (Jacobson & Stein, 1966) and the debates over the oceans (and, then, the atmosphere) turned the displacement of negative externalities onto the commons into a major justification for global rules (Soroos, 1977; Wijkman, 1982). While some of the advocates of regimes for the commons were motivated by a desire to address distributive issues, others advanced solutions that could well aggravate maldistribution in the name of environmental efficiency. It is also worth noting here that the concept of the commons as it appeared in the 1970s and the 1980s referred largely to spaces and resources outside of state jurisdiction—more properly speaking, open rather than shared spaces. It was not until the mid-1980s and beyond that the commons started including anything that was shared and, increasingly, ought to be shared.

In addition to states and international governmental organizations (IGOs), more militant societal forces also rose to prominence during this period. Non-governmental organizations had long played a key role in environmental and resource politics going as far back as the nineteenth century (Boardman, 1981; McCormick, 1989). Starting around the time of the Stockholm Conference, however, we see the rise of environmental organizations with a globalist rhetoric, prominent among them being Greenpeace and Friends of the Earth but, also, the network around the magazine *The Ecologist* (Goldsmith, 1972). While existing organizations, such as IUCN and WWF, may be considered too scientistic and technical in their approach, this new wave of organizations was more militant in placing ecological principles into a political agenda. Some of these societal entities, such as *The Ecologist*, did adopt a strong scarcity approach while others, such as Greenpeace and Friends of the Earth, a more tempered one. It is important to note in any case that while social movement organizations did contribute to globalizing the environment, they were relative latecomers compared to IGOs and the older IUCN and WWF (see Boardman, 1981).

By the late 1970s scarcity views had lost some of their wind as environment-development issues were rising in prominence. In any event, if one were to go back in time it is apparent that the idea of a global and a globalized environment was right in the middle of environmental debates. The developments of the subsequent period, therefore, built on the past and were not a break from it.

Globalization from Above and Below

During the 1980s the discourses of the previous few decades fused into those of global environmental change and sustainable development. As noted, large scientific projects, largely led by the North and/or coordinated by IGOs, had been common since the late 1950s. The earliest ones were led by ecologists and biologists in search of the ecosystemic properties of the globe (Golley, 1993; Mooney, 1999). By the early 1980s developments in space sciences, in selected core countries, generated an impetus towards a comprehensive approach to the earth, largely led by physical scientists (see Clark & Munn, 1986; Price, 1990; Turner, 1990; Redclift, 1992). The overall agenda is known under the rubric of 'global environmental change'. While one may be tempted to separate large scientific projects from the overall political economy that would certainly be unfortunate and can generate strong criticisms (Boehmer-Christiansen, 1994a, 1994b; for more sociological accounts of science see Litfin, 1994; Taylor & Buttel, 1992). This is not to say that scientific establishments, particular scientific organizations and specific individuals are not often critical of other parts of the state. Rather, it is to say that they are part of a larger whole, as a result of organizational and resource matters, in which the overall power structure of the political economy plays a central role. Thus, the 'global environmental change' agenda does reflect both the critical stance of many environmental scientists as well as the more opportunistic uses of new technologies and the appeal of the environment by other scientists.

There is no denying that various environmental processes are global and ought to be treated as such. The global, however, has also tended to obscure the persistent significance of subglobal environmental dynamics while it also promotes an aggregate, non-distributive approach very similar to that of the scarcity views of decades past (for various views see Buttel et al., 1990;

Jacobson, 1992; Redclift, 1992; Yearley, 1996). Even though the use of sophisticated technologies allows global change researchers to localize the causes and impacts of environmental harm, they have not been as sensitive to the power relations central to environmental practices, as with all human activities, resulting in rather mechanistic causal claims (for a critique see Van Buren, 2002). But this is a shortcoming that can be rectified with the proper political will. It does require an important shift in the politics of science, however, and it is not a simple technical matter.

As noted earlier, the aggregate bias of scarcity views offered a golden opportunity to the developmentalists of the South during the early 1970s. I have also suggested, however, that many analysts as well as practitioners realized that it is possible to take into account distributive issues as well as protect the environment. The debates over the fusion of environmental sustainability and development have covered the last three decades. During the 1970s and early 1980s the fusion went under the rubric of 'ecodevelopment'. With the publication of *Our Common Future* (World Commission on Environment and Development, 1987), however, the term sustainable development became the dominant one.

More so than global environmental change, sustainable development is applicable to all spatial levels. Both as a result of the global debates that gave birth to the term as well as subsequent political developments such as the Rio Conference and the UN Commission on Sustainable Development, debates over sustainable development have become entrenched at the global level.

Various analysts have compellingly argued that sustainable development hides more than it reveals as far as the environment is concerned (see Redclift, 1987; Becker & Jahn, 1999; Harrison, 2000; Bruyninckx, 2005). One can also point to the fact that the World Summit on Sustainable Development that took place in Johannesburg during 2002 did not even include environment in its title. Yet sustainable development does allow for the possibility of recognizing a social dimension as well as the variability of levels of environmental and social processes. In that respect it is much more open than the global environmental change discourse which is biased towards large processes, tends to be more techno-environmentalist and obscures the autonomous dynamics of various levels of environmental processes (for a treatment of both see Redclift, 1992).

In the Shadow of the Grand Narratives

Global environmental change and sustainable development may be considered as the grand narratives of environmental politics since the late 1980s. There have been important developments in their shadow, however, since the early 1990s. The two most important ones are the renewed focus on the impacts of specific social processes and the influence of the globalization discourse.

At the social level we can highlight the political and the economic. Politically, and following the prominence of the accords to protect the ozone layer, there has been a decisive focus on global governance (Vogler, 2000; Bernstein, 2002; Jasanoff & Martello, 2004; Elliott, 2004 for overview; Biermann, 2005). This move received additional impetus at the Rio Conference and subsequent successes and failures with respect to climate change and biodiversity. The argument that global problems require global governance is persuasive, but one cannot help but notice that global governance does come in different shades—ranging from technical management to social regulation. One must also note that the global governance discourse does obscure the fact that many agreements are largely international rather than supranational. Without wanting to underestimate some of the successes with respect to ozone, climate change, and biodiversity, it is worth noting that many analysts and practitioners consider the International Labour Organization as the model towards which to strive. This is sobering both because this is the oldest IGO and because its tripartite structure was considered a compromise aimed at weakening the social-democratic union movement of the time.

In addition to this move towards global environmental governance there has also been a renewed debate over the impacts of specific economic processes, particularly with the global liberalization of trade promoted by the GATT/WTO (Neumayer, 2000; Williams, 2001; Clapp, 2005). Programmatically, the GATT/WTO system seeks to put in place global rules for the movement of products. With the failure of the Multilateral Agreement on Investment, moreover, it has taken on an important role with respect to investment, as well as trade. While some analysts have argued that environmental provisions are not inimical to the WTO, provided that they are not discriminatory, the truth of the matter is that the WTO aims to liberalize rather than environmentally regulate trade. The environmental opportunities that it offers are residual rather than proactive. Regional agreements, particularly the North American Free Trade Agreement and the Free Trade Area of the Americas, are fairly consistent with the WTO in that respect (Audley, 1997). Environmentalists have sought to include environmental provisions in trade agreements as well as to ensure that global (and local) environmental agreements have equal or superior standing. As a result, we have seen a very clear shift of the debate to the global level between those who seek liberalization and those who seek regulation.

Related to the political and economic processes that were just mentioned there has been a rise in the prominence of global societal environmental organizations (see Betsill, 2005). As has been noted, international or global conferences have long provided an opportunity for societal organizations to make their interests known. As one moves into the past we encounter various single-issue organizations or networks seeking to abolish slavery, empower women and protect various species and habitats (Keck & Sikkink, 1998). One also notes, however, the important role of political parties and unions with broad political agendas. Rather than try to avoid engagement with the state, these entities sought to control and change the state—stated differently, to change overall social relations in more or less reformist or revolutionary directions (Stevis, 1998).

Increasingly, global environmental organizations are not only single issue ones but, more importantly, hold visions of sectoral change that only marginally address the overall political economy. In this sense, we have observed the spread of USA-type interest group environmental politics over the globe. As a number of analysts have suggested, the time is ripe to place environmental and other societal entities within the political economy rather than situate them within a civil society or networks presumed to be at odds or independent of states and capital (Kamal Pasha & Blaney, 1998; Stevis, 2002).

The resurgence of societal processes of environmental globalization has taken place at the same time that the increased spread and intensity of economic and communication interactions led to the concept of globalization, in general (Yearley, 1996). As we noted earlier, the concept of globalization has been strongly based on presumed 'subpolitical' exchanges. In the same sense that economic exchanges have served to 'naturalize' the integration of the world political economy, the natural dynamics of the environment have served to naturalize the globalization of the environment. This is not to say that natural dynamics are not central to the spread of environmental harm. Rather, that social processes are often as important while natural dynamics vary in terms of their scope. Undifferentiated evocations of the natural media tend to take environmental harm out of the political economy, leading us to focus on the medium rather than the structural causes that produce an environmental problem.

Conclusions

My goal has not been to provide an exhaustive account of all the framings of environmental globalization. Rather, I have sought to show that the framings of globalization have changed over time, suggesting that holistic views are themselves the product of historical dynamics. I have also pointed out that different framings of the global/ized environment have been contesting for discursive hegemony throughout the period discussed.

In this sense I hope to have contributed to that analysis of global integration that uses the term 'globalization' in a heuristic sense and recognizes that processes of global integration are uneven, subject to political choices, and serve to depict real processes as well as marginalize alternative interpretations. Not only, then, must we continue interrogating the content and goals of different framings of globalization but we must also recognize that globalized processes are intimately articulated with localizing ones, as social forces draw political lines in an effort to shape and resist the history of which they are part.

The debates over the causes of the September 2005 destruction of New Orleans by a tropical storm highlight the need to make the history of human choices central to our analyses of environmental harm. Following the disaster a number of analysts focused on the central role of global warming in strengthening the storm. Others focused on the maldistribution of environmental harm as the poorer segments of the population were less able to leave the city, amongst other factors. It is necessary, in my view, to take into account the impacts of human practices on the climate and to recognize the maldistribution of harm. I strongly agree with those, however, who point out that this disaster, and other such disasters, are the products of long term choices that place humanity at odds with nature or, stated differently, reshape nature in ways that are often difficult to control. Bringing in history will serve us well by situating the environment within the broader political economy since it is only by changing our political economy that we can achieve sound environmental practices.

References

Alker, H., Jr. & Haas, P. (1993) The rise of global ecopolitics, pp. 133–171 in Choucri, N. (ed.) *Global Accord* (Cambridge, MA: MIT Press).
Audley, J. J. (1997) *Green Politics and Global Trade: NAFTA and the Future of Environmental Politics* (Washington, DC: Georgetown University Press).
Becker, E. & Jahn, T. (eds) (1999) *Sustainability and the Social Sciences* (Paris: Unesco).
Bernstein, S. (2002) *The Compromise of Liberal Environmentalism* (New York: Columbia University Press).
Betsill, M. (2005) Transnational actors in international environmental politics, in Betsill, M., Hochstetler, K. & Stevis, D. (eds) *Palgrave Advances in International Environmental Politics* (Basingstoke: Palgrave).
Biermann, F. (2005) Global governance and the environment, in Betsill, M., Hochstetler, K. & Stevis, D. (eds) *Palgrave Advances in International Environmental Politics* (Basingstoke: Palgrave).
Boardman, R. (1981) *International Organization and the Conservation of Nature* (Bloomington, IN: Indiana University Press).
Boehmer-Christiansen, S. (1994a) Global climate protection policy: the limits of scientific advice: part 1, *Global Environmental Change*, 4(2), pp. 140–159.
Boehmer-Christiansen, S. (1994b) Global climate protection policy: the limits of scientific advice: part 2, *Global Environmental Change*, 4(3), pp. 185–200.
Brown, H. (1954) *The Challenge of Man's Future; an Inquiry Concerning the Condition of Man During the Years That Lie Ahead* (New York: Viking Press).
Bruyninckx, H. (2005) Sustainable development: a contested policy concept, in Betsill, M., Hochstetler, K. & Stevis, D. (eds) *Palgrave Advances in International Environmental Politics* (Basingstoke: Palgrave).
Buttel, F. H., Hawkins, A. P. & Power, A. G. (1990) From limits to growth to global change: constraints and contradictions in the evolution of environmental science and ideology, *Global Environmental Change*, 1(1), pp. 57–66.

Caldwell, L. K. (1972) *In Defense of Earth: International Protection of the Biosphere* (Bloomington, IN: Indiana University Press).
Charney, J. I. (1982) *The New Nationalism and the Use of Common Spaces: Issues in Marine Pollution and the Exploitation of Antarctica* (Totowa, NJ: Allanheld Osmun).
Clapp, J. (2005) International political economy and the environment, in Betsill, M., Hochstetler, K. & Stevis, D. (eds) *Palgrave Advances in International Environmental Politics* (Basingstoke: Palgrave).
Clark, W. C. & Munn, R. E. (1986) *Sustainable Development of the Biosphere* (Cambridge: Cambridge University Press).
de Araujo Castro, J. A. (1972) Environment and development: the case of the developing countries, *International Organization*, 26(2) (International Institutions and the Environmental Crisis), pp. 401–416.
di Castri, F. (1985) Twenty years of international programmes on ecosystems and the biosphere: an overview of achievements, shortcomings and possible new perspectives, in Malone, T. F. & Roederer, J. G. (eds) *Twenty Years of International Programmes on Ecosystems and the Biosphere: An Overview of Achievements, Shortcomings and Possible New Perspectives* (Cambridge: Cambridge University Press).
Ehrlich, P. R. (1968) *The Population Bomb* (New York: Ballantine Books).
Elliott, L. M. (2004) *The Global Politics of the Environment*, 2nd edn (New York: New York University Press).
Falk, R. A. (1971) *This Endangered Planet: Prospects and Proposals for Human Survival* (New York: Random House).
Falk, R. A. (1975) *A Study of Future Worlds* (New York: Free Press).
Farvar, M. T. (1974) *International Development and the Human Environment: An Annotated Bibliography* (New York: Macmillan Information).
Gills, B. (ed.) (2000) *Globalization and the Politics of Resistance* (New York: St. Martin's Press).
Goldsmith, E. (1972) *Blueprint for Survival* (Boston, MA: Houghton Mifflin).
Golley, F. B. (1993) *A History of the Ecosystem Concept in Ecology: More Than the Sum of the Parts* (New Haven, CT: Yale University Press).
Goodrich, C. (1951) The United Nations Conference on Resources, *International Organization* 5(1), pp. 48–60.
Hardin, G. J. & Baden, J. (1977) *Managing the Commons* (San Francisco: W. H. Freeman).
Harrison, N. (2000) *Constructing Sustainable Development* (Albany, NY: SUNY Press).
Held, D. & McGrew, A. (eds) (2003) *The Global Transformations Reader: An Introduction to the Globalization Debate*, 2nd edn (Cambridge: Polity Press).
Jacobson, H. K. (1992) Institutions—human dimensions of global environmental change program. *Environment*, 34(5), pp. 44–45.
Jacobson, H. K. & Stein, E. (1966) *Diplomats, Scientists, and Politicians; the United States and the Nuclear Test Ban Negotiations* (Ann Arbor, MI: University of Michigan Press).
James, J. (1978) Growth, technology and the environment in less developed countries: a survey, *World Development*, 6, pp. 937–965.
Jasanoff, S. & Martello, M. L. (eds) (2004) *Earthly Politics: Local and Global in Environmental Governance* (Cambridge, MA: MIT Press).
Kamal Pasha, M. & Blaney, D. (1998) Elusive paradise: the promise and peril of global civil society, *Alternatives* 23(4), pp. 417–440.
Keck, M. & Sikkink, K. (1998) *Activists Beyond Borders: Advocacy Networks in International Politics* (Ithaca, NY: Cornell University Press).
Keohane, R. O. & Ostrom, E. (1995) *Local Commons and Global Interdependence: Heterogeneity and Cooperation in Two Domains* (London: Sage).
Kütting, G. & Rose, S. (2005) The environment as a global issue, in Betsill, M., Hochstetler, K. & Stevis, D. (eds) *Palgrave Advances in International Environmental Politics* (Basingstoke: Palgrave).
Litfin, K. (1994) *Ozone Discourses: Science and Politics in Global Environmental Cooperation* (New York: Columbia University Press).
McCormick, J. (1989) *Reclaiming Paradise: The Global Environmental Movement* (Bloomington, IN: Indiana University Press).
Meadows, D. H., Richardson, J. M. & Bruckmann, G. (1982) *Groping in the Dark: The First Decade of Global Modelling* (New York: Wiley).
Mooney, H. (1999) On the road to global ecology, *Annual Review of Energy and the Environment*, 24(1), pp. 1–31.
Neumayer, E. (2000) Trade and the environment: a critical assessment and some suggestions for reconciliation, *Journal of Environment & Development*, 9(2), pp. 138–159.
Nicholson, M. (1970) *The Environmental Revolution: A Guide for the New Masters of the World* (New York: McGraw-Hill).

Onuf, N. (1983) Reports to the Club of Rome, *World Politics* 36(1), pp. 121–146.
Ophuls, W. (1977) *Ecology and the Politics of Scarcity: Prologue to a Political Theory of the Steady State* (San Francisco: W. H. Freeman).
Orr, D. W. & Soroos, M. S. (eds) (1979) *The Global Predicament: Ecological Perspectives on World Order* (Chapel Hill, NC: University of North Carolina Press).
Osborn, F. (1948) *Our Plundered Planet* (Boston, MA: Little Brown).
Osborn, F. (1953) *The Limits of the Earth* (Boston, MA: Little Brown).
Pearce, D. (2002) An intellectual history of environmental economics, *Annual Review of Energy and the Environment*, 27, pp. 57–81.
Price, M. F. (1990) Humankind in the biosphere: the evolution of international interdisciplinary research, *Global Environmental Change*, 1(1), pp. 3–13.
Redclift, M. (1987) *Sustainable Development: Exploring the Contradictions* (London: Methuen).
Redclift, M. (1992) Sustainable development and global environmental change: implications of a changing agenda, *Global Environmental Change*, 2(1), pp. 32–42.
Soroos, M. S. (1977) The commons and lifeboat as guides for international ecological policy, *International Studies Quarterly*, 21(4), Special Issue on International Politics of Scarcity, pp. 647–674.
Steger, M. (2005) *Globalism: Market Ideology Meets Terrorism*, 2nd edn (Lanham, MD: Rowman & Littlefield Publishers).
Stevis, D. (1998) International labor organizations, 1864–1997: the weight of history and the challenges of the present, *Journal of World-Systems Research*. Available at http://jwsr.ucr.edu/4, pp. 52–75.
Stevis, D. (2002) Agents, subjects, objects or phantoms? Labor, the environment and liberal institutionalization, *Annals of the American Academy of Political and Social Science*, 581(1), pp. 91–105.
Stevis, D. (2005) The trajectory of the study of international environmental politics, in Betsill, M., Hochstetler, K. & Stevis, D. (eds) *Palgrave Advances in International Environmental Politics* (Basingstoke: Palgrave).
Taylor, P. & Buttel, F. H. (1992) How do we know we have global environmental problems? Science and the globalization of environmental discourse, *Geoforum*, 23(3), pp. 405–416.
Turner, B. L. (1990) *The Earth as Transformed by Human Action: Global and Regional Changes in the Biosphere over the Past 300 Years* (Cambridge: Cambridge University Press).
Van Buren, M. (2002) The archaeology of El Niño events and other 'natural' disasters, *Journal of Archaeological Method and Theory*, 8(2), pp. 129–149.
Vogler, J. (2000) *The Global Commons: Environmental and Technological Governance* (New York: Wiley).
Vogt, W. (1948) *Road to Survival* (New York: William Sloane Associates).
Ward, B. (1966) *Spaceship Earth* (New York: Columbia University Press).
Wijkman, M. (1982) Managing the global commons, *International Organization*, 36(3), pp. 511–536.
Williams, M. (2001) In search of global standards: the political economy of trade and the environment, pp. 39–61 in Stevis, D. & Assetto, V. (eds) *The International Political Economy of the Environment: Critical Perspectives* (Boulder, CO: Lynne Rienner Publishers).
Woodhouse, E. J. (1972) Re-visioning the future of the third world: an ecological perspective on development, *World Politics*, 25(1), pp. 1–33.
World Commission on Environment and Development (1987) *Our Common Future* (Oxford: Oxford University Press).
Yearley, S. (1996) *Sociology, Environmentalism, Globalization: Reinventing the Globe* (London: Sage).

Dimitris Stevis is professor of international politics at Colorado State University. His research focuses on the social regulation of global and regional integration with an emphasis on environment and labor. He has served as chair of the Environmental Studies Section and of the Sprout Award Committee of the International Studies Association. He has recently published chapters and articles on international environmental and labor politics and has co-edited (with Valerie Assetto) *The International Political Economy of the Environment: Critical Perspectives* (Lynne Rienner, 2001). He is currently completing a book entitled *Globalization and Labor: Democratizing Global Governance?* (with Terry Boswell) and is researching the views of labor unions towards global environmental issues.

Environmental Globalization and Tropical Forests

ALAN GRAINGER

Introduction

Globalization is often portrayed as contested but inexorable, and discussions of its relationships with the environment tend to focus on the environmental impacts of economic globalization. This paper offers a different perspective, exploring environmental globalization as a distinct dimension of globalization and the culmination of a long-term evolution of international intervention. It shows how, in the case of tropical forests, it is being resisted by the governments of developing countries. The paper consists of three parts. Part one provides an outline of key concepts. Part two describes early external initiatives to manage and conserve tropical forests. Part three interprets more recent initiatives within the framework of environmental globalization.

Environmental Globalization

There have been numerous studies of the environmental impacts of economic globalization (e.g. Gibbs, 2000; Bridge, 2002; Reed, 2002; Lejour, 2003) and of the rise in environmental governance (Johal and Ulph, 2002), both as a form of globalization and as a corrective to economic globalization.

Few authors, however, have tackled environmental globalization directly. Clark (2000) was one of the first to do so, but appears to have been constrained by editorial reasons to conform to an overarching definition of globalization as an increase in 'globalism': 'a state of the world involving networks of interdependence at multi-continental distances' (Keohane and Nye, 2000). He identified three sorts of global linkages involving: (a) global flows of energy, materials and organisms; (b) the formulation and global acceptance of ideas about the global environment; and (c) environmental governance. These are valuable perspectives but only deal, in the view of this author, with the superficial artefacts of environmental globalization, rather than addressing it directly. For instance, while the rise of environmental globalization is promoted and facilitated by the expansion of global environmental governance, which involves an increasing density of voluntary and binding regimes linking nation states that facilitates the copying of regulations, it is not an inevitable consequence of this.

Globalization is a multi-dimensional process with interactions between its various dimensions, one of which is the environment. Globalization in each dimension can be defined similarly as:

> The transformation over time of the spatial organization of the complex, contradictory, and thus ambiguous social relations, institutions and transactions—assessed in terms of their extensity, intensity, velocity, and impact—generating transcontinental or inter-regional flows and networks of activity, interaction, and the exercise of power. (Held et al., 1999; Kellner, 2002)

Environmental globalization therefore becomes apparent in an increasing spatial uniformity and connectedness in regular environmental management practices. Similar trends in administration, production or consumption practices are found in other dimensions. The contradictory and ambiguous features of globalization are evident in interactions between its various dimensions. Thus, concern about the environmental impacts of economic globalization, apparently driven by transnational corporations and other interests of international capital, generates globalizing responses by non-governmental organizations (NGOs), governments and intergovernmental organizations aimed at controlling or regulating these.

Narratives, Discourses, Institutions and Globalization

The spread of globalization, and resistance to this, can be understood using the concepts of narrative, discourse and institution. Narrative refers here to a meaningful totality of past and future events (Labov, 1972; Ricoeur, 1981; Barton, 2000). Each actor assembles its narrative within its own frame of reference, or discourse. Discourse is defined in a Foucauldian way (Sharp and Richardson, 2001) as 'a historically, socially and institutionally specific structure of statements, terms, categories and beliefs' (Scott, 1988) which 'gives meaning to physical and social relations' (Hajer, 1995).

Institutions, the regular formal or informal practices found in a society, are fundamental to globalization. They are not mere techniques that can be adopted and changed at will, but are socially configured and, according to one strand of neo-institutionalism (e.g. North, 1990), historically contingent. As Fairclough (1992) explained, an institution is 'an order of discourse [which] simultaneously facilitates and constrains the social action of its members', while for Schmidt and Radaelli (2002), institutions are 'socially constructed, historically evolving, and/ or interest-based roles of interaction that represent incentives, opportunities, and/or constraints for individual and collective actors'.

Focusing on globalization as the developing outcome of historical processes, and not a causal factor in its own right, avoids generating another 'folly' of globalization theory (Rosenberg, 2000). It also shines the spotlight on a fundamental mechanism of globalization—the institutionalization of globally optimal preferences through repetitive actions. The need for such actions to be upwardly nested through different orders of compatible discourses (Rein and Schoen, 1994) if they are to become institutionalized helps to explain how resistance can occur to various dimensions of globalization (see below). It also shows why attempts to interpret behaviour in one society within the framework of institutions found in another can lead to problems, as in the recent focus by environmentalists on so-called 'illegal logging' in tropical countries. Viewing disparities between logging practices and the legal codes enshrined in the modern state in a developing country overlooks the fact that the actual structure of power may reside elsewhere. Things may therefore not be as simple as they seem (e.g. McCarthy, 2002), and such practices may not be perceived within the country as illegal at all.

Tropical Forests and their Management

Tropical forests account for about 60% of world forest area. They have received considerable international attention in recent decades in response to claims that they contain half of all species on the planet (Myers, 1985) and 20–40% of all carbon in terrestrial vegetation (Brown et al., 1989), which gives them a significant role in attempts to manage the global carbon budget to combat climate change. They are mainly composed of broadleaved trees and can be divided into two main groups:

1. *Closed forests.* Closest to the Equator are found tropical rain forests, which mainly consist of evergreen broadleaved trees with valuable hardwoods, such as mahogany. These give way at higher latitudes, where rainfall is still heavy but more seasonal, to tropical moist deciduous forests, which shed their leaves in the dry season and also contain valuable hardwoods, such as teak. These are the two main types of tropical moist forest. Some closed forests also occur in the dry tropics.
2. *Open forests and woodlands.* At higher latitudes, where rainfall is relatively low and even more seasonal, are found open forests and woodlands, also known as savannas. These are mixtures of trees, shrubs and grasses of varying densities.

Tropical forests are subject to two main types of human impacts: *deforestation*, in which forest is cleared, mostly for agriculture, and *degradation*, in which the forest remains but canopy cover, tree density and/or biomass density is reduced, e.g. by selective logging, which removes the largest commercial trees but leaves the vast majority of trees behind (Lanly, 1981). (The meanings of these two terms are, however, contested.)

Tropical forests covered a total of 1,785 million ha in the year 2000. About 60% of this was closed forest—the majority of which is tropical moist forest—and the remainder open forest. As a result of deforestation this area was 7.5% lower than in 1990 (Table 1). The overall annual deforestation rate in the 1990s was only slightly lower than in the 1980s (Table 2) (FAO, 2001).

Table 1. Areas of forest in tropical countries, 1980, 1990 and 2000 (thousand ha) as shown in successive Forest Resource Assessments of the UN Food and Agriculture Organization (FAO). FRA 1990 and FRA 2000 contain a corrected set of estimates for the previous assessment in addition to the current estimates

	FRA 1980	FRA 1990		FRA 2000	
	1980	1980	1990	1990	2000
Africa	703,079	568,600	527,576	682,233	627,894
Asia-Pacific	336,458	349,600	310,595	311,926	263,776
Latin America	930,659	992,200	918,121	936,093	893,238
Total	1,970,196	1,910,400	1,756,292	1,930,252	1,784,908
Countries	76	90	90	90	90

Sources: FAO Forest Resource Assessments from 1980, FRA 1980 (Lanly, 1981); 1990, FRA 1990 (FAO, 1993); and 2000, FRA 2000 (FAO, 2001).

As most tropical closed forests are on public lands, ultimate responsibility for managing and conserving them lies in the hands of state forestry departments. Operational management of closed forests in the humid tropics for tropical hardwood production has normally been delegated through concession systems to private firms, whose performance is monitored and regulated by forestry departments. However, since 1990 decentralizing operational responsibility to local communities has become increasingly popular (Ribot, 2002).

Tropical hardwood has become an increasingly important part of world trade in wood products since the end of World War II but the organization of logging and international trade in tropical hardwood is not typical of a sector undergoing economic globalization. Exports rose 14-fold between 1950 and 1980, with most of the increase coming from forests in Southeast Asia, whose share of exports rose to 83% by 1980, though it has declined slightly since then. The global trend in logging location has generally corresponded to an economically optimum pattern, with low unit extraction cost reserves (concentrated in Southeast Asia) being exploited before higher cost reserves in Africa and Latin America. However, this spatial optimization appears to have been achieved more by the operation of market forces than by the planning

Table 2. Deforestation rates for 90 tropical countries 1980–1990 and 1990–2000 (thousand ha·a^{-1})

	Deforestation rates	
	1980–1990	1990–2000
Africa	4,102	5,434
Asia-Pacific	3,901	4,815
Latin America	7,408	4,286
Total	15,411	14,534

Source: FAO (2001).

of transnational corporations, whose direct role in logging has been relatively limited (Grainger, 1993).

Sustainable forest management ensures a continuing flow of products and services from a given area of forest indefinitely. By definition this requires that the forest concerned is effectively protected from deforestation. The traditional productivist forest sustainability paradigm, based on sustained commercial timber yield, has now been superseded by a post-productivist sustainability paradigm, recognized in the Statement of Forest Principles (1992) and the 2nd International Tropical Timber Agreement (1994) (see below). This also requires that forestry operations undermine neither the sustainability of environmental services nor that of local and national communities (Mather, 2001).

Insufficient attention has been paid to how new paradigms of this kind emerge from specific 'higher order' discourses in particular countries and how attempts to introduce a new paradigm elsewhere may fail if similar higher order discourses are absent. For example, the introduction of modern 'scientific forestry' by colonial powers in developing countries was incompatible with indigenous traditional discourses; and the post-productivist sustainability paradigm which has emerged from the higher order discourses of 'post-modern states' may not be compatible with those of states that are only partially modernized.

The Prelude to Environmental Globalization

The historical process of environmental globalization can be divided, in the case of tropical forests, into three eras: colonial, modern and post-modern.

Colonial Era

In the colonial era the need to conserve and manage tropical forests was deduced from an environmental crisis narrative portraying the soil degradation, flooding, irregular water supplies and even climate change that could result from deforestation (Troup, 1940; Millington, 1987). This, in turn, emerged from a colonial environmental discourse, adopted in British and French colonial forestry circles and called an ecological 'science of empire' by Robin (1997), that linked together deforestation, desertification and changes in climate (Fairhead and Leach, 1998). Central to colonial environmental discourse was 'scientific forestry', a system of managing forest ecosystems based on scientific observation of the growth of trees and requiring the establishment of forest reserves free from all uses except commercial timber production (Lanz, 2000). When applied to tropical countries this led to antagonism on the part of indigenous people who were expelled from the new reserves and prevented by law from practising traditional uses within them.

Given the vast extent of the British and French empires the spread of scientific forestry in the colonial era could be regarded as an early stage of environmental globalization. There are parallels too with economic globalization, e.g. the contribution of trade to the British economy peaked in 1913 and has never been equalled subsequently (Knox and Agnew, 1994). However, in common with Dicken (1998) we distinguish contemporary globalization from that in the colonial era by its greater intensity and depth (as in the above definition), as well as by its contradictory, ambiguous, fragmented and pluralistic features, which are typical of post-modernity and theories of this (Best and Kellner, 1991).

Modern Era

In the modern era, tropical deforestation was a key element of the Neo-Malthusian narrative, in which the planet's natural resource stocks were being depleted and its environments despoiled by population growth and economic growth. This contested narratives emerging from modernization theory which privileged the latter. In the late 1960s concern about forests expanded to the global scale. Helped by space exploration, people could now conceive of how the planet as a whole was being affected their activities.

The notion of 'Spaceship Earth', that was central to the UN Conference on the Human Environment held in Stockholm in 1972 (Ward and Dubois, 1972), led almost imperceptibly to a globalist environmental discourse that challenged all countries to protect their environments to save the planet as an ethical concern external to the development of national economies, and to be judged by the same standards. Although improving the balance between environment and development was intended to be one of four main themes discussed at the Stockholm Conference it was overshadowed by the other three themes: improving human settlements, slowing natural resource depletion and reducing pollution (Caldwell, 1990). As a result, environmental protection was privileged over the needs and rights of the people of developing countries to attain a higher standard of life through economic development. These countries were expected to play a major part in conservation because they contained a large share of the planet's remaining pristine environments, unspoiled by industrialism. In this discourse, tropical deforestation was seen as a 'problem', not an inevitable consequence of development as had been experienced in temperate countries in the past.

Three major initiatives to tackle the tropical forest 'problem' were launched in this era:

1. World Conservation Strategy. The World Conservation Strategy (WCS), was published by the International Union for the Conservation of Nature (IUCN, 1980) as a framework for conserving all major global ecosystems, including tropical forests. Each country was invited on a voluntary basis to devise its own national conservation strategy and 35 countries did so (World Resources Institute, 1988).

2. Tropical Forestry Action Plan. During the second half of the 1980s efforts to conserve tropical forests generally focused on supporting the Tropical Forestry Action Plan (TFAP), first published in 1985 by the World Resources Institute, the World Bank and the UN Development Programme. Although its main goal was supposed to be controlling deforestation, most of its recommendations concerned forestry and conservation activities, and it largely ignored the agriculture sector, which is the major cause of deforestation (Grainger, 1993). However, 74 tropical countries participated in the TFAP and formulated National Forestry Action Plans, and overseas aid to tropical forestry doubled between 1984 and 1988 (Winterbottom, 1990).

3. First International Tropical Timber Agreement. The First International Tropical Timber Agreement (ITTA1) was finalized in 1983, ratified over the next two years, and became operational in 1986. It provided a framework within which tropical hardwood producing and importing countries could work together to improve the sustainability of forest management, the effectiveness of conservation, and the diversification of the tropical hardwood trade and processing industries, with projects being funded by the importing countries (Poore, 2003). The signatories of ITTA1 (21 producing countries and 25 importing countries) held regular meetings of the International Tropical Timber Council, approved numerous collaborative projects, commissioned a major study of the extent of sustainable management (Poore, 1989), and devised criteria for measuring the sustainability of tropical forest management. In contrast to the other two 'action programmes' listed above, ITTA1 was a binding international regime, a regime being 'a social institution with ... agreed principles, norms, rules, procedures and programmes that govern the activities and shape the expectations of actors in a specific issue area' (Greene, 1997). Yet all three initiatives were intended to support the development of national capabilities in tropical countries and did not impose any duties on governments in respect of how they managed their forests.

The Post-Modern Era: the Spread of Environmental Globalization

In the post-modern era, the debate on tropical forests has become more fractured, complex, ambiguous and discursive. Most leading actors in the tropical forest debate now have a public voice, no matter how small. Since the mid-1980s there has been a distinct shift from voluntary and collaborative schemes towards adopting a more coercive and regulatory approach to the activities of the governments of developing countries in managing tropical forests. This has been led by national and international donor organizations, and by non-governmental organizations (NGOs) which increased their influence by forming international networks to become a major part of 'global civil society' (Keane, 2001). However, it has been resisted by developing countries, through (a) ambiguity, and (b) direct confrontation—sometimes with the help of their own networks.

Imposition of Environmental Conditions by Donor Organizations

1. Direct Environmental Conditionality. The earliest initiative contributing to environmental globalization was probably the introduction in the 1980s of environmental conditions for development projects funded by multilateral and bilateral donor organizations. Among the former, the World Bank developed policies on protecting indigenous peoples and conserving biodiversity (Ledec and Goodland, 1988). If it funded the building of a road through an area of tropical rain forest then it imposed conditions on the route and construction methods. These may have required the establishment of new protected areas, such as national parks. Environmental conditionality has encouraged the global spread of environmental impact assessment procedures too (Hironaka, 2002).

2. Indirect Environmental Conditionality and Resistance by Ambiguity. International donor organizations have also pressed the governments of developing countries to adopt more environmentally sustainable policies as a condition for receiving aid in general. Some governments, however, have resisted this through the instrumental use of ambiguity, for while the published, or stated, forest policy of a government may have the goal of sustainable management this does not necessarily accord with its actual policy, which may be exactly the opposite (Grainger and Malayang, 2005). Thus, in 1980 the government of Sierra Leone asked the UN Food and Agriculture Organization (FAO) to undertake a Forest Sector Review, as the last Forest Ordinance had been passed in 1912. The FAO made detailed proposals for a new Forest Act (FAO, 1982), but when the government showed reluctance to follow the FAO's advice, donor agencies implied that they would not fund any more forestry projects in the country. To assuage them the government published the Forest Act of 1988, following the FAO's proposals virtually word for word (GOSL, 1988). The government then proceeded to ignore the Act entirely. A subsequent administration was obliged to publish a comprehensive National Environmental Policy (MLHE, 1992) in return for receiving assistance from the World Bank, but this stated policy suffered a similar fate (Grainger and Konteh, 2005).

Non-Governmental Organization Schemes

Frustrated at the lack of successful action by governments and international organizations to control deforestation, NGOs increased the scope of their activities, even to the extent of adopting roles previously reserved for governments.

1. Debt for Nature Swaps. For instance, NGOs used 'debt for nature swaps' to complement efforts by the governments of developed countries to relieve the severe debt crisis faced by developing countries in the 1980s. Initiated by the US NGO Conservation International, debt for nature swaps involved NGOs purchasing the national debt of tropical countries in US dollars from banks, provided that the governments of these countries agreed to put an equivalent amount of local currency into the conservation of tropical forests and other environmentally important areas (Dunne, 1989). This parallels the indirect form of environmental conditionality discussed above.

2. Forest Certification Schemes. A second initiative involved encouraging the establishment of organizations to identify which forests were managed sustainably so that timber extracted from these could be given labels recognized as authoritative by overseas wholesalers, retailers and consumers (Upton and Bass, 1995). Here NGOs were using market mechanisms to put pressure on the governments of tropical countries to improve the sustainability of forest management, rather than attempting to influence them directly. A pioneer in this field was the Forest Stewardship Council, initially launched in 1990 with support from the Worldwide Fund for Nature (WWF) and leading retailers, such as B&Q, the British DIY store. B&Q agreed that by the year 2000 it would only sell timber accredited by FSC as coming from sustainably managed forests. In order to meet demand for tropical hardwood controlled by merchants recognizing the authority of these certification organizations, governments would have to follow the international set of rules required by each organization for the certification of sustainability. Of the four approaches with the potential for globalization listed so far, this one had the most chance of success because it was based on results rather than just intentions, which governments could later disavow, although the establishment of national certification systems within the framework of FSC principles (Elliott and Schlaepfer, 2001) could be seen as a modest resistance to international intervention.

Although sustainable forest management necessarily requires the protection of forest from deforestation by farmers, the growth of forest certification is linked to other factors. Unlike WWF, environmentalist pressure groups, such as Friends of the Earth and Greenpeace, were latecomers to the tropical forest field, and when they did arrive in the late 1980s they brought with them preconceived notions, e.g. that deforestation is mainly caused by logging (Thomson, 1988), and made various attempts to persuade governments to ban imports of wood taken from tropical forests that were not sustainably managed (Grainger, 1993). This focus on logging partly reflected their suspicion about the economic and political power wielded by transnational corporations, which was widespread among the 'alternative' movement at the time. (This hegemony was also the subject of extensive academic analysis by economic geographers in the 1970s and 1980s (Winters, 1985; Healey and Ilbery, 1988) that was the forerunner of studies of globalization.) NGOs also wrongly assumed that logging in tropical countries requires clearfelling, as in temperate countries. Whether this is true or not is not important, because in our media-dominated post-modern world NGOs are often able to impose their interpretations through their superior symbolic skills (Tsoukas, 1999). Ironically, experience so far suggests that the spread of certification does not guarantee an end to deforestation (Nebel et al., 2005).

Lobbying at International Institutions

1. International Tropical Timber Council. WWF and other NGOs continued to lobby governments to become more proactive on tropical forests. By participating in meetings of the International Tropical Timber Council they persuaded developed country governments to ensure that the Second International Tropical Timber Agreement (ITTA2), signed in January 1994, was more coercive than its predecessor. For instance, it required producing countries to commit themselves to adopting by the year 2000 policies whose goals would include sustainable management. In return, developed country members agreed to set appropriate guidelines for sustainably managing their own forests, using standards agreed at the Ministerial Conference on the Protection of European Forests in Helsinki in 1993.

Most of the now 29 producing country members actually fulfilled their obligation by enacting by 2000 new policies with sustainable management as their primary goal (Poore, 2003), though they were not obliged to implement these. Signatories to ITTA2 agreed to focus on implementation under their Yokohama Action Plan 2002–2006, but whether much progress towards achieving sustainable management will be achieved in so short a time is doubtful. The use of policy ambiguity is widespread and the gap between ideal indicators of the sustainability of tropical forest management and current logging practices is still very wide (McDonald and Lane, 2004). Negotiations on a Third International Tropical Timber Agreement were, at the time of writing, expected to be completed in early 2006.

2. World Trade Organization. NGOs also lobbied member governments of the World Trade Organization (WTO) to add environmental conditions to world trade rules in order to, among other things, prevent tropical countries from exporting wood extracted from unsustainably managed forests. However, they have not been very successful. Under trade rules inherited by WTO from its predecessor, the General Agreement on Tariffs and Trade (GATT), it is an unfair restriction on trade for one country to restrict imports from other countries that do not share its environmental laws, or to discriminate between imports on the basis of the *process* by which a particular *product* was made, e.g. the sustainability of harvesting. Greenpeace responded to these judgements by calling GATT an organization 'subservient to multinational corporations' (Dunne, 1992). WWF opposed the creation of the WTO, calling it incompatible with the goal of sustainable development. It believed the new body should recognize 'the need to set limits on trade in order to adequately protect the environment' (Williams, 1993).

The campaign to integrate environmental standards into world trade rules continued at the WTO meeting in Seattle in November 1999 that was intended to launch a new round of trade liberalization talks. The European Union was keen to promote discussion about environmental standards, partly to deflect criticism from other countries about its farm subsidies. Unfortunately, the meeting ended in acrimony, as WTO member states were heavily divided on many issues and a consensus could not be reached. At the request of the EU, environmental conditionality was again placed on the agenda of the next WTO Ministerial Meeting held in Doha, in Qatar, in November 2001, but was not given a high priority. The resulting 'Doha Declaration' merely 'took note' of 'efforts by members to conduct national environmental assessments of trade policies on a voluntary basis' and asked its Trade and Environment Committee to check if there was any conflict between WTO rules and trade obligations in environmental agreements. The environment was given an even lower priority at the next meeting, in Cancun, Mexico in September 2003. Attempts at the World Summit on Sustainable Development in Johannesburg in 2002 to include in the 'Johannesburg Declaration' a clause to give WTO primacy over links between trade and environment were also defeated.

Direct Resistance to Environmental Globalization: Blocking a Forest Convention

The governments of developing countries engaged in direct confrontation to defeat an attempt by NGOs and the governments of some developed countries to get a Forest Convention signed at the UN Conference on Environment and Development (UNCED), held in Rio de Janeiro in 1992. This was intended to be a set of common guidelines for forest management in all countries, though the main aim was to regulate tropical forest management. If successful, this would have been an important step towards extending environmental globalization (Pearce, 1992). However, developing countries fought hard before UNCED to prevent agreement on a Forest Convention because they thought it would undermine their sovereign right to choose how to balance the economic, social and environmental dimensions of their development. According to Dr Mahathir Mohamad, then Prime Minister of Malaysia, 'A convention would only be fair if we could also tell the North that they could not have this or that factory' (Anon, 1992). The Kuala Lumpur network of governments of forested countries stated at their meeting before UNCED that the developed countries were using the convention as 'an attempt to spread the blame for the greenhouse problem', because of carbon dioxide emitted by tropical deforestation (Goldemberg, 1994). Developed countries even offered to support a Convention on Desertification, which was a priority for African countries, in return for support for the Forest Convention. However, the much larger network of all developing countries active at UNCED—the 'Group of 77'—was sufficiently cohesive and powerful to gain agreement to negotiate a Convention on Desertification without having to compromise in this way.

Accordingly, only voluntary Statement of Forest Principles was approved at UNCED, and its text was bland and limited in scope. For example, at the request of the Group of 77:

1. All references to a future Forest Convention were removed from the preamble. So it referred only to 'appropriate internationally agreed arrangements to promote international cooperation'.
2. No mention was made of the 'global' importance of forests, in order not to encroach on national sovereignty, so the text spoke only of forests being 'essential to the economy as a whole'. According to Kamal Nath, the Indian Environment Minister at the time, 'We do not talk about the globalization of oil. Yet oil has a greater impact than forests on the global environment' (Anon, 1992). The text also outlawed unilateral boycotts on 'unsustainable' forest products (Lamb, 1992).

Although a series of meetings was held after UNCED to try to bridge the gap between developing and developed countries on a Forest Convention, no substantive progress was made. However, an Intergovernmental Panel on Forests was established by the UN Commission on Sustainable Development, and this led in turn to the creation of the UN Forum on Forests.

In 2001 this launched an initiative to implement National Forest Programmes worldwide, with the aim of applying to forest policy making the participatory approach of Agenda 21— the 'action plan' for sustainable development agreed at UNCED. A number of countries have since established these programmes (Schanz, 2002).

Clean Development Mechanism of the Framework Convention on Climate Change

One of the most globally uniform set of rules for forestry projects yet adopted is probably the set of regulations for determining how carbon sequestration by afforestation and reforestation projects is accounted for under the Kyoto Protocol of the Framework Convention on Climate Change agreed at UNCED. Article 3.3 of the Protocol allows carbon uptake by afforestation and reforestation and carbon emissions by deforestation to be included when calculating a country's net emissions of greenhouse gases. Developing countries are not currently required to comply with the Protocol, but Article 12 allows developed country signatories to receive credits under the Clean Development Mechanism for assisting developing countries to sequester more carbon, e.g. by expanding their forest plantations, and so the regulations would apply to such projects. Following a detailed study of definitions and accounting procedures by the Intergovernmental Panel on Climate Change (IPCC, 2000), the rules were agreed at the Sixth Conference of the Parties (COP 6), held in Bonn in 2001, COP 7 in Marrakesh in 2002, and COP 10 in Buenos Aires in 2004, and they continue to be refined.

Informal Environmental Globalization

This paper has focused on attempts to spread environmental globalisation to the management of the commercially important closed forests in the humid tropics by imposing formal rules through government agency. Yet NGOs have also long been involved in funding and implementing small scale community afforestation projects for environmental protection and the supply of fuelwood, fodder and other basic needs in drier areas (Grainger, 1984). While the practices involved vary considerably, they reflect a post-modern environmental ethos, are usually channelled directly to grassroots level with limited government impediment and, significantly, reflect considerable national, regional and global networking between NGOs (Grainger, 1990). Consequently, their overall impact can be considered an informal form of environmental globalization which deserves further study.

Conclusions

This has only been an initial exploration of the spread of environmental globalization. However, because tropical forests have been an important issue in international environmental politics for so long, the development of overseas pressures to first assist and then coerce the governments of developing countries to control deforestation and manage tropical forests more sustainably provides a useful context for assessing the effectiveness of attempts to impose globally uniform sets of rules for environmental management. This experience shows that environmental globalization has been resisted by the governments of developing countries through: (a) policy ambiguity, and (b) collective action to directly contest the imposition of new institutions, most notably in defeating plans for a Forest Convention. It also suggests that environmental globalization will only spread slowly in future, at least as far as tropical forests are concerned.

64   A. Grainger

Acknowledgement

The author is indebted to Jan Oosthoek for drawing his attention to the importance of informal environmental globalization.

References

Anon. (1992) Third World fends off controls on forests, *Financial Times*, 20 June.
Barton, E. (2000) Sanctioned and non-sanctioned narratives in institutional discourse, *Narrative Inquiry*, 10, pp. 341–375.
Best, S. & Kellner, D. (1991) *Postmodern Theory: Critical Interrogations* (Basingstoke: Palgrave).
Bridge, G. (2002) Grounding globalization: the prospects and perils of linking economic processes of globalization to environmental outcomes, *Economic Geography*, 78, pp. 361–385.
Brown, S., Gillespie, A. J. R. & Lugo, A. E. (1989) Biomass estimation methods for tropical forests with applications to forest inventory data, *Forest Science*, 35, pp. 881–902.
Caldwell, L. K. (1990) *International Environmental Policy* (Durham, NC: Duke University Press).
Clark, W. C. (2000) Environmental globalization, pp. 86–108 in Nye, J. S., Jr. & Donahue, J. D. (eds) *Governance in a Globalising World* (Washington, DC: Brookings Institution Press).
Dicken, P. (1998) *Global Shift*, 3rd edn (London: Paul Chapman).
Dunne, N. (1989) Ecuador in $9 million debt-for-nature swap, *Financial Times*, 10 April.
Dunne, N. (1992) Fears over 'Gattzilla the trade monster', *Financial Times*, 30 January.
Grainger, A. (1993) *Controlling Tropical Deforestation* (London: Earthscan).
Elliott, C. & Schlaepfer, R. (2001) Understanding forest certification using the Advocacy Coalition Framework, *Forest Policy and Economics*, 2, pp. 257–266.
Fairclough, N. (1992) *Discourse and Social Change* (Cambridge: Polity Press).
Fairhead, J. & Leach, M. (1998) *Reframing Deforestation* (London: Routledge).
FAO (1982) Joint Inter-Agency Forestry Sector Review Mission, Sierra Leone. Issues Paper (Rome: UN Food and Agriculture Organization).
FAO (1993) *Forest Resources Assessment 1990: Tropical Countries*, FAO Forestry Paper No. 112 (Rome: UN Food and Agriculture Organization).
FAO (2001) *Forest Resources Assessment 2000*, FAO Forestry Paper No. 140 (Rome: UN Food and Agriculture Organization).
Gibbs, D. (2000) Globalization, the bioscience industry and local environmental responses, *Global Environmental Change*, 10, pp. 245–257.
Goldemberg, J. (1994) The road to Rio, pp. 175–186 in Mintzer, I. & Leonard, J. A. (eds) *Negotiating Climate Change. The Inside Story of the Rio Convention* (Cambridge: Cambridge University Press).
GOSL (Government of Sierra Leone) (1988) The Forest Act, 1988, Supplement to the Sierra Leone Gazette Extraordinary (Freetown: Government Printers).
Grainger, A. (1984) Activating policies for increasing the effectiveness of afforestation policies in the tropics involving non-governmental organizations, pp. 375–385 in Wiersum, K. F. (ed) *Proceedings of an International Symposium on Strategies and Designs for Afforestation, Reforestation and Tree Planting* (Wageningen, Netherlands: Pudoc).
Grainger, A. (1990) *The Spreading Desert: Controlling Desertification* (London: Earthscan).
Grainger, A. (1993) *Controlling Tropical Deforestation* (London: Earthscan).
Grainger, A. & Konteh, W. (2005) Autonomy, ambiguity and symbolism in African politics: the development of forest policy in Sierra Leone, *Land Use Policy* (in press).
Grainger, A. & Malayang, B. (2005) A model of policy changes to secure sustainable forest management and control of deforestation in the tropics, *Forest Policy and Economics* (in press).
Greene, O. (1997) Environmental issues, pp. 313–338 in Baylis, J. & Smith, S. (eds) *The Globalization of World Politics* (Oxford: Oxford University Press).
Hajer, M. A. (1995) *The Politics of Environmental Discourse. Ecological Modernization and the Policy Process* (Oxford: Clarendon Press).
Healey, M. J. & Ilbery, B. W. (1988) *Location and Change: Perspectives on Economic Geography* (Oxford: Oxford University Press).
Held, D., McGrew, A., Goldblatt, D. & Perraton, J. (1999) *Global Transformations: Politics, Economics and Culture* (Cambridge: Polity Press).

Hironaka, A. (2002) The globalization of environmental protection: the case of environmental impact assessment, *International Journal of Comparative Sociology*, 43, pp. 65–78.

IPCC (2000) *Special Report on Land Use, Land Use Change and Forestry* (Geneva: Intergovernmental Panel on Climate Change).

IUCN (1980) *World Conservation Strategy* (Gland: International Union for the Conservation of Nature (World Conservation Union)).

Johal, S. & Ulph, A. (2002) Globalization, lobbying and international environmental governance, *Review of International Economics*, 10, pp. 387–403.

Keane, J. (2001) Global civil society?, pp. 121–145 in Anheier, H., Glasius, M. & Kaldor, M. (eds) *Global Civil Society 2001* (Oxford: Oxford University Press).

Kellner, D. (2002) Theorizing globalization, *Sociological Theory*, 20, pp. 285–305.

Keohane, R. O. & Nye, J. S., Jr. (2000) Introduction, pp. 1–41 in Nye, J. S., Jr. & Donahue, J. D. (eds) *Governance in a Globalising World* (Washington, DC: Brookings Institution Press).

Knox, P. & Agnew, J. (1994) *The Geography of the World Economy* (London: Edward Arnold).

Labov, W. (ed) (1972) The transformation of experience in narrative syntax, pp. 354–396 in *Language in the Inner City* (Philadelphia, PA: University of Pennsylvania Press).

Lamb, C. (1992) Forest set fire to world passions, *Financial Times*, 15 June.

Lanly, J. P. (ed) (1981) *Tropical Forest Resources Assessment Project (GEMS): Tropical Africa, Tropical Asia, Tropical America*, 4 Vols. (Rome: UN Food and Agriculture Organization/UN Environment Programme).

Lanz, T. (2000) The origins, development and legacy of scientific forestry in Cameroon, *Environment and History*, 6, pp. 99–120.

Ledec, G. & Goodland, R. (1988) *Wildlands: Their Protection and Management in Economic Development* (Washington DC: World Bank).

Lejour, A. (2003) Globalization and the global environment: four quantitative scenarios, *Transportation Planning and Technology*, 26, pp. 9–40.

Mather, A. S. (2001) Forests of consumption: postproductivism, postmaterialism, and the postindustrial forest, *Environment and Planning C*, 19, pp. 249–268.

McCarthy, J. F. (2002) Turning in circles: district governance, illegal logging, and environmental decline in Sumatra, Indonesia, *Society and Natural Resources*, 15, pp. 867–886.

McDonald, G. T. & Lane, M. B. (2004) Converging global indicators for sustainable forest management, *Forest Policy and Economics*, 6, pp. 63–70.

Millington, A. C. (1987) Environmental degradation, soil conservation and agricultural policies in Sierra Leone 1895–1984, pp. 229–248 in Anderson, D. & Grove, R. (eds). *Conservation in Africa: People, Policies and Practice* (Cambridge: Cambridge University Press).

MLHE (1992) National Report for Sierra Leone to the United Nations Conference on Environment and Development (Freetown: Ministry of Lands, Housing and the Environment).

Myers, N. (1985) *The Primary Source* (New York: W. W. Norton).

Nebel, G., Quevedo, L., Jacobsen, J. B. & Helles, F. (2005) Development and economic significance of certification: the case of FSC in Bolivia, *Forest Policy and Economics*, 7, pp. 175–186.

North, D. C. (1990) *Institutions, Institutional Change and Economic Performance* (Cambridge: Cambridge University Press).

Pearce, F. (1992) How green was our summit? *New Scientist*, 27 July, pp. 12–13.

Poore, M. E. D. (ed.) (1989) *No Timber Without Trees* (London: Earthscan Publications).

Poore, M. E. D. (2003) *Changing Landscapes: The Development of the International Tropical Timber Organization and its Influence on Tropical Forest Management* (London: Earthscan Publications).

Reed, D. (2002) Poverty and the environment: can sustainable development survive globalization? *Natural Resources Forum*, 26, pp. 176–184.

Rein, D. & Schoen, M. (1994) *Frame Reflection* (New York: Basic Books).

Ribot, J. (2002) *Democratic Decentralization of Natural Resources: Institutionalizing Popular Participation* (Washington DC: World Resources Institute).

Ricoeur, P. (1981) *Hermeneutics and the Human Science* (Cambridge: Cambridge University Press).

Robin, L. (1997) Ecology: a science of empire?, pp. 63–75 in Griffiths T. & Robin L. (eds) *Ecology and Empire: Environmental History of Settler Societies* (Keele: Keele University Press).

Rosenberg, J. (2000) *The Follies of Globalization Theory* (London: Verso).

Schanz, H. (2002) National forest programmes as discursive institutions, *Forest Policy and Economics*, 4, pp. 269–279.

Schmidt, V. & Radaelli, C. (2002) Europeanisation, discourse and policy change: mapping the new research agenda, Paper presented at the ECPR Joint Sessions, 5 March, Turin.
Scott, J. (1988) Deconstructing equality-versus-difference: or the uses of poststructuralist theory for feminism, *Feminist Studies*, 14, pp. 33–50.
Sharp, L. & Richardson, T. (2001) Reflections on Foucauldian discourse analysis in planning and environmental policy research, *Journal of Environmental Policy and Planning*, 3, pp. 193–209.
Thomson, K. (1988) The Friends of the Earth tropical rain forest campaign, pp. 58–61 in McDermott, M. J. (ed) *The Future of the Tropical Rain Forest* (Oxford: Oxford Forestry Institute).
Troup, R. S. (1940) *Colonial Forest Administration* (Oxford: Oxford University Press).
Tsoukas, H. (1999) David and Goliath in the risk society: making sense of the conflict between Shell and Greenpeace in the North Sea, *Organization*, 6, pp. 499–528.
Upton, C. & Bass, S. (1995) *The Forest Certification Handbook* (London: Earthscan).
Ward, B. & Dubois, R. (1972) *Only One Earth* (Harmondsworth: Penguin).
Williams, F. (1993) Green group calls for limits on world trade, *Financial Times*, 1 June.
Winterbottom, R. (1990) *Taking Stock: The Tropical Forestry Action Plan After Five Years* (Washington DC: World Resources Institute).
Winters, A. (1985) *International Economics*, 3rd edn (London: George Allen &Unwin).
World Resources Institute, World Bank & UN Development Programme (1985) *Tropical Forests: A Call for Action* (Washington DC: World Resources Institute).
World Resources Institute (1988) *World Resources 1988–89* (New York: Basic Books).

Alan Grainger is Senior Lecturer in Geography at the University of Leeds. He is the author of *The Spreading Desert: Controlling Desertification* (1990) and *Controlling Tropical Deforestation* (1993), and co-editor of *Exploring Sustainable Development: Geographical Perspectives* (2004). He has been Editor of the *Journal of Forest Policy* (formerly the *Journal of World Forest Resource Management*) since 1984.

The Sustainability Debate: Idealism versus Conformism—the Controversy over Economic Growth

S. W. VERSTEGEN AND J. C. HANEKAMP

Introduction

Since the publication of *Our Common Future* in 1987, scientists have struggled with the concept of sustainability and many definitions are now in existence. In 1989, Pezzey counted 60 (Kula, 1998, p. 147), Kastenholz could find even more than 60 in 1996 (Steurer, 2002, p. 244). A comparison of the 57 definitions the MIT listed in 1997 (Murcott, 1997) shows, however, that one can differentiate between a much smaller series of themes. Working from these definitions, we focus on six such themes; these are presented here not as a means to reach a final decision as to what sustainability is. On the contrary, what we will show is that these themes are the battleground for two opposing worldviews within Western society that are not complementary and thereby rule each other out. We will further reorganize the discussion on sustainability by distinguishing two political opposites.

The first, the *idealistic strand*, operates in clear opposition to mainstream politics. Its adherents depict the present state of our society in different gradations from grey to pitch-black, and are therefore usually called 'pessimists'. Economic growth in their view cannot continue because in the end it will destroy nature and with it human society. Here we can discriminate three themes: 1) conservation of resources and nature 2) the quality of life and 3) cultural conservation.

However, an *idealistic* conception lies underneath. 'Pessimism' is a political tool to persuade us to accept the idealistic framework and so make possible a political climate to reach what the Club of Rome once called 'a harmonious state of global economic, social and ecological equilibrium' (Meadows and Meadows, 1972, p. 198). It is a line of thought that focuses on a better world and it is a variation on the theme of the search for the 'good society' (Hollander, 1998).

By contrast, the *conformist strand* are contemporary 'optimists', whose analyses of today's society is not so bleak. They focus on 1) technological progress, 2) economic growth and 3) fighting poverty. They also use all kinds of definitions of sustainability. Real concern is uttered as well as lip service paid to the seriousness of the environmental crisis. However, they do not envision a break with the past but try to fit solutions to environmental problems in the existing political, social and technological framework of economic growth, which has dominated Western society at least since World War II. The agenda here is that of political and economic continuity.

In essence the debate about sustainability is one between *revolution*, be it a peaceful and gradual one, and *evolution*. The revolutionary character in the sustainability debate was best formulated by Maurice Strong in 1992 (cited in Murcott, 1997, 36), who defined sustainable development as 'a process of deep and profound change in the political, social, economic, institutional, and technological order, including redefinition of relations between developing and more developed countries'. On the other end of the spectrum we find the 'business as usual' definition of David Pearce, formulated in 1993, in which all moot issues in the sustainability debate are put aside: 'Sustainable economic development is continuously rising, or at least non-declining, consumption per capita, or GNP, or whatever the agreed indicator of development is' (cited in Murcott, 1997, 44).

The sustainability discussion is an emotional one, full of complaints and irritations (Myers and Simon, 1994). 'Greens' accuse the conformists of being irresponsible, short-sighted, materialistic and anthropocentric people who are ready to sacrifice nature, native peoples and the next generation for the sake of one short-lived cornucopia of material pleasures and profits. According to the conformist strand however, 'greens' are not interested in the fate of poor people in the Third World who are reaching out for Western comforts and income levels. 'Greens', in their view, are the spoiled, rich middle-class, suburban children of the 1960s (Douglas and Wildavsky, 1982) who idealize nature and focus on a 'stabilized' society, at present by political application of the precautionary principle which tries to eliminate technology induced changes which might affect health, nature or the environment (Hanekamp et al., 2005; Pieterman and Hanekamp, 2002).

Within the scientific community, these emotional aspects of contrasting ideologies are mostly hidden since in the end, without being 'reasonable' no political compromise is possible. Idealists as well as conformists tend to be members of the same social class: i.e. the educated elite who are strongly rooted in the Judeo-Christian tradition as well as in the Enlightenment. Even if they reject this tradition and operate in opposition to it, for example like Earth First activists

(Bramwell, 1994, pp. 84–86), there are no deep prejudices based upon race, class or religion that actually keep conformists and idealists apart; nothing like the gap in opportunities that separates blacks and whites, Muslims and Christians, labourers and businessmen or natives and colonialists. The struggle between idealism and conformism is an intellectual clash within Western civilization in which the ideas of Saint Francis, Jean-Jacques Rousseau, Henry Thoreau, John Stuart Mill, John Maynard Keynes, John Kenneth Galbraith and Rachel Carson, to name but a few, are used to support divergent political worldviews and ambitions. The aim of this article is to explain, by looking at the past and present of the hotly debated issues mentioned above, why, as with East and West, the twain have never really met, and probably never will.

The Idealistic Worldview

Resources

In the last chapter of his book *The Wonderful Century*, Alfred Wallace lamented in 1898 the chaotic and wasteful 'plunder of the earth' in a surprisingly modern fashion (Wallace, 1898). Such laments have proven to be even older. Van Zon was able to trace them back to the fifteenth century when a fictional trial between a devastated mother earth and greedy mankind was published (Van Zon, 1996). In the twentieth century the 'plunder of the earth' has developed into one of the main themes in the environmental debate, so many other books on this issue could be mentioned (McNeill, 2000; Van Zon, 2002; Zwaan et al., 2003; Diamond, 2004). Central in the sustainability debate, however, is the question of whether or not 'mining' mother earth is, besides damaging nature, a historical cul-de-sac for humanity.

Resources, so the argument goes, with the exception of renewables, are finite so, one day, standards of living must decline. In England, in 1865, William Stanley Jevons predicted that (admittedly) the use of coal had strongly enhanced the power and prosperity of England but that within some decades this would all be over, as the country would run out of coal resources (Kula, 1998). In the Dutch republic the same fears were uttered in the eighteenth century about the exhaustion of peat reserves (Verstegen, 2005a).

The basic idea here is that resources are somehow 'given'. *Limits to Growth* (Meadows and Meadows, 1972) visualized this in a graph by setting (all) resources in the year 1900 at 100%. Exhaustion, in this line of thought, is unavoidable, even if more resources are discovered. In our view, the fear of exhausting resources is the basic reason why the sustainability debate always focuses on 'future generations'. We hear the echoes of *Limits to Growth* when writers talk about 'Minimizing resource depletion', terms used by Barbier in 1987 (cited in Murcott, 1997, 9) or, as Tolba wrote in 1987, the necessity of operating 'within natural resource constraints' (cited in Murcott, 1997, 12). The most outspoken in terms of thrift are Opschoor and Reijnders, who stated in 1991 that 'use of relatively rare non-renewable resources, such as fossil carbon or rare metals, should be *close to zero* [our italics], unless future generations are compensated for current use by making available for future use an equivalent amount of renewable resources' (cited in Murcott, 1997, 32; see also Verstegen, 2005a).

This idea clearly aims at balancing present and future resource use. New technologies are used only to replace present resources. Goodland and Ledoc wrote in 1987 that resource use should not 'eliminate', 'degrade', 'diminish' or 'deplete' (cited in Murcott, 1997, 10). As an alternative to the use of non-renewables, which by definition must lead to a downfall of society either by exhaustion or by pollution, we see the idealistic notion that sustainability means a complete switch to renewables and, to start with, a slowing down of the pace of consuming non-renewables

(Meadows and Meadows, 1972). Economics should be aimed at a reasonable standard of living for 'future generations'. Some are more modest than others in this respect. Carpenter in 1995 (cited in Murcott, 1997, 54) limited this ambition to 'at least several decades', but Brown in 1988 (cited in Murcott, 1997, 14) opted for 'the indefinite survival of the human species'. Costanza, Waigner, Allaby and Norgaard (cited in Murcott, 1997) write about an economic behaviour that can be sustained *indefinitely* (our italics). O'Riordan and Yaeger (cited in Murcott, 1997, 48) dream about a 'redistribution of resources and power in a manner that guarantees adequate conditions of liveability for *all* [our italics] present and future generations'.

Since threatening with resource-exhaustion is an argument in support of an idealistic programme, playing down that risk is a way for conformists to try to remove this sting out of the debate. The conformist side is not aiming at some kind of stabilization or continuity. It has its roots in the scientific optimism of the twentieth century and the idea that resources are not so much 'given', but are discovered, made, invented and developed. Resource use evolves, driven by curiosity, technology and the price mechanism, which might stimulate (or slow down for that matter) the search for alternatives and new resources. What is considered a resource in one stage of economic development might be useless at another stage. This worldview, it seems, condemns, deplores, and even recompenses, but does not fear the destruction of nature in the sense that exhaustion of non-renewables is not the main problem, especially not in the long run.

Against the idea that sustainability should lead to less extreme forms of thrift, we see the idea that sustainability means finding new opportunities in due time so that growth can continue. For this reason, *Our Common Future* and Brundtland herself deemed it necessary within the scope of fighting poverty to say that sustainability should aim at both maintaining *and* enhancing the resource assets of society (cited in Murcott, 1997). Howe, already in 1979 (cited in Murcott, 1997, 2) wrote about a resource base 'to maintain *or expand* [our italics] production possibilities'.

Quality of Life

As 'growth' is considered to be one of the strongest ideological concepts operating within Western societies and growth is also considered to be the main problem in the environmental crisis, idealists have tried to create a compromise in which the ideology of 'growth' is redefined. In 1979, the ante-Brundtland definition of Coomer (cited in Murcott, 1997, 1) read: 'The sustainable society is one that lives within the self-perpetuating limits of its environment. That society ... is not a "no growth" society ... It is rather, a society that recognises the limits of growth ... [and] looks for alternative ways of growing'. The idea is that material progress might be subject to limits; immaterial progress is not. A couple of definitions on sustainability argue that improving the human condition in the end would mean, as Allen wrote in 1980 (cited in Murcott, 1997, 4), 'improvement of the quality of human life'. In 1989 Robert Goodland wrote in a paper to the World Bank: 'We must shift our goal from quantitative growth to qualitative improvement' (cited in Murcott, 1997, 10). The term 'quality of life' can be found in official documents of the International Union for the Conservation of Nature, United Nations Environment Programme and the WWF as well as the Australian government in the early 1990s. The enthusiasm of nature conservationists for this aspect of sustainability is that it tries to bridge the gap between the strong urge for 'progress' in society and their own ambitions to conserve nature. They hope that if 'progress' can mean something else than economic growth or material progress, nature could be left in peace.

The idea of qualitative growth as a way out, however, is much older than the sustainability debate *Our Common Future* instigated. *Limits to Growth* already dedicated a special paragraph on the quality of life under the heading of 'Growth in the equilibrium state'. Meadows and Meadows (1972) used a statement of John Stuart Mill from 1857, who wrote 'the stationary condition of capital and population implies no stationary state of human improvement' (pp. 180, 182) and used the terms 'improvement of the quality of life' as well. John Stuart Mill was sincerely concerned about a human future in which material progress would dominate everything else and was convinced that this would be impossible in the end because of limited resources (Kula, 1998, pp. 43–46).

Given that the struggle for material progress of the working class dominated the political debate for a long time, it was not until the mid-1950s that improvement in 'quality of life' was again put on the political agenda. This started in the United States and two developments lay behind it. After the defeat in the 1952 and 1956 elections, the American Democratic Party was looking for a new issue that might attract voters. Now that the main struggle for material well-being was over for the bulk of Americans, immaterial progress might do the job. Real concern about environmental degradation played its part, as well as a dislike for modern society, large scale industry and consumerism as formulated for instance in the famous study by John Kenneth Galbraith, *The Affluent Society*, published in 1958 (Rome, 2003).

The historicity of the 'qualitative growth' argument within the sustainability debate in the US is best illustrated by quoting from the study published in 1953 by Fairfield Osborne, *The Limits of the Earth*. His 'quality of life' argument not only contained an element of dissatisfaction with consumer society but also the assumption that further material growth is impossible:

> The day is here when we Americans need to clarify what we mean by a 'standard of living' and in doing so give greater recognition to the immeasurable values of social, and not merely economic, criteria. We may dismiss Thoreau, who preached restriction of wants instead of increase of material goods—but we cannot forget him. As time goes on we may be compelled to take at least a portion of his philosophy as our own—even though it is not of our choice. (Osborne, 1953, p. 76)

This idea underpins the model developed by Dennis Meadows in the early 1970s; he tried to prove that further economic growth would inevitably lead to a breakdown of society. The model gave room for a 'decent standard of living' if economic growth stopped in time and income per capita could be frozen at the European level which was half the level of the United States (Meadows and Meadows, 1972, p. 171). Further qualitative growth could only be accomplished within the boundaries of an 'equilibrium state'. In this way, Meadows supported a moral appeal for a better world with a scientific model. This idea is still operating as a key element in the sustainability debate, as Boersema shows. He cited a 1997 survey by the World Bank which showed no addition of well-being once income per capita has surpassed a level of about $15,000 per year (in 1995). So, his argument goes, at some point, income growth becomes rather useless. If growth is no longer necessary we can focus on the 'quality of life', making way for a 'green' society (Boersema, 2004).

Cultural Conservation

In an emotional appeal to the World Commission on Environment and Development in 1985, Jaime da Silva Araujo of the National Council of Rubber Tappers, complained about the deterioration of the tropical rainforest in Brazil. The rainforests he knew comprised 15 native products. When the trees were felled, only one resource remained: cattle, which hardly needed labour. So, deforestation means job losses and the now jobless people have to move into the cities and stimulate urbanization. In his situation, 'development' came down to the building of roads, 'and the roads bring destruction under a mask called progress' (WCED, 1987, p. 58).

Especially since *Our Common Future* gave attention to the fate of native peoples, alongside nature and biodiversity, their future has become part of the debate about sustainability. An essential aspect of the culture of the native peoples is that they have been around for ages, without modern technology, without 'development', without 'progress', without 'economic growth' and yet they still exist. So, it seems rather obvious that, from this point of view, their way of life could be called 'sustainable'. Nowadays, they are threatened with extinction as Western 'development' destroys the economic basis of their existence. Because of their proven ways of keeping alive in harsh environments, many NGOs consider these peoples not just as victims, but rather as an example, an alternative to today's modern society.

In *Beyond Brundtland: Green Development in the 1990s*, a publication of Dutch NGOs, we see a couple of examples of this admiration of what once were dubbed 'primitive' societies: 'a motorcar provides speed, power and status. A camel provides food, milk, dung, transport, shadow, warmth. A camel is trustworthy and cheaper, part of a tradition of desert folks and perfectly adapted to the local environment' (Court, 1990). In some cases, this idealization of native peoples has become unhistorical, as in the famous pseudo-chief-Seattle speech, written by the Hollywood scenario writer Ted Perry (Budiansky, 1995), in which a native American chief complained about the destruction of the bison, nature in general and the Western preoccupation with 'property'. In this case, environmentalism pays, unconsciously perhaps, honour to Rousseau, who was also in strong opposition to society and held property to be the basis of inequality (Rousseau, 1754/1996, p. 107).

Myths notwithstanding, native cultures really are threatened by Western style economic growth and for that reason the protection of native cultures is in a couple of instances explicitly mentioned in definitions about sustainability. Barbier (cited in Murcott, 1997, 9) wrote in 1987 that sustainable development also means protecting people against 'cultural disruption'. One year later Norgaard (cited in Murcott, 1997, 18) said that whether or not an economy could be called sustainable meant asking if agricultural and industrial practices would not 'destroy ... the local people and their cultural system'. Norgaard uses the phrase 'culturally sustainable' in order to be able to insert the voice of native populations in the environmental debate. We see the same attempt by Munasinghe and Shearer (cited in Murcott, 1997, 52), who in 1995 used the term 'cultural diversity' alongside 'biological diversity' and so made a strong association between one of the main issues of sustainability and the fate of native peoples. In practice, many international agreements indeed pay homage to this idea by giving native peoples, like the Inuit, juridical protection to maintain their way of life under the banner of 'sustainability'.

But the idea that saving the cultural heritage has something to do with sustainability does not limit itself to the Third World. In the Western world as well, we sometimes see a tendency within the environmental debate to add the protection of monuments, or our cultural heritage in general, to the list of nature protection and *environmental* desirabilities. In an historical overview of environmental jurisdiction in Norway for instance, Aall (2005) added a building regulation of 1845 aimed at the protecting the cultural heritage as an example of early environmental policy in his country. As we all know, landscape protection includes not only the conservation of old agricultural parcellation for the sake of species protection, but also of old farms, mills, (ruined) castles and old churches. In the sustainability definition used by Vavrousek in 1994 (cited in Murcott, 1997, 46) each civilization is summoned to respect 'its own cultural roots'.

There exists a link between the idealists' approach to environmental problems on the one hand and their distrust of modernity, at least against an unchecked modernity ('opposition to blind progress' as the Sierra Club called it, cited in Meadows and Meadows, 1972, p. 160) on the other. It is a predilection of the past, or things past that sometimes comes very close to an all-out glorification of country life and the world we have lost, as in the opening lines of Rachel Carson's *Silent Spring*. In this sense, the call for cultural sustainability is an inseparable part of the cultural-ecological critique that dominates idealistic thinking (Hanekamp et al., 2005).

The Conformist Worldview

Technology

Whether or not we can believe that technological solutions lie at the heart of a sustainable future, is one of the most basic questions in the environmental debate. On the one hand we see within the environmental movement a deep distrust of technology. Without the technological revolution of the last century, many environmental disasters would not have been there: the changeover to fossil fuels causes the enhanced greenhouse effect and air pollution, CFCs damage the ozone layer. DDT, Bhopal and Chernobyl have become symbols of the failure of modern technology to create a safe and nature-friendly environment.

A list of the environmental havoc caused by modern technology will be endless and so this distrust can be found in many 'classics' in the environmental library like *Silent Spring*. Under the influence of pessimistic writers such as Galbraith and Mishan (Steurer, 2002), the evils of modern society are blamed on technology: 'historically mankind's long record of new inventions has resulted in crowding, deterioration of the environment and greater social inequality', wrote Dennis Meadows (Meadows and Meadows, 1972, p. 182). Back-to-the-land movements, organic farming and the exemplary features of native peoples living in harmony with nature are the direct result of the distrust modern society has generated against technology (Veldman, 1994). It is also clear that the criticism focuses on big technology: large power plants, nuclear energy, fishing nets longer than ever, broad highways, enormous agricultural machines etc. or, according to Weart, even on every new technology (Weart, 2003, p. 69).

Small is Beautiful, published in 1973 by Ernst Schumacher, was the direct answer to the perceived havoc wrought by big technology and capitalism (Bramwell, 1994, pp. 50–53). Nevertheless, it has been admitted by many critics as well as supporters that technology is capable of many goods things resulting in, above all, a much longer life expectancy. And it is recognized by all that sophisticated 'clean' technologies are needed to reach the sustainable world (Ausubel, 1996; Meadows and Meadows, 1972, pp. 181, 182; Grübler, 1998, pp. 365, 366).

So, one of the prerequisites of the operation of technology in a sustainable society must be that it causes no harm, or in more euphemistic terms only 'acceptable environmental impacts', as Schultink stated in 1992 (cited in Murcott, 1997, 37). The distrust against technology is echoed in the stronger words of O'Riordan and Yaeger in 1994 that technological advance must be part of a policy that 'guarantees' the 'liveability' of future generations (cited in Murcott, 1997).

This is the classical contradictory position on science and technology found within the idealistic strand of sustainability. Though it is recognized that knowledge is never complete and certain, science and technology have to prove that new technologies are 'safe'. Within the world of definitions, no author dares to be absolutely against technological progress but one can rather easily distinguish between the careful and the daring. The careful approach is the core of the so-called precautionary principle which tries to prohibit complicated technologies like nuclear energy and genetic engineering or conceptualizes the entire chemical industry as a 'historical mistake'.[1]

It is a reaction against the optimism of technological possibilities generated by the industrial revolution. This optimism has survived two world wars, the horrors of the gas chambers, nuclear warfare and the defoliation in Vietnam to name but a few of the reproaches it has to deal with. Instead of a backtracking attitude, conformists can be identified for their use of words like advance, expansion, technological development, improvement and the like. The WCED itself set an example here. It rejected a gloomy outlook on the future and considered technological progress, 'powered by a continuing flow of wealth from industry' to be a prerequisite to reach sustainability (WCED, 1987, pp. 1, 9, 16).

Nevertheless, there exists a strong unimaginative tendency in the sustainability debate which opts for stability, continuity, or even conservatism, as in the recent Dutch definition of the Royal Institute for Public Health and Environment: 'possibility to continue the (here and now) chosen quality of life' (RIVM, 2004, p. 39). Moreover, the opposing sides in the debate have a difference of opinion on the meaning of the word 'change'. In the idealistic worldview, when 'change' is considered a necessity to reach a sustainable society, it is envisioned as a change in opinion, a change in mentality. In a technocratic worldview, 'change' is something that happens in the real world as a consequence of technological breakthroughs or adjustments. The idea that 'We have sensed that our ways of living are very unsustainable but we haven't been able to change our practices and move towards more sustainable ones' (Simon, 2003, p. 1), differs from the idea of Howe (cited in Murcott, 1997, 2), formulated in 1979, that sustainability 'implies not an unchanging resource base but a set of resource reserves, technologies, and policy controls that maintain or expand the production possibilities of future generations'.

To use a metaphor, it is the difference between the presumed wisdom of stepping on the brakes or on the accelerator. It is also the difference between using technology to contain, to conserve and maintain, against using technology to reach new horizons. It is the fight of the 'new' pessimism of the late 1960s and 1970s against the 'old' optimism, which reigned in the 1950s and early 1960s, a struggle which turned the meaning of being 'progressive' upside down. 'Progress' now has a conservative connotation.

Economic Growth

To understand the sustainability debate better we should realize that, though without explicitly mentioning 'pessimistic' studies like *Limits to Growth* or *Blueprint for Survival*, 'Sustainable growth' was the 'optimistic' answer the Brundtland commission developed in response to the idea that further economic growth was impossible. *Our Common Future* was also a reaction to the recession of the 1970s and 1980s and wanted strong growth in material production: 'sustainable development is not a fixed state of harmony' and 'a five to tenfold increase in manufacturing output will be needed'. Levels of 5–6% annual growth for developing and 3–4% for developed countries were deemed necessary (WCED, 1987, pp. 1, 9, 15, 50, 51).

It is quite remarkable however that though nobody seemed to be openly in opposition to the Brundtland *definition* of sustainability, the application of what 'sustainability' should be operates in the idealistic world view often diametrically opposed to this idea of strong economic growth. Munn, for instance, said in 1989 (cited in Murcott, 1997, 26): 'If development is equated with economic growth, this criticism is indeed justified: Malthusian limits prevent sustained growth in a finite world'. The exclusion of economic growth as an option for the future can also be read in the study of Reijnders and Opschoor in 1992: 'Maintenance of a steady state is one of the operational definitions of sustainable development. A steady state is a dynamic state in which changes tend to cancel each other out' (cited in Murcott, 1997, 32). They clearly took this idea from the concept of 'dynamic equilibrium' in *Limits to Growth* (Meadows and Meadows, 1972, p. 156).

A kind of steady state economy is also implied in the definition given by Costanza and Wainger in 1991 (cited in Murcott, 1997, 35): 'The amount of consumption that can be sustained indefinitely without degrading capital stocks, including natural capital stocks'. We could argue that these writers, as well as others, at the same time also try to prevent being accused of wanting 'zero growth'. The basic contrast between idealists and conformists as far as living standards are concerned is that the first want to create an economic system which prevents a future diminishing of living standards and look for 'growth' as something that should happen outside the materialistic world, i.e. in 'qualitative growth', while conformists want to assure that living standards will continue to grow. Pezzey (cited in Murcott, 1997, 25) for instance wrote in 1989: 'Our standard definition of sustainable development will be *non-declining per capita utility* [our italics]—because of its self-evident appeal as a criterion for inter-generational equity'. Idealist definitions can be recognized easily by the fact that they stress the dangers ahead and use words like 'eroding', 'undermine', 'degrading', 'decreasing', 'destruction' and so on (Murcott, 1997). Daly in 1980 (cited in Murcott, 1997) talked about sustainability as based on the idea 'that it is both morally and economically wrong to treat the world as a business in liquidation'. According to IUCN, WWF and UNEP, 'maintenance' lies at the heart of sustainability (cited in Murcott, 1997, 52). The idealists in the sustainability debate thus talk about *the impossibility* of growth in the long run and therefore about *the injustice* for future generations. The economists and their 'growth-fetishism' are seen in this worldview as culpable for the destruction of nature and the pollution of the environment (McNeill, 2001, p. 336).

An aspect that is missed in most discussions about 'stopping' economic growth, however, is the question of whether it would be politically possible to do so (Steurer, 2002). Just a few economists have given that important point some thoughts, one of them being the Dutch economist Jan Pen. He argued that stopping growth would need a deliberate and complete control of the credit system by the state—an anti-Keynesian policy—to prevent investments that could cause growth. The idea of stopping growth as suggested by Meadows in *Limits to Growth* would mean, according to Pen, that the state should *force* investments in the direction of recycling, cleaning up the environment and thrift in resource use and away from the production of more consumer goods. Such a policy no non-communist state could ever dream of (Pen, 1972).

What Pen made clear was that, from an idealistic point of view, sustainability involves a strong policy of controlling the future. It is in opposition to the post-bellum ideology of limitless economic growth, but took over from the optimists the idea, the wish, or maybe just the hope, that the future can be made or even planned. This idealistic idea can be traced back to Wallace in 1898 and Meadows in the twentieth century. In 1995 this is most clearly stated by Munasinghe and Shearer (cited in Murcott, 1997) who talked about 'planning and action at local, regional and global scales'. The same idea we can find in the 'orderly society transition' of Goodland and Ledoc formulated in 1987 or the opposition of Munn in 1989 against *uncontrolled* (our italics) economic growth (both cited in Murcott, 1997).

The historical roots of 'growth fetishism' lay in the 1930s when the lack of it led to mass unemployment, extreme poverty and the rise of fascism in Europe. After World War II, economists stimulated growth to achieve rising living standards and full employment (Steurer, 2002). This concern is always left out within the idealistic strand of thinking, according to Pearce. He commented angrily: 'Antigrowth advocates are embarrassingly silent or unrealistic on how they would solve problems of poverty and unemployment' (cited in Kula, 1998, p. 149).

Growth, according to Steurer, is moreover needed to give elected governments room for political manoeuvring. It means more income from taxes and more government spending on health, schooling and social security. Without growth no money can be generated to finance environmental politics (Steurer, 2002, p. 466). Moreover, because of continuing technical progress and rising productivity, zero growth would generate unemployment, lower income levels, a downward economic spiral and rising inequality. Therefore, the experience of the economic recession of the 1970s and 1980s quickly led to a reappraisal of economic growth within the environmental movement, at least in the Netherlands (Cramer, 1989, p. 78; Tellegen, 1983, p. 44).

A deliberate policy of zero growth would limit the financial scope for any political action which would in turn lead to a shift in the vote towards parties who are ready to stimulate growth. Therefore, some writers argue, we are dealing not with 'limits to growth' but with 'limits to politics' (Steurer, 2002, p. 487; see also Van der Pot, 1985, pp. 902–907). Thus, an increase of GNP per capita is a social necessity, a prerequisite for social stability and development. Protecting jobs is sometimes explicitly mentioned as one of the important conditions for accepting the whole idea of sustainable growth (Steurer, 2002; Verstegen, 2005b). 'Growth fetishism' is therefore deeply rooted in the pre- and post-war history of Western society. No growth is in fact no longer a political option, even for Green parties (Steurer, 2002, pp. 400, 404–410, 460). For Pearce it will result in poverty and unemployment on a massive scale creating major social problems by widening inequalities (Kula, 1998, p. 147). What makes such a vision 'conformist' is that it does not so much anticipate a future crisis but is a reaction to past crises, the nightmare of the 1930s and the recessions of the 1970s and 1980s.

The preferred solution to such crises is never-ending growth. This can be fairly openly seen in the idea of Allaby in 1988: 'Sustainable development—economic development that can continue indefinitely because it is based on the exploitation of renewable resources and causes insufficient environmental damage for this to pose an eventual limit' (cited in Murcott, 1997, 13). Conformists use optimistic words like 'enhance', 'improvements', 'increase', 'rising' (Murcott, 1997) or, as in the case of Braat in 1991 (cited in Murcott, 1997, 33): 'development . . . directed towards maximum welfare'. Indeed a different world than the one of Brown in 1988 that tries to safeguard at least 'a quality of life beyond mere biological survival' in the face of nature's destruction (cited in Murcott, 1997).

Poverty

Right from the start Gro Brundtland made it absolutely clear that talking about the environment meant talking about poverty. Poverty is the main obstacle to environmental protection and so economic growth is absolutely necessary. This is a moot point within the idealistic mind-set as low consumption levels seem to be more in line with an environmentally friendly way of life than material abundance. This culminates in the idea that Saint Francis should be an example for the environmental movement: being poor as well as able to talk with animals (Ponting, 1991, pp. 145, 146).

In Wackernagel, the author behind the idea of the ecological footprint, we see even an idealization of poverty. He found what he called a 'model society' in Kerala in south-west India (Wackernagel and Yount, 2000). Here people have a life expectancy of about 70 years, a high level of literacy and an income of (*sic*!) one dollar a day. According to Wackernagel, three ideals of sustainability have been accomplished here: almost Western levels of health, literacy and 'low consumption levels'. He did not mention, check or see that his model society in reality is full of social ills: alcoholism, poverty, foeticide, gender selection and unemployment.[2]

However, mainstream thinking about sustainability wants poverty to be eliminated. The question, of course, is how. Here lies a difference between idealists and conformists. Conformists stick to the idea that economic growth is necessary to lift the standard of living among the poor. It is a conformist idea because it is the solution Western society had formulated as the cure against the poverty as well as the high unemployment rates among the working classes before World War II.[3]

The basic alternative line of thought, as formulated by, e.g., O'Riordan and Yaeger in 1994 and Hossain in 1995 (cited in Murcott, 1997) is that living standards in the West are now high enough and that to eliminate poverty we should stimulate a more even distribution of the material spoils of industrial society, i.e. more equality is the answer, not necessarily more growth. A 'fairer' distribution of income is also considered highly desirable among the advocates of strong growth, like Pearce. Pen and Pearce both wrote that a more even distribution of income is only feasible when there is economic growth. A voluntary transfer of money from rich to poor nations will rather quickly reach its political limits, especially within a zero growth situation. No growth would only stimulate the fight over the spoils between rich and poor, the powerful and powerless, a battle the poor surely will lose.

So, here the discussion ends; both sides claiming the strategy of the other as impossible. 'To many', Kula wrote: 'relentless or sustainable economic growth, no matter how one measures it, appears to be an unsustainable idea itself. Sooner or later it must fall flat on its face' (Kula, 1998, p. 148). On the other side Pearce says:

> Fanciful ideas abound, including one that suggests that economic growth in the 'north' should be sacrificed for the benefit of the south, as if not demanding goods and services in the rich countries would somehow release the poor countries. The actual outcome, of course, is that they will not be produced at all, and everybody loses. (Kula, 1998, p. 149)

Mentality, Individualism, and a Culture without Ambition: Concluding Remarks

The conformist–idealist concept is a viable one in the fundamental analysis of the issue of sustainability. To grasp why, we should start with Bramwell, who has argued that ecological thinking in the political sense of the word has changed from 'soft right' before World War II to 'soft left' afterwards (Bramwell, 1994, p. 2). This remark makes clear why 'being progressive' has nowadays an entirely different meaning than in the 1950s. 'Redefining progress' are the words Wackernagel uses to illustrate his idealistic conception of the sustainable society. It aims at conservation of past objects and cultures, on lowered resource use and stable, non-growing equal living standards in the material sense; it also aims at the prevention of a future crisis. It is the reformulation of the model of *Limits to Growth*. Modern times have made this future collapse an ostensible possibility and so the idealistic vision tends to romanticize the world before 'modernity' arrived. It was this conservative, anti-modern ring, which kept green thinkers in the right camp before the war. It glorifies the world which existed before 'big' mechanized technology crushed nature, the world where people, despite their poverty, lived more or less in a stable relationship with the environment.

During the revolutionary 1960s the political world turned upside down. What was once the programme of the progressives, planned or at least controlled industrialization, fighting poverty, lifting the material well-being of the masses and full employment, became suspect. Adherents of such a policy suddenly found themselves on the defensive. A new green idealism took over, declaring the former progressive policy a danger for the future. This distrust of the future eventually found its expression in the precautionary principle which shifts the burden of proof to those who want 'old-fashioned' progress. Adherents of this older concept of being progressive now became suspect conformists.

The idealist alternative, however, has so far failed to attract much support in practice. Civilians, whether 'green' consumers or otherwise, are too deeply committed to technological progress and its prerequisite: economic growth to which all contribute. On the practical level, in other words, everybody has a stake in growth and nobody will do without this objective, which brings in the necessary money and technological development to bring about a more 'sustainable society'. Society is thus willing and able to counter pollution and secure parts of nature, but it is not willing to give up the idea of further material progress and rejects the social consequences of a 'no growth' policy. We might see, as a spin-off of environmental thinking and the cultural critique of Western society, people admiring foreign cultures and their way of life (De la Court, 1990; Bramwell, 1994, p. 51), but without seriously trying to give up the Western high standard of living themselves, thereby acquiring the best of both worlds.

On the other hand, the conformist worldview does not have anything to offer but more of the same now that in the Western world most people have reached a standard of living and a life expectation the socialists of the nineteenth and early twentieth century could only have dreamed of. The conformist strand can only offer a 'business-as-usual' approach, as the recent G8-2005 meeting showed, which has a much stronger appeal to most Western civilians as it does not rock the political and societal boat too much. The conformists counter the idealists by trying to defuse the ideological struggle through technology and science in service of the environment. For the conformist, the future is an extrapolation of the present. Yet results achieved in the past cannot guarantee future gains, to paraphrase a recent Dutch advertisement slogan.

Where do we stand intellectually speaking, now that the sustainability debate has reached a stalemate between uninspiring alternatives, of which, as was said, the conformist side of the debate is the socio-economic reality we all take part in? As Steurer wrote, the discussion about sustainability has fallen victim to a repetitive loop where, as in the more recent discussions about 'strong' and 'weak' sustainability, the possibility or impossibility of further economic growth is endlessly debated (Steurer, 2002, pp. 260–271, 356–360). It is clear that both the conformist and the idealistic strand of the sustainability discussion lack vision for the society of tomorrow, and have an uneasy relationship with this future, which is inherently uncertain. In our view, the present global society faces no greater difficulties, or complexities, than in the past (the plague pandemics or the era of religious warfare come to mind, McNeill, 1976; Rabb, 1975). Yet it has seemingly lost its sense of ambition, of the need to develop a broader realistic vision, and of the paramount importance of the will to explore and experiment. A society that appears so riddled by self-doubt and fears (Furedi, 2002; Durodië, 2003) has become afraid of taking risks either way and is hence unable to establish trust. As Jacoby remarks: 'Few envision the future as anything but a replica of today—sometimes better, but usually worse. ... A new consensus has emerged: There are no alternatives' (Jacoby, 1999). This is the wisdom of our times, an age of political exhaustion and retreat. Such a view, of course, is not any kind of 'solution' to the environmental and social problems we are facing at present. In order to find a way forward we need to rekindle our political and economic inspiration.

Notes

1 W. van Dieren & L. Reijnders in the Dutch Newspaper *NRC Handelsblad*, 24 May 1995.
2 Soma Wadhwa, 'And he can keep it', *Outlook India*, Monday 12 July 2004.
3 See the paragraph about 'growth'.

References

Aall, C. (2005) The ups and downs in the history of local environmental policy in Norway, Conference paper European Society for Environmental History, Florence, February.
Ausubel, J. J. (1996) Can technology spare the earth?', *American Scientist* (April).
Boersema, J. (2004) *Het goede leven is te weinig groen* (Amsterdam: Blaise Pascal Institute).
Bramwell, A. (1994) *The Fading of the Greens. The Decline of Environmental Politics in the West* (New Haven, CT & London: Yale University Press).
Budiansky, S. (1995) *Nature's Keepers. The New Science of Nature Management* (London: Weidenfeld & Nicholson).
Cramer, J. (1989) *De Groene golf. Geschiedenis en toekomst van de milieubeweging* (Utrecht: Van Arkel).
De la Court, Th. (1990) *Beyond Brundtland: Green Development in the 1990's* (New York: New Horizon Press).
Diamond, J. (2004) *Collapse. How Societies Choose to Fail or Succeed* (New York: Viking).
Douglas, M. & Wildavsky, A. (1982) *Risk and Culture. An Essay on the Selection of Technological and Environmental Dangers* (Berkeley, CA: University of California Press).
Durodié, B. (2003) Limitations of public dialogue in science and the rise of new 'experts', *Critical Review of International Social and Political Philosophy*, 6(4), pp. 82–92.
Furedi, F. (2002) *Culture of Fear: Risk-Taking and the Morality of Low Expectations* (London: Continuum).
Grübler, A. (1998) *Technology and global change* (Cambridge, New York & Melbourne: Cambridge University Press).
Hanekamp, J. C., Verstegen, S. W. and Vera-Navas, G. (2005) The historical roots of precautionary thinking, *Journal of Risk Research*, 8(4), pp. 295–310.
Hollander, P. (1998) *Political Pilgrims. Western Intellectuals in Search of the Good Society*, 4th edn (New Brunswick & London: Transaction Publishers).
Jacoby, R. (1999) *The End of Utopia. Politics and Culture in an Age of Apathy* (New York: Basic Books).
Kula, E. (1998) *History of Environmental Economic Thought* (New York & London: Routledge).
McNeill, J. (2000) *Something New under the Sun. An Environmental History of the Twentieth Century* (London, etc.: Penguin).
McNeill, W. H. (1976) *Plagues and Peoples* (London & New York: Penguin).
Meadows, D. H. & Meadows, D. L. (1972) *The Limits to Growth* (Washington, DC: Potomac Associates).
Myers, N. & Simon, J. (1994) *Scarcity or Abundance? A Debate about the Environment* (New York: Norton & Company).
Murcott, S. (1997) Appendix A: Definitions of Sustainable Development. AAAS Annual Conference, IIASA 'Sustainability Indicators' Symposium, Seattle 16 February. Massachusetts Institute of Technology, http://www.sustainableliving.org/appen-a.htm.
Osborne, F. (1953) *The Limits of the Earth* (Boston, MA: Little Brown).
Pieterman, R. & Hanekamp, J. C. (2002) *The Cautious Society? An Essay on the Rise of the Precautionary Culture* (Zoetermeer: HAN).
Ponting, C. (1991) *A Green History of the World* (London, etc.: Penguin).
Pen, J. (1972) De onbekende consequenties van het model van Forrester en Meadows voor de economische politiek, *Economisch Statistische Berichten*, 16 February, pp. 159–162.
Rabb, Th. K. (1975) *The Struggle for Sustainability in Early Modern Europe* (New York: Oxford University Press).
RIVM (2004) *Kwaliteit en toekomst. Verkenning van duurzaamheid* (The Hague: SDU).
Rome, A. (2003) 'Give Earth a chance'. The environmental movement and the sixties, *The Journal of American History* (90), pp. 525–554.
Rousseau, J.-J. (1996/1754) *Discours sur l'origine et les fondements de l'inégalité parmi les hommes* (Paris: Librairie générale Française).
Simon, S. (2003) Sustainability indicators. *Internet Encyclopaedia of Ecological Economics*, http://www.ecoeco.org/publica/encyc_entries/SustIndicator.pdf
Steurer. R. (2002) *Der Wachstumsdiskurs in Wissenschaft und Politik. Von der Wachstumseuphorie über 'Grenzen des Wachstums' zur Nachhaltigkeit* (Berlin: Verlag für Wissenschaft und Forschung).

Tellegen, E. (1983) *Milieubeweging* (Utrecht: Het Spectrum).
Van der Pot, J. H. J. (1985) *Die Bewertung des technischen Fortschritts. Eine systematische Übersicht der Theorien* (Assen & Maastricht: Van Gorcum).
Van der Zwaan, B. & Petersen, A. (eds) (2003) *Sharing the Planet: Population–Consumption–Species* (Delft: Eburon Academic Publishers).
Van Zon, H. (1996) Oude wegen naar de Club van Rome, *Amsterdams Sociologisch Tijdschrift* (June).
Van Zon, H. (2002) *Geschiedenis en duurzame ontwikkeling. Duurzame ontwikkeling in historisch perspectief, enkele verkenningen* (Rotterdam: Netwerk Duurzaam Hoger Onderwijs).
Veldman, M. (1994) *Fantasy, the Bomb and the Greening of Britain. Romantic Protest, 1945–1980* (Cambridge: Cambridge University Press).
Verstegen, S. W. (2005a) Fuel resources and wastelands in the Netherlands around 1800, in Whited, T. L. (ed.) *Northern Europe An Environmental History* (Santa Barbara, CA: ABC-Clio).
Verstegen, S. W. (2005b) Thinking about sustainability: the reception of the Brundtland report in the Netherlands 1987–1991. Unpublished conference paper European Society for Environmental History, Florence, February.
Wackernagel, M. & Yount, J. D. (2000) Footprints for sustainability: the next steps, *Environment, Development and Sustainability*, 2, pp. 21–42.
Wallace, A. R. (1898) *The Wonderful Century, its Successes and its Failures* (London: Swan Sonnenschein).
WCED (World Commission on Environment and Development) (1987) *Our Common Future* (Oxford: Oxford University Press).
Weart, S. R. (2003) *The Discovery of Global Warming* (Cambridge MA & London: Harvard University Press).

S.W. Verstegen is a lecturer in economic, social and environmental history at the Free University, Amsterdam. He has published on landed elites, the history of industrial innovations, and the environmental debate.

J.C. Hanekamp works at the HAN Foundation, a Dutch academic think tank focusing on public issues related to such areas as the environment, agriculture, biotechnology, and chemistry. These topics border more or less with issues of sustainability and precautionary thinking. This article is the second instalment of a series of articles dealing with these themes. The preceding article, published in *Journal of Risk Research*, dealt with the history of the precautionary principle.

The European Union as an Environmental Leader in a Global Environment

ANTHONY R. ZITO

Introduction

The environmental sector has witnessed the transformation and internationalization of the problems, processes and actors that compose it. The policy problems of global warming, for example, contain many cross-border issues of uncertainty and complexity that require international responses and leadership. Since the 1970s the European Union (EU)—referring to the overall political entity as opposed to the European Community (EC) governing aspects of the Common Market—has evolved into a supranational actor of international standing in its own right (Jupille and Caporaso, 1998). The EU arguably now surpasses the United States as an environmental driver (Sbragia with Damro, 1999; Vogel, 2003).

This article conceptualizes the EU's potential for international leadership, examining the EU institutional context and historical opportunities. It asks this question: how have the institutional and ideational complexities of the European policy-making structure defined both the scope and the impact of EU efforts?

Using the institutionalist, ideational and organizational learning literatures, the paper studies the opportunities and conflicts that this historical process has embedded within both the internal and external faces of the environmental area. The article explores the EU's institutional nature and offers a future research agenda highlighting a number of important means (involving both direct and indirect processes) for international environmental influence.

Analytical Perspectives

The EU's complexity is fundamental in driving its international potential (Geyer, 2003). Studying this complexity in the environmental sector is not new (e.g. Weale, 1996; Bretherton and Vogler, 2000), but further elaboration is required to unravel the different implications.

This paper emphasizes the EU's institutional and ideational dimensions. Institutions are 'collections of interrelated rules and routines that define appropriate actions in terms of relations between roles and situations' (March and Olsen, 1989). Institutions provide rules and norms that create conditions under which certain policy choices are selected or excluded (Weale, 1992). Because (1) institutional actors operate with limited information, (2) institutions gradually alter the thinking of actors operating within the institutions and (3) institutional decisions lead down unanticipated paths, actors find it difficult to change the policy direction or wider institutional norms (Pierson, 1996).

Ideas provide the means for making choices and establishing the rules of the game; they provide a focus for new policies and political coalitions (Goldstein and Keohane, 1993). In contrast to institutions, ideational explanations posit the possibility for substantial change as old ideas are challenged. Ideas can exist as a larger set of beliefs (which may be quite amorphous) or as more specific notions operating within a particular belief system. Rein and Schön (1994) offer a useful conceptualization of 'policy framing': framing isolates how actors organize and interpret the complex reality confronting them in order to develop guideposts and maps for understanding and acting.

Learning theory helps explain how institutional structures and policy ideas change: organizations make inferences on the basis of history and transform them into structures of belief and organizational routines that guide behaviour (Levitt and March, 1988, p. 320). The actors normally perceive some mismatch between the expected course of action and the reality (Argyris and Schön, 1996); alternatively, a separate coalition of actors holding a different set of policy principles seizes policy control (Sabatier, 1998). As organizations resist dramatic value changes, more incremental changes of procedures and instruments are more likely in any given political situation. Substantial change in world views is possible, particularly if the political actors face a substantial crisis/challenge to their certainties (Sabatier, 1998).

Complexity and Tensions

The complex nature of the EU institutional system generates a number of inherent tensions, which affect (positively or negatively), the EU's potential as a global environmental leader. This paper concentrates on four tensions, but first explains the EU institutional array that, with the 25 member states, induces this complexity.

The Commission, led by its President and a College of Commissioners, acts to some degree as ministers with portfolios overseeing a number of bureaucratic directorate-generals. It proposes EC environmental legislation and oversees its implementation. The Commission requires approval for the proposals from the Council of Ministers, which each member state chairs for six months as EU President. Although the Council represents the ministers of each country, the Council structure involves a number of working groups and committees including the critical Committee of Permanent Representatives (Hayes-Renshaw and Wallace, 1997). The only directly elected institution remains the European Parliament (EP), and its increasing policy significance signifies that environmental legislation must also get through the Parliament, which has the ability to block legislation if it has a sufficient majority (Bomberg and Burns, 1999). The Parliament's organization includes rather amorphous catch-all European party groups and specialist committees that provide policy expertise. The last main body, the European Court of Justice (ECJ), has the power to uphold the EU Treaties and law while having some scope to interpret law (often in a way favourable to environmental protection, see Cichowski, 1998).

The complex EU system, when combined with the activities of the member states and other actors in such policy matters as implementation, generates numerous tensions. First, the EU shares a characteristic of federal systems: the inherent institutional tension between territorial concerns of the individual member states versus the more supranational concerns of the political system. Despite the striking success of the EU environmental policy sector, there remains an outlook within some member states that seeks the devolution of policy-making power away from the supranational level (Golub, 1996; Flynn, 2003).

Closely associated with this point is the tension between the prioritization of efficiency versus control (Kerremans, 1998). Territorial representation of member states is embedded consciously in all EU institutions (Sbragia, 1993). Particularly with the 2004 accession of ten states, there is a struggle to maintain the voice and control of individual states while ensuring efficiency in the supranational decision-making process through greater qualified majority voting in the Council (i.e. states lose their individual vetoes).

Second, while territorial concerns partly define the EU organizational structure, the heavy institutional orientation towards policy sectors (single market, environment, etc.) cuts across the territorial dimension. The institutional emphasis on policy sectors allows for the possibility of institutional specialization, but it also creates the potential conflict between different sectoral interests and bureaucratic politics (Peters, 1992). Policy priorities, values and frames of the individual sectors shape EU actors and how they interact. Sectoralization means that both the Commissioners and individual directorates have their own specific policy duties and priorities. These priorities are built around particular policy frames, bureaucratic interests and policy constituencies. The environment ministers may share more in common with their counterparts in the EU Commission and the other member states than with the finance ministers of their own country (Hill, 1993). Many view the Commission Environment Directorate-General as being less influential than the more senior DGs and co-opted by environmental interests (Wurzel, 2002).

One of the most difficult EU environmental objectives has been the integration of environmental priorities into other EU policy sectors despite its explicit policy prominence (Schout and Jordan, 2003). The Commission has created a number of operating principles to integrate environmental concerns more effectively, but the results have been limited due to conflicting operational approaches and philosophies within the EU institutions. The Common Agricultural Policy, which continues to result in over-intensive farming despite well-publicized environmental consequences, illustrates this problem (Lenschow and Zito, 1998).

Third, EC policy specialization creates its own set of complexities and tensions. With a supranational organization containing a bureaucracy (the Commission) no larger than that found in a medium sized city, such as Aarhus in Denmark, EC actors require technical expertise from the member states to operate regulations (Majone, 1997; Zito, 2004). This and limited financial resources force Commission reliance on technical support from both member state representatives and willing interest groups. Much of the Commission activity heavily involves member state representatives who sit on committees with the Commission representatives (Demmke, 1998). Although the Commission is both the key agenda setter and compliance monitor, it relies on the knowledge, expertise and support of the actors that it regulates. Heavy consultation and significant involvement with various interested parties also helps the Commission to build the consensus necessary to get Council and Parliament agreement.

External experts are involved from the very start of the policy process, which normally is conducted behind closed doors. This reality limits the non-expert ability to monitor or influence such deliberations (Beetham and Lord, 1998). Thus the EU policy-making system is in one sense extremely open but simultaneously is perceived as being extremely closed: while the formal structures for civil society and popular input are quite limited, interest group participation is important for environmental governance.

The fourth policy complexity is related in that it limits the influence of less organized and knowledgeable environmental actors: the sheer complexity of the EU institutional process. The EC policy process involves a number of institutions (Commission, Council of Ministers, European Parliament, individual member states and other bodies) in the creation, negotiation, decision-making and implementation stages. The Commission shares executive functions: i.e. policy leadership, with the Council of Ministers, and implementation with the member states. This and the sharing of the traditional legislative functions of ratification and accountability (between the European Parliament and the Council of Ministers) create a complex system.

This complex institutional chain has a number of implications for placing issues on the EC environmental agenda and then manufacturing a policy consensus. Various actors and interest groups have numerous opportunities to find favourable institutional actors and access points. It is easy to place new and innovative definitions of the policy problem and the solution onto the EC decisional agenda (Zito, 2000). Nevertheless, each important actor within this long policy chain is a veto point, and any actor promoting a particular goal must build consensus and compromise across all the veto points (Weale, 1996). It is relatively easy to influence the EC agenda, but much harder to maintain the issue on the agenda and achieve agreement—i.e. 'agenda maintenance' (Zito, 2000).

Policy Complexity within the Environmental Sector

In order to understand how the tensions mentioned above manifest themselves in EU global behaviour, it is important to study the history and evolution of the EU environmental sector. Offering only a snapshot of the enormous sector, the article focuses (1) on the administrative structures and procedural arrangements that develop and implement policy; and (2) on policy goals, often based on a framework of ideas, that inform EU policy content (Hall, 1993). This section identifies how the tensions in the EU institutional framework are embedded in the evolution and the current dimensions of environmental policy.

Institutional Structure

One sees the immediate tension between EU policy frames in the very creation of EU environmental policy. The main EU constitutional basis, the Treaties signed by the member states, did not mention environmental policy until the 1987 ratification of the Single European Act, but environmental policy was one of the most dynamic Community areas two decades before this

(Hildebrand, 1993, Jordan, 1999). Before 1987, the Commission primarily based legislation under Treaty Article 100 (harmonizing national regulations that inhibit common market trade) or Article 235 (permitting the pursuit of Community objectives in the course of operating the common market where the Treaty has not provided the necessary powers). Accordingly, an important rationale for Community environmental activity was protecting the common market from national environmental legislation that act as trade (non-tariff) barriers.

Consequently the environment had to be inserted into a pre-existing European Treaty and ideational/institutional structure that explicitly prioritized other objectives (Lenschow and Zito, 1998). The policy frame of environmental sustainability and protection had to compete against pre-existing priorities, particularly economic ones. The subsequent Treaties have included the environmental priority, explicit mentions of environmental policy integration and the enhancing of the power of certain supranational bodies—i.e. the EP—held to be pro-green, but the tension remains.

In addition to the sectoral policy and value conflict, the Treaties contain rules to protect member state autonomy (the territorial dimension); these rules place strong limits on EU environmental action. Significantly, member state governments retain the EU budget setting powers although the supranational institutions have a role. Consequently, the member states have imposed significant constraints on the EU budget; this budget spending is quite limited beyond the traditional agricultural and regional funding. This necessarily limits the range of EU environmental activities; it creates a political dynamic where member states support EU frugality (Sbragia, 2000).

The EU ability to act in its own right as an environmental actor is a by-product of the historical evolution of complex institutional forces. Just as the EU was expanding its environmental policy scope, it was also enhancing enormously its international profile. The original Treaty of Rome creating the EC contained specific provisions allowing the Community to exercise external competence in the areas of foreign commercial trade (Jordan, 1999). The 1970s saw not only the threat of national environmental policies to the common market, but also member states becoming signatories to multilateral conventions protecting the environment that might create non-tariff barriers (Sbragia, 1998). The Commission used this economic imperative to expand the Community role and seek international status (Sbragia with Damro, 1999).

The ECJ affirmed this by ruling in the 1971 European Road Transport Agreement (ERTA) case that the ability of the Community to legislate a common policy within the market enables it to also have external powers. The ruling left ambiguous whether the Commission or the Council Presidency represented the EU; moreover, member states continued to have their international status when participating in such negotiations (Sbragia, 1998). Evidence of the political conflict present has been in the continued prohibition of separate Community participation in the Convention on International Trade on Endangered Species (CITES). There has been a move to reclaim some of the exclusive competence on the trade front in the 1990s (Meunier, 2000).

Environmental treaties are termed 'mixed agreements' as they involve the ratification of both the Community and the individual member states, thus thoroughly enmeshing territorial considerations with the system's supranational thrust. A rather elaborate EU negotiation procedure ensues at the international level in mixed competence areas. The Commission serves as negotiator under a mandate unanimously approved by the Council (without the participation of the EP) and consults continuously with the member state representatives (Krämer, 2003). Member states retain the right to negotiate on their own where they retain jurisdiction, but often the Commission (in areas of exclusive competence) or the Council President (in areas of mixed competence) will be asked to speak on the Community's behalf. Where the Commission does have a mandate, member states also participate in negotiations and sometimes carry far greater clout. This creates an international actor lacking the clear unitary negotiator found more typically in the international arena (Sbragia with Damro, 1999).

Policy Content

Institutional constraints as noted above have pushed the Community towards more command and control solutions, specifying the emissions limits or the means of environmental protection. The EU differs substantially from the traditional state in its highly limited budgetary powers (and police powers etc.—see Sbragia, 2000; Majone, 1997). EU law-making consequently has gravitated towards creating rules which require no budgetary expenditure on the actors who formulate them. In the early expansion of Community environmental legislation, regulation dominated the Community process although this has altered over time (Weale, 1999; Jordan et al., 2003).

Since 1992 the output has changed; there has been more exploration of 'new' policy instrument types. This partially reflects internal learning by the Commission and other policy actors about the limitations of traditional regulation and the potential benefits of alternatives and of stakeholder involvement. The tensions mentioned above also helped create this opportunity: (1) several member states led a push towards using the subsidiarity principle (i.e. an attempt to redress the territorial balance) in environmental policy (Flynn, 2003); and (2) various actors promoting economic competitiveness as a competing policy frame to that of enhancing the environment (Jordan et al., 2003, pp. 563–564).

The selection of instruments and the specification of standards create a parallel tension that shapes the nature of EU policy. A frequent Council dynamic occurs when certain states take a particular lead on a given issue, pushing for a Council decision or for a Commission initiative (Liefferink and Andersen, 1998). 'Regulatory competition' drives much of this process: member states seek to impose their own national standards at the EC level, in order to minimize the adjustment costs for their own economic sector relative to other member states (Héritier et al., 1996). Successful 'regulatory competition' can lead to tensions as certain states are forced to 'follow' the lead adopted by the whole EC. Thus the EU territorial units seek to 'upload' their own national preferences, which have to be 'downloaded' by other member states (Padgett, 2003, pp. 228–229). To successfully upload a policy, ideas must be pushed onto the EU agenda and past the various veto points, but how a policy is downloaded is equally important. This depends on how well the policy idea fits with domestic institutions and interests and the domestic institutional configuration within each member state.

The adoption of EU measures may redistribute resources and affect the political balance within the domestic constituency (Padgett, 2003, pp. 242–243). Over EC environmental history there has developed a tension felt particularly by the 'Southern' states: namely that the substantial EC legislation reflects a 'Northern' outlook towards goals and standards and not Southern priorities (Weale et al., 2000).

The Global Impact of EU Environmental Policy and Leadership

Having analysed how the EU complexity has shaped its environmental policy, we now theorize how this system's complexity shapes the EU's global environmental impact. Extensive scholarship has noted how the EU role as an external trade actor and a promoter of environmental protection values has led to internal conflict, often resolved in favour of the trade interests (Bretherton and Vogler, 2000). However, these tensions do not necessarily work against the EU's efforts. This article's thesis is that there are circumstances where the EU actually benefits from this complex process.

While this contradicts the conventional wisdom concerning EU foreign relations lacking a single voice, both EU trade and environmental scholars argue that, in particular circumstances, complexity can work to the EU advantage against an opponent such as the United States which has a more cohesive negotiating team. There are circumstances in which the EU can negotiate trade initiatives against US wishes (Clarke et al., 2000; Meunier, 2000; Rhinard and Kaeding, 2005). The diverse range of EC actors and member states force the EU towards a very inclusive pre-negotiation process; while problematic, the successful achievement of this stance may make the convention ratification process easier than the one confronting the US executive when it seeks Congressional ratification (Sbragia with Damro, 1999).

Finally, organizations look for ways around complex formal structures that inhibit necessary change. Héritier (1999) argues that the EU policy process has witnessed the utilization of a range of informal mechanisms to progress policy and to gain political legitimacy. The EU may conduct symbolic and rhetorical exercises in order to mask policy change, buy off particular internal or external actors by offering compensation, structure the sequence of policy negotiations to gain agreement in a more favourable arena before tackling more difficult ones, shifting a deadlocked issue from one EU institutional arena to another, and so forth.

The EU is a complex system that provides both procedural challenges and opportunities. To get some sense of how this system may influence EU international environmental negotiations and external relations more generally, we turn to the wide range of potential EU roles. Rather than offering detailed empirical analyses, the article offers some different conceptual permutations created by the complex EU process.

EU Global Leadership Roles

EU as Negotiator

A wide scholarship has examined the issue of EU global leadership, particularly concerning the EU as an active player shaping world events and negotiations. There has been a substantial discussion of the nature of EU power. Given its previous difficulties of developing a military capability, many have focused on the notion of the EU as a civilian power with international clout backed by its economic resources. Manners (2002) argues that the EU's hybrid status and supranational development give it a unique prominence to inculcate the global society with several key international norms (including democracy) and fundamental freedoms (including sustainable development). Manners suggests that there are a number of different vehicles by which the EU can diffuse its norms to third party actors, including procedural agreements, trade interaction and so forth. This emphasis about diffusion resonates with the roles articulated in this article.

However, the tensions and complexity found in the EU system severely complicate the EU effort to act as a normative leader. Taking the complexities in turn, the EU has endeavoured to promote the frames of sustainable development and the need for global environmental protection. The EU can develop a cohesive negotiating stance and sustain this with a complex institutional process. The Kyoto Protocol history reveals how domestic concerns motivated member state governments while the Commission and other EU actors saw an opportunity to expand EU influence (Damro and Luaces Méndez, 2003a). The respective EU Council President brokered a deal between the member states during and after the Kyoto negotiations which allowed the EU to develop a more coherent identity (Sbragia with Damro, 1999). As noted above, the EU has found it easier to ratify its Kyoto commitments than the US.

The fact that the EU has diverse actors and voices may be an advantage in dealing with complex problems as the variation of perspectives and voices that EU actors have may be attractive to counterparts. Taking a non-environmental example, the record of neutrality of some EU member states has helped reassure certain third parties (wary of NATO and US influence) about the likely direction taken by EU foreign relations. Equally, certain EU actors may engage third parties with more sympathy in environmental negotiations than the overall EU organization. This may not make the final negotiation easier but it may help to get opposing actors to the negotiation table.

While the Kyoto process is seen as a great success in the EU global environmental leader bid, EU complexity can hinder this effort. The EU participation in the World Summit on Sustainable Development reveals the negative impact of the EU tensions (Lightfoot and Burchell, 2005). While the EU managed to achieve some of its environmental objectives, the discussions on trade quickly fell foul of two of the core EU tensions: (1) the policy frame prioritizing trade competitiveness and economic growth was strongly embedded in many key EU actors and (2) policy integration across sectors (with their differing frames) proved extremely difficult. Commission officials in the Trade and the Development Directorates ended up promoting textual changes that conflicted with the environmental stance (Lightfoot and Burchell, 2005, pp. 85–88).

The EU also can play a negative environmental role, especially as it needs to satisfy the concerns of 25 very different member states. The tension between environmental protection and economic costs/fears can lead to a suboptimal EU negotiation stances (in environmental terms). In the agreements to protect the ozone layer, the Community fought to gain the contracting party status (Sbragia, 1998, pp. 296–298). After gaining that status, certain member state (particularly Greece) positions led the EC to join the international coalition pushing for less stringent regulations concerning particular substances (Jupille, 1999, pp. 416–419).

EU as Innovator

One of the key means through which the EU can take global leadership is by creating innovative solutions to the complex global policy problems. In the 1980s, both the OECD (Organization for Economic Co-operation and Development) and UNEP (United Nations Environment Programme) adapted regulatory ideas for governing hazardous waste that the EC originated (Zito, 2000). Given its current environmental status and the Single Market's perpetual clout, the EU has significant global agenda setting ability.

The institutional tension results in the EU having numerous actors who can veto innovation when that seems to threaten the balance of resources in favour of that particular state or organization. However, the global complexity and uncertainty of many of the problems (such as climate change) may make it harder for actors to have a clear sense of the direct and indirect consequences of particular solutions. Organizations facing complex uncertainty also may move away from formal routines and understandings (Levitt and March, 1988, p. 327). This may create more flexibility and potential for innovation, but there is a risk of such activities feeding into a separate EU tension, namely the concern about how distant and opaque this EU process is for the greater EU polity. While conditions of environmental uncertainty may lead the wider population to defer to the complex EU policy process and its solutions, various groups will resist discernible costs, as has been seen in the petrol tax protests (this fiscal instrument being heavily used by European governments, partly under the rationale of protecting the environment and stopping global emissions).

Besides acknowledging the legitimization problem, it is important to conceptualize how such a complex system might constitute a learning organization. With its diverse actors and processes, the EU should find it easier to create a diversity of theories and gather knowledge than simple national systems to solve transnational problems. Complex institutions are more likely to be able to learn and formulate approaches to complex problems as their separate constituent units follow different learning paths and perhaps even compete to find the best solutions to problems (Weir, 1992, pp. 192–194).

The tradable permits scheme within the Kyoto accord provides a useful example of a new environmental policy instrument, one that may bridge frame conflicts. Originally, individual states within the US took the lead in developing practical versions of this instrument. With the change in the US approach to Kyoto, the EU has taken over the leadership role and has embraced the tradable permits solution initially promoted by the USA (Damro and Luaces Méndez, 2003b; Jordan et al., 2005). The tradable permits system, which establishes markets that allow polluters to trade in a limited supply of 'pollution rights' to reduce emissions, addresses market competitiveness concerns as well as demands for cutting emissions through the setting of overall market emission limits. The Netherlands and the UK have been seeking to develop their ideas on this system in order to gain some first mover advantage and 'upload' their ideas within the larger EU debate and prevent disruption to their domestic systems (Jordan et al., 2005). Here member states sought advantage from new solutions and have helped to push EU innovation overall in this direction.

EU as Market

As already indicated, the EU market is extremely important in giving the EU political and economic influence. Bretherton and Vogler (2004) focus on how this can shape the EU as a foreign policy actor that can use exclusion from access and membership to influence other actors. This dynamic holds true for the environment as global business and actors fear the kinds of regulations that such an attractive market may place on economic activities. This explains the enormous international attention being devoted in 2004–2005 to the EU internal negotiations to reform the chemical regulations (Ochs and Schaper, 2005). In the past there is clear evidence of actors such as Australia seeking to globalize EU chemical regulation by getting the issues shifted to a more sympathetic international environment where these countries can directly protect their interests and concerns (Kellow and Zito, 2002). The wide range of diverse actors and policy frames within the EU context can aid lobbying efforts by third parties.

By agreeing regulations about genetically modified organisms at an early stage, the EU has set a number of rules that have become the global standard, despite US opposition. The EU managed to insert the Precautionary Principle into the Cartagena Protocol on Biosafety and have been taken to the World Trade Organization dispute settlement panel by the United States (Rhinard and Kaeding, 2005; Ochs and Schaper, 2005).

There is another dimension to this market activity that goes beyond exclusion: namely the EU ability to use the power of its market to penetrate other markets and force compatibility within EU norms or practices. Nicolaïdis and Egan (2001) argue that the EU effort to complete the single market has led to a number of externalities which have changed the environment for non-EU actors. The creation of a set of common standards, including environmental ones, has forced other actors to respond to EU efforts in bilateral and multilateral fora. EU firms also have a strong incentive to push the EU standards and standardization norms at the international level and within other regions (Nicolaïdis and Egan, 2001). Thus the process of the competitive advantage seen within the Common Market is also operative at the international level with the EU actors being willing to work with international organizations in a two way exchange that entrenches the EU influence.

While these dynamics suggest the EU should undertake global leadership and enhance international competitiveness, this does not necessarily mean a commitment to the highest level of environmental protection. Furthermore, although the EU endeavoured to protect the standardization process from being deadlocked by national perspectives through such tools as mutual recognition, the tension remains, particularly when the standards in question involve politically or socially sensitive areas.

EU as Model

Another potentially significant means for influencing other international actors and consequently outcomes is through the role of teacher and/or model. Here the multiplicity of EU actors can have a considerable impact on a wide range of objectives. Thus the Commission and the member state environmental ministries can offer their insights and experiences at international fora while other EU actors can engage with different levels of society.

An example of the latter effort is that of European environmental non-governmental organizations (ENGOS) seeking to promote environmental governance and democratic participation. In the mid-1990s, the European Environmental Bureau (or EEB, which is partly funded by the Commission) was heavily oriented to tackling North–South questions and made a major effort concerning Latin America and Mercosur environmental groups (ENGO interview, 23 September 2003). With the onset of Eastern European enlargement, ENGOs such as the EEB have concentrated substantial effort in building the knowledge and capacity of ENGOS to help make them become more effective EU policy participants and national lobbyists (Bomberg, 2003). The EU also offers a model of a democratic regional system with active environmental groups; elements of the Latin American population view positively regional integration as a result of their attitude to the EU (Jacobs and Zito, 2003).

Nevertheless, this effort to build civil society actors to further global environmental aims runs into the EU systemic tensions. Many of the external political elites as well as general populations are focused on the implications of the European Single Market and view the success story in terms of economic competitiveness. Programmes such as the Common Agricultural Policy suggest different norms and lessons from those emphasizing environmental concerns.

Summary and Future Research

This article has explained how the nature of the EU institutional/ideational structure has shaped the internal and external dimensions of EU environmental policy. Inherent in that structure are a number of core tensions. The EU contains a constant territorial tension between its national and EU elements. There are strong differences in policy values and frames located within the system. The strong emphasis on policy sectoralization reinforces these differences, which EU actors have found difficult to ameliorate and integrate. There is a tendency to include a wide range of experts in an open system that nevertheless lacks transparency and thus suffers under questions of legitimacy. Finally, the sheer size of the policy process creates a number of significant veto threats that must be overcome.

Although this set of tensions can lead to internal deadlock and incoherence in the approach to external relations, it can nevertheless create opportunities. This article does not offer a comprehensive list of potential EU global roles, but rather suggests some of the more significant ones and how they might be affected by the EU institutional tensions. One must realize that, in the context of any given global environmental problem, the EU may be influencing the other actors in at least four different ways. This direct and indirect influence may not create coherent pressures to protect the environment.

The EU may face deadlocks or conflicting policy frames that lead to one policy priority triumphing over another. However, they also may create opportunities for shrewd players that other international actors will not expect. The arguments explored here suggest that political entrepreneurship that understands both the EU process and the policy problem may be able to achieve their objectives in a way conventional wisdom will not expect. Part of the key is being able to define the international problem and provide a plausible solution early enough in the process to gain the advantage over other actors (Nicolaïdis and Egan, 2001; Ochs and Schaper, 2005). However, the aftermath of the Katrina hurricane suggests that all complex institutions and policy processes may face rapid policy change as environmental crises dramatically alter the policy perspectives of the policy elite and the general population.

References

Argyris, C & Schön, D. (1996) *Organizational Learning II: Theory, Method, and Practice* (Wokingham: Addison-Wesley Publishing).
Beetham, D. & Lord, C. (1998) *Legitimacy and the EU* (Longman: London).
Bomberg, E. (2003) Environmental NGOs, NEPIs and EU enlargement, Paper prepared for the 2nd Annual ECPR Conference, 19–21 September (Marburg).
Bomberg, E. & Burns, C. (1999) The Environment Committee of the European Parliament: new powers, old problems, *Environmental Politics*, 8(4), pp. 174–179.
Bretherton, C. & Vogler, J. (2000) The European Union as trade actor and environmental activist: contradictory roles? *Journal of Economic Integration*, 15(2), pp. 163–194.
Bretherton, C. & Vogler, J. (2004) Constructing the EU as an actor: implications for foreign policy analysis, paper for Fifth Pan-European SGIR Conference, 9–11 September (The Hague).
Cichowski, R. (1998) Integrating the environment: the European Court and the construction of supranational policy, *Journal of European Public Policy*, 5(3), pp. 387–405.
Clark, W., Duchesne, E. & Meunier, S. (2000) Domestic and international asymmetries in United States–European Union trade negotiations, *International Negotiation*, 5(1), pp. 69–95.
Damro, C. & Luaces Méndez, P. (2003a) Emissions trading at Kyoto: from EU resistance to Union innovation, *Environmental Politics*, 12(2), pp. 71–94.
Damro, C. & Luaces Méndez, P. (2003b) The Kyoto Protocol's emissions trading system: an EU–US environmental flip-flop (Working Paper # 5, UCIS, University of Pittsburgh).
Demmke, C. (1998) The secret life of comitology or the role of public officials in EC environmental policy, *EIPASCOPE* 1998(3), pp. 1–10.
Flynn, B. (2003) Subsidiarity and the evolution of EU environmental policy (Ph.D. thesis, University of Essex).
Geyer, R. (2003) European integration, complexity and the revision of theory, *Journal of Common Market Studies*, 41(1), pp. 15–35.
Goldstein, J. & Keohane, R. (1993) Ideas and foreign policy: an analytical framework, pp. 3–30 in Goldstein, J. & Keohane, R. (eds) *Ideas and Foreign Policy: Beliefs, Institutions and Political Change* (Ithaca, NY: Cornell University).
Golub, J. (1996) British sovereignty and the development of EC environmental policy, *Environmental Politics*, 5(4), pp. 700–728.
Hall, P. (1993) Policy paradigms, social learning and the state, *Comparative Politics*, 25(3), pp. 275–296.

Hayes-Renshaw, F. & Wallace, H. (1997) *The Council of Ministers* (Houndmills, Basingstoke: Macmillan).
Héritier, A. (1999) *Policy-making and diversity in Europe: Escape from Deadlock* (Cambridge: Cambridge University Press).
Héritier, A., Knill, C. and Mingers, S. (1996) *Ringing the Changes in Europe: Regulatory Competition and the Transformation of the State* (Berlin: Walter de Gruyer).
Hildebrand, P. (1993) The European Community's environmental policy, 1957 to '1992': from incidental measures to an international regime, pp. 13–44 in Judge, D. (ed.) *A Green Dimension for the European Community: Political Issues and Processes* (Portland, OR: Frank Cass).
Hill, A. (1993) EU Rottweiler both petted and panned, *Financial Times*, 13 December, p. 2.
Jacobs, J. & Zito, A. (2003) A cross-regional comparison of civil society in the environmental policy-making of the MERCOSUR and the European Union, paper presented at the UACES 33rd Annual Conference and 8th Research Conference, 2–4 September (Newcastle).
Jordan, A. (1999) Editorial introduction: the construction of a multilevel environmental governance system, *Environment and Planning C*, 17(1), pp. 1–27.
Jordan, A., Wurzel, R., Zito, A. & Brückner, L. (2003) European governance and the transfer of 'new' environmental policy instruments, *Public Administration*, 81(3), pp. 555–574.
Jordan, A., Wurzel, R. & Zito, A. (2005) The rise of 'new' policy instruments in comparative perspective: has governance eclipsed government? *Political Studies*, 53(3), pp. 477–496.
Jupille, J. (1999) The European Union and international outcomes, *International Organization*, 53(2), pp. 409–425.
Jupille, J. & Caporaso, J. (1998) States, agency, and rules: the European Union in global environmental politics, pp. 213–229 in Rhodes, C. (ed) *The European Union in the World Community* (Boulder, CO: Lynne Rienner).
Kellow, A. & Zito, A. (2002). Steering through complexity: EU environmental regulation in the international context, *Political Studies*, 50(1), pp. 43–60.
Kerremans, B. (1998) The political and institutional consequences of widening: capacity and control in an enlarged Council, pp. 87–109 in Laurent, P. & Marescau, M. (eds) *The State of the European Union (Vol. 4): Deepening and Widening* (Boulder, CO: Lynne Rienner).
Krämer, L. (2003) *EC Environmental Law* (London: Sweet & Maxwell).
Lenschow, A. & Zito, A. (1998) Blurring or shifting of policy frames? Institutionalization of the economic–environmental policy linkage in the European Community, *Governance*, 11(4), pp. 415–441.
Levitt, B. & March, J. (1988) Organizational learning, *Annual Review of Sociology*, 14, pp. 319–340.
Liefferink, D. & Andersen, M. S. (1998) Strategies of the 'Green' member states in EU environmental policy-making, *Journal of European Public Policy*, 5(2), pp. 254–270.
Lightfoot, S. & Burchell, J. (2005) The EU and the World Summit on Sustainable Development, *Journal of Common Market Studies*, 43(1), pp. 75–95.
Majone, G. (1997) From the positive to the regulatory state: causes and consequences of changes in the modes of governance, *Journal of Public Policy*, 17(2), pp. 139–167.
Manners, I. (2002) Normative power Europe: a contradiction in terms? *Journal of Common Market Studies*, 40(2), pp. 235–258.
March, J. & Olsen, J. (1989) *Rediscovering Institutions: The Organizational Basis of Politics* (New York: Free Press).
Meunier, S. (2000) What single voice? European institutions and EU–US trade negotiations, *International Organization*, 54(1), pp. 103–135.
Nicolaïdis, K. & Egan, M. (2001) Transnational market governance and regional policy externality: why recognise foreign standards? *Journal of European Public Policy*, 8(3), pp. 454–473.
Ochs, A. & Schaper, M. (2005) Conflict or cooperation? Transatlantic relations in the environmental field, paper presented at the EUSA Conference, 31 March to 2 April (Austin, Texas).
Padgett, S. (2003) Between synthesis and emulation: EU policy transfer in the power sector, *Journal of European Public Policy*, 10(2), pp. 227–245.
Peters, B. G. (1992) Bureaucratic politics and the institutions of the European Community, pp. 75–122 in Sbragia, A. (ed.) *Euro-politics* (Washington, DC: Brooking Institute).
Pierson, P. (1996) The path to European integration: a historical institutionalist analysis, *Comparative Political Studies*, 29(2), pp. 123–163.
Rein, M. & Schön, D. (1994) *Frame Reflection: Toward the Resolution of Intractable Policy Controversies* (New York: BasicBooks).
Rhinard, M. & Kaeding, M. (2005) The international bargaining power of the European Union in 'mixed' competence negotiations, paper presented at the EUSA Conference, 31 March to 2 April (Austin, Texas).

Sabatier, P. (1998) The Advocacy Coalition Framework: revisions and relevance for Europe, *Journal of European Public Policy*, 5(1), pp. 98–130.
Sbragia, A. (1993) The European Community: a balancing act, *Publius: The Journal of Federalism*, 23(1), pp. 23–38.
Sbragia, A. (1998) Institution-building from below and above: the European Community in global environmental politics, pp. 283–303 in Sandholtz, W. & Stone Sweet, A. (eds) *European Integration and Supranational Governance* (Oxford: Oxford University Press).
Sbragia, A. (2000) The European Union as coxswain: governance by steering, pp. 219–240 in Pierre, J. (ed.) *Debating Governance* (Oxford: Oxford University Process).
Sbragia, A. with Damro, C. (1999) The changing role of the European Union in international politics: institution building and the politics of climate change, *Environment and Planning C: Government and Policy*, 17(1), pp. 53–68.
Schout, A. & Jordan, A. (2003) Coordinated European governance: self-organizing or centrally steered? *Public Administration*, 83(1), pp. 201–220.
Vogel, D. (2003) The Hare and the Tortoise revisited: the new politics of consumer and environmental regulation in Europe, *British Journal of Political Science*, 33(4), pp. 557–580.
Weale, A. (1992) *The New Politics of Pollution* (Manchester: Manchester University Press).
Weale, A. (1996) Environmental rules and rule-making in the European Union, *Journal of European Public Policy*, 3(4), pp. 594–611.
Weale, A. (1999) European environmental policy by stealth: the dysfunctionality of functionalism? *Environment and Planning C*, 17(1), pp. 37–51.
Weale, A., Pridham, G., Cini, M., Konstadakopulos, D., Porter, M. & Flynn, B. (2000) *Environmental Governance in Europe* (Oxford: Oxford University Press).
Weir, M. (1992) Ideas and the politics of bounded innovation, pp. 188–216 in Steinmo, S., Thelen, K. & Longstreth, F. (eds) *Structuring Politics: Historical Institutionalism in Comparative Analysis* (Cambridge: Cambridge University Press).
Wurzel, R. (2002) *Environmental Policy-making in Britain, Germany and the European Union: The Europeanization of Air and Water Pollution Control* (Manchester: Manchester University Press).
Zito, A. (2000) *Creating Environmental Policy in the European Union* (Macmillan/St. Martin's Press/Palgrave).
Zito, A. (2004) EU Environmental Governance, paper presented at 'Environmental Policies in Decentralized Governmental Systems: A Blueprint for Optimal Governance', University of Turin, Italy.

Anthony R. Zito is a Reader in Politics at the University of Newcastle, specializing in European Union decision making and policy making. He has written a monograph, entitled *Creating Environmental Policy in the European Union*, as well as numerous articles on the themes of EU public policy and on environmental policy. He has recently completed a UK Economic and Social Research Council Future Governance Programme research grant focusing on new environmental policy instruments with Ruediger Wurzel and Andrew Jordan.

Global Indigenism and Spaceship Earth: Convergence, Space, and Re-entry Friction

JIM IGOE

Introduction

In 1969 Inuit Activist William Willoya made the following appeal to conservation groups in his native Alaska (Catton, 1997, p. 194): 'We Eskimos would like to join the Sierra Club. The first thing we would like is the testing of tankers coming to load oil through the Northwest Passage.' Ensuing alliances between Inuit and conservationists contributed to the creation of Gates of the Arctic National Park, one of the few US parks in which indigenous communities are allowed to live. Increasingly, western conservationists were also beginning to acknowledge the potential of such alliances (Dassman, 1976; Redford and Stearman, 1993; Turner, 1993; Catton, 1997; Igoe, 2004a). In the 1970s, alliances between aboriginal groups and conservationists blocked uranium mines in the Northern Territory and established Kakadu National Park (Allen, 1981; Lawrence, 2000). In the 1980s, transnational conservation NGOs worked with indigenous groups in Latin America to protect rainforests ecosystems (Turner, 1993; Chapin, 2000).

By the 1990s such alliances were being institutionalized.[1] Conservation interventions targeting indigenous peoples were proliferating rapidly (Chapin, 2004). Indigenous peoples and indigenous issues became increasingly common at international conservation events. A position paper published by the WWF (World Wildlife Fund) in 1997 posited a global overlap between areas of high biodiversity and high cultural diversity and suggested that indigenous resource management and environmental knowledge were essential to conservation (cf. Stepp et al., 2004). Conservation's mission, therefore, should to be extended to include the protection of indigenous peoples.

The idea of protecting biodiversity by protecting cultural diversity enjoyed a brief but intense popularity. Its appeal was its apparently seamless weaving together of two powerful universal ideals: 1) the ideal of 'spaceship earth', a global community brought together by our common dependence on the fragile biodiversity of our planet (Nugent, 1994; Escobar, 1996), and 2) the ideal of universal human rights, including the rights of people to live according to their own cultural traditions without fear of political or economic retribution (Niezen, 2003).

The global spread of the institutions and funding associated with these ideals presented indigenous activists with new opportunities for transnational activism and 'space making', especially with the global proliferation of NGOs in the wake of the Soviet collapse (Li, 2000; Muehlebach, 2001; Hodgson, 2002; Niezen, 2003; Igoe, 2004a, 2004b). These developments accompanied the rise of what Niezen (2003, pp. 4–5) calls 'indigenism', a nascent global ideology premised on the common experiences of the world's 'first peoples'—those who are 'strongly attached to the world's last "wild places"' and who 'share the claim to have survived on their land through the upheavals of colonialism and corporate exploitation'. The association of 'first peoples' with 'wild places' suggested a close association of indigenous rights and biodiversity and opportunities for 'space making' within transnational structures like the World Conservation Union (IUCN).

These processes engendered more systematically global encounters between conservationists and indigenous peoples and the generation and 'discovery' of new kinds of knowledge, of community-based conservation and indigenous environmental wisdom—and ultimately the proposition that global biodiversity is inextricably linked to global cultural diversity. At the same time, however, the universal ideals that informed these encounters began to encounter what Tsing (2004, p. 1) has labeled 'friction'—as they were 'charged and enacted in the sticky materiality of practical encounters'. Tsing cautions us against assuming that such collaborations are based on similar goals or viewpoints, or that they will necessarily result in compromise. 'Collaborations create new interests and identities, but not to everyone's benefit.'

Encounters between conservationists and indigenous peoples are never between equals. Inuit who worked to create 'Gates of the Artic' have found themselves increasingly excluded from the park (Catton, 1997). Aboriginal groups in the Northern Territory found themselves being used as pawns between mining companies and conservationists (Allen, 1981). Transnational conservation NGOs aggressively pursued alliances with indigenous groups in Latin America, but then wound up with the lion's share of the funding (Chapin, 2004). Transnationally, the putative link between indigenous peoples and biodiversity placed tremendous pressure on indigenous leaders to cultivate certain images that were difficult to live up to in practice (Niezen, 2003).

Through the conflicts and negotiations of conservation targeting indigenous peoples, conservationists learned that indigenous ways of valuing and using nature were frequently out of step with their own (Niezen, 2003). Furthermore, most of the conservation interventions were widely coming to be regarded as failures (Chapin, 2004, p. 20). All this friction sparked a backlash known as 'back to the barriers' (Roe et al., 2003), advocating a return to conservation excluding local people and human needs (Bruner et al., 2001; Leakey, 2003; Sanderson, 2004). Relationships between conservationists and indigenous leaders became increasingly hostile. Back-to-the-barriers conservationists accused indigenous activists and their supporters of invoking 'the ecologically noble savage' (Redford, 1990) and dressing environmental issues up in 'Indian blankets'.[2] Indigenous peoples in many places have become disdainful of anything labeled conservation.[3]

Chapin (2004) has recently outlined reasons for the increasing tensions between these groups in an article entitled *A Challenge to Conservationists*.[4] The article, which caused a minor furor at the 2004 World Conservation Congress, reveals that people on each side of this debate accuse the other of using spurious science and sexy imagery to support their position. Neither is completely wrong in the respect, as debates over the relative merits of 'fortress conservation' and 'people-centered' approaches are frequently formulated with very little empirical evidence.

Much research needs to be done on the relationship between western conservation and indigenous peoples. This article hopefully represents a small beginning, by outlining the institutional and historical context of the convergence and frictions of global conservation and global indigenism. In so doing it emphasizes both the opportunities and dangers they present to indigenous movements and biodiversity conservation.

The Expanding Common Ground: The Scaling Up of Biodiversity Conservation and Indigenous Movements

The Historical Basis for the Common Ground

The common ground between indigenous peoples and western conservationists is linked to the history of western conservation in the context of European expansion—and more specifically to the emergence of the 'Fortress Conservation' in the USA in the late nineteenth century. The forceful creation and protection of 'pristine wilderness', which emerged in this context, became the model for 'preservationist efforts and native dispossession around the world' (Spence, 1999, p. 85).[5]

Neumann (2005, pp. 134–135) takes this argument further, asserting that protected areas are linked to the expansion of state control. Certainly parks are often closely associated with the control and containment of indigenous communities. However, they are also frequently spaces uniquely beyond the realm of state control. Parks in Africa and Latin America have become staging grounds for guerrilla movements (Dunn, 2003; Tapia, 2005), as well as for drug trafficking (Stepp, 2005; Tapia, 2005). US parks shelter marijuana plantations and meth amphetamine labs, as well as people seeking to enter the country illegally.[6] Parks also sometimes provide opportunities to indigenous peoples to elude state control, as with the Ute Mountain Tribal Park in Colorado (Igoe, 2004a) and the Xingu National Park in Brazil (Turner, 1993).

As contested spaces, sometimes beyond the reach of states and global capitalism, parks have brought together indigenous communities and western conservationists in landscapes around the world. In an effort to protect these landscapes, sometimes from each other, both groups have sought support and resources from distant but powerful institutions. Over time, their externally oriented strategies have engendered transnational structures like the IUCN and the UN Forum on Indigenous Issues. Relationships that emerged in the context of parks have been reproduced in these structures, with the added complexity of distance, funding cycles, and institutional survival.

Large Organizations and Large Landscapes

In the 1970s, conservation became a growth industry and organizations like the WWF and Nature Conservancy grew rapidly. During the 1980s, individuals from these groups left to form Conservation International, which quickly became a major player in international conservation. Competition between these organizations intensified as they sought to raise money for overlapping causes and from overlapping constituencies and in a field of rapidly proliferating conservation organizations (Bonner, 1993; Chapin, 2004).

For the most part, however, these changes remained unaddressed until Chapin's controversial article in 2004, which described in excruciating detail the impacts of funding competition on transnational conservation. The resulting changes, Chapin argues, have come at the expense of indigenous communities. He traces these shifts to the 1990s, during which conservation funding decreased by 50%. At the same time funding to WWF, the Nature Conservancy, and Conservation International increased dramatically (Chapin, 2004, p. 22). This was achieved through diversification of funding sources to include corporate, bilateral, and multi-lateral funding.

To capture this funding, Chapin explains, large conservation organizations 'reformulated their missions to focus on large-scale conservation'. Large-scale approaches require large sums of money, and must be overseen by organizations large enough to administer them effectively. Every large conservation organization has its own special term for this approach to conservation, which is something like a registered trademark (Redford et al., 2003).

Large landscape conservation is also closely linked to recent increases in the global conservation estate. The area of the world's surface enclosed by protected areas has increased threefold in recent years. The 2004 World Database on Protected Areas listed 105,344 protected areas, covering 19.67 million km^2. Fifteen million km^2 of lands are protected, covering 10% of the world's land area. More expansion is planned, as the IUCN target of 10% of each ecosystem has not been met for several ecosystems (Brockington et al., in press). This expansion of the global conservation estate will intensify encounters between conservationists and indigenous communities, undoubtedly producing new types of frictions in the process.

The Roots of Global Indigenism

Transformations in the Global Environmental Movement have been paralleled by the emergence of the Global Indigenous Peoples' Movement. While transnational indigenous activism has been going on for as long as transnational environmental activism, it has taken place on a smaller scale, with fewer resources, and remains less intensively centralized and coordinated. Nevertheless, indigenous movements have become a force that conservationists must regularly engage.

The transnational structures of global indigenism have their roots in colonial policies of assimilation and indirect rule, which accompanied the consolidation of European empires and westward expansion in North America. Stung by the obvious contradictions between liberal ideals of citizenship and legal rights on the one hand, and the treatment of their peoples by European settlers on the other, indigenous leaders lobbied distant imperial authorities to resolve these contradictions (Sanders, 1980, p. 2). This pattern of activities continued and intensified throughout the twentieth century, influencing the creation of international laws promoting indigenous sovereignty in the years following World War II. In 1974, indigenous leaders from North America, Latin America, Australia, and New Zealand established the World Council of

Indigenous Peoples, the first of 11 indigenous NGOs with official UN consultative status (Sanders, 1980). These groups were instrumental in establishing the UN Forum on Indigenous Issues in 2003.

However, it was not until participation in 'international consultations and standard-setting exercises [was extended] to self-identifying indigenous peoples from Africa and Asia in the 1990s that the indigenous peoples movement became more fully global' (Niezen, 2003, p. 26, also see Hodgson, 2002). The reasons for the inclusion of African and Asian groups in the Global Indigenous Peoples' Movement are complex and controversial (see Li, 2000; Sylvaine, 2002; Kuper, 2003; Niezen, 2003; Igoe, in press). They are closely tied to the global spread of NGOs, which presented activists in Africa and Asia with unprecedented opportunities for gaining access to international fora (Niezen, 2003; Igoe, in press).

While these developments have clearly increased the political clout of indigenous activists from around the world, it has also presented indigenous movements with a fundamental paradox:

> The clearest expression of human diversity can be found in a category now widely referred to as 'indigenous peoples'; yet the very creation of this category involves common origin, is predicated on the global sameness of experience, and is expressed through the mechanisms of law and bureaucracy, the culprits most commonly associated with the steady gains of cultural uniformity. (Niezen, 2003, p. 2)

We now turn to the reasons for this paradox, and its implications for representation and action.

'The Shifting Middle Ground': Issues of Distance and Representation

Simple Narratives and Complex Realities

Much has been written about the discrepancies between the complex realities of ecosystems and human communities and the simplifying tendencies of bureaucracies that administer them. Recent academic discussions have been dominated by Foucauldian scholars, who emphasize 'the production of knowledge', how this knowledge shapes the realities of bureaucrats, and how their thoughts and actions contribute in turn to the production of further 'knowledge'— thereby reinforcing specific ways of understanding the world. While 'constructed realities' are frequently out of step with empirical reality, they are extraordinarily powerful and difficult to refute—in large part because of their links to policy and funding (Ferguson, 1990; Escobar, 1995).

Others have emphasized the importance of incentive structures and funding imperatives. The imperative of moving money within a stipulated period places significant pressure on bureaucrats and community leaders to simplify problems so that their funding proposals appear viable (Tendler, 1975; Chambers, 1984). Because an admission of failure spells almost certain doom in a highly competitive funding environment, this in turn places pressures on individuals to embellish or even to fabricate outcomes of interventions that were too simple and inflexible to engage the complexities of problems they were designed to solve (Chambers, 1984; Maren, 1997; Brechin et al., 2003; Igoe, 2003, 2004a). Herein lies a central source of friction in biodiversity conservation, where the complexities of both ecosystems and human communities demand approaches that are flexible enough to engage specific local circumstances, while accounting for more universal forces and processes.

Unfortunately the demands of conservation bureaucracies present inconsistencies and contradictions that are frequently at odds with such approaches. For example the AWF's (African Wildlife Foundation) ivory ban campaign influenced policies that contributed to the recovery of East Africa's decimated elephant populations. However, it also contributed to conditions in Southern Africa, where elephant populations became so large that they were destroying their own habitat (Bonner, 1993). Both the AWF and the WWF describe indigenous environmental knowledge and resource management systems as essential to biodiversity, while simultaneously sponsoring interventions designed to transform these systems (Goldman, 2003; Igoe, 2004b). Finally, the creation of parks without considering their impacts on local resource management frequently threatened the very biodiversity that they were designed to protect (Igoe, 2004a).

Wilderness Ideals and Corporate Agendas

In the realm of conservation, these kinds of problems, paradoxes, and frictions are rendered discursively invisible by the ideal of wilderness. The fundraising activities of conservation organization frequently invoke what Nugent (1994) has termed 'ecodomains': putative a-social landscapes that loom large in the western imagination (e.g. Amazonia, the Serengeti, and the Grand Canyon). With the possible exception of small hunter/gatherer groups, humans are not envisioned as part of 'ecodomains'. Human conflicts are notably absent in their construction.

The idea of 'ecodomians' has made it possible to imagine places 'where nature might be left alone to flourish by its own pristine devices' (Cronon, 1996, p. 82). It is strengthened by the notion that protecting such areas is as easy as writing a check. It also promotes ideas that the only places worth taking care of are those locked away in wilderness areas. In order to be effective, however, 'ecodomains' must describe distant and exotic environments. This keeps people from seeing the importance of more mundane environments and the environmental impacts of their day-to-day activities (Cronon, 1996; Adams, 2004). Ultimately, it obscures the interconnections of human communities, both to each other and to the physical environment.

Such discrepancies have become increasingly visible in the rhetoric and action of large conservation organizations. Fierce funding competition has engendered an environment in which claims about how best to protect biodiversity are based more on ideas than empirical reality (McShane, 2003). It has also resulted in inconsistencies in the ways in which these organizations do business. While leaders of large conservation organizations assert that poverty alleviation is not conservation's responsibility, they are increasingly funded by agencies and organizations whose missions revolve around poverty alleviation (Chapin, 2004).

Funding from bilateral and multilateral donors, essentially diplomatic agencies, has also reduced their ability to take political stances in countries whose governments are facilitating environmental destruction (Chapin, 2004, p. 25). Increasing corporate sponsorship compounds this problem.[7] A recent expose in the *Washington Post* revealed that Conservation International was reluctant to criticize 'the environmental records of its corporate board members' (Stephens and Ottaway, 2003). As such, it has avoided taking a strong stance on issues such as global warming and oil drilling in the Arctic Wildlife Refuge. In my own work I recently assessed a development project in which an international conservation organization supported the introduction of genetically modified seeds to Tanzania by an international corporation. The project would settle local people onto a mechanized rice scheme in a wetland of international significance.[8]

While some conservationists claim that they are engaging corporations to be more 'ecologically responsible' (Sanderson, 2002), critics counter that they are supplying corporate sponsors with a 'green fig leaf'. Whatever the case, large conservation organizations are currently more inclined to identify local people as a threat to the environment than large-scale commercial interests. Meanwhile, indigenous activism has become increasingly geared to the reified standards of transnational bureaucracies (Niezen, 2003; Igoe, 2003, in press).

Indigenous Activism and the Limits of Strategic Essentialism

Like conservationists, indigenous activists find themselves having to describe the complex problems of their communities in simplified narratives that distant audiences will recognize and support. While this kind of strategic essentialism is an important component of all political activism (cf. Robins, 2003), Niezen (2003, p. 187) argues that 'indigenous nationalism is shaped more significantly by the demands of consumer export than any other group identity ... [and] usually shapes itself around values that resonate most strongly with the non-indigenous public'.

This is compounded by the fact that western conservation organizations operating in developing countries are controlling more and more of the funding upon which indigenous activists depend for their advocacy activities (Chapin, 2004). As a consequence, indigenous activists are increasingly finding themselves needing to spin their activities according to the agendas of these organizations. Conklin and Graham (1995, p. 695) describe this process as the creation of discursive 'middle ground' through which indigenous peoples and western conservationists construct a 'mutually comprehensible world'. Unfortunately, the inequitable terms of this relationship usually mean that this middle ground is defined more by the ideas and agendas of western conservationists than by those of indigenous communities. Consequently, indigenous activists must assert that their environmental values are consistent with western conservation principles (Alcorn, 1993; Turner, 1993; Catton, 1997; Brosius, 2001; Li, 2000; Igoe, 2004a).

In the process, they often wind up setting discursive standards for themselves that are impossible to achieve in practice. They must be 'noble, strong, spiritually wise, and above all, environmentally discreet', while coming from communities where 'addictions are rampant, economic desires are unfulfilled, and political frustration pushes regularly against the barriers preventing violence' (Niezen, 2003, p. 186). Furthermore, effective indigenous activists must be able to negotiate the complex discourses and structures of international bureaucracies— they must be simultaneously modern and traditional (Li, 2000; Hirtz, 2003; Niezen, 2003; Igoe, in press).

These contradictory conditions open indigenous peoples to criticisms by western conservationists that they are not 'ecologically noble'. Any attempts to bring commercial development to impoverished indigenous communities are likely to result in assertions that these communities are no longer worthy 'conservation partners' (Redford, 1990; Redford and Sanderson, 2000; Niezen, 2003; Chapin, 2004). 'Noble savage' ideals also obscure the fact that indigenous identity is not 'a simple reflection of timeless values and practices; it is based in large measure on a compendium of cultural facts and artifacts intended for consumption within a dominant national society and international audience' (Niezen, 2003, p. 191).

As such there is a tendency to conflate the various levels (local, national, and transnational) at which indigenous activism occurs, while ignoring how the distances and differences between these levels influence indigenous politics. This conflation springs from assertions that indigenous peoples represent a 'self-ascribed polythetic class' (Colchester, 2002, p. 2) who need only show up in Geneva to become part of a global indigenous community. Once part of this community, they will enjoy the benefits of a new body of international law, which recognizes their collective right to control their land and territory (Colchester, 2002; Niezen, 2003; Igoe, in press). These activities are thereby conflated with local struggles for the control of collective land and territory, so that 'indigenous cultural politics are always also the politics of land ... and all struggles for and about land are also struggles about identity and culture' (Muehlebach, 2001, p. 425).

While international indigenous activism is irrefutably tied to local land struggles, the idea of indigenous peoples as a 'self-ascribed polythetic class' ignores the exclusivity of the transnational forums in which 'space making' by indigenous activists takes place. When this exclusivity is ignored, whether or not a group of people becomes indigenous appears as a matter of choice. Colchester's (2002, p. 2) discussion of this issue smacks surprisingly of Sartrean free will: 'Not all marginalized ethnic groups choose to consider themselves indigenous. Some apparently see greater advantage in assimilating into the national mainstream.'

As Li (2000, p. 151) demonstrates, however, not all marginal groups can 'choose' to be indigenous: 'A group's self-identification as indigenous is not natural or inevitable, but neither is it simply invented, adopted, or imposed. It is a positioning, which draws upon historically sedimented practices, landscapes, and repertoires of meaning, and emerges through particular patterns of engagement and struggle.' Li conceptualizes an 'indigenous slot' with which some groups are able to articulate. Certain preconditions are necessary for this articulation, three of which are apropos to this article: outsiders interested in helping indigenous groups; a capacity to make local cultural identity intelligible to outsiders; and individuals mandated to speak on behalf of the group (Li, 2000, p. 169).

It is also important not to underestimate the extent to which indigeneity represents an important form of symbolic capital, which indigenous leaders use to make alliances with, and leverage resources from, transnational institutions, including conservation NGOs. Arguments about 'indigenous self-identity' notwithstanding, effective use of this symbolic capital often depends upon meeting externally defined criteria of indigenous legitimacy and community needs, which may be quite different from local ideas of what these mean (Conklin and Graham, 1995; Igoe, 2000; Hodgson, 2002; Niezen, 2003; Igoe, 2004a).

Finally, indigenous struggles are not always about land (cf. Sylvain, 2002, p. 1076). Increasingly, they are also about monetary resources associated with interventions targeting indigenous peoples. These external resources are crucially important to communities that have been impoverished by the historical alienation of their natural resources. Tribal governments and indigenous NGOs represent one of the few opportunities for gainful employment in many indigenous communities.

There are two inequities inherent in this situation: 1) between indigenous groups and 2) between indigenous groups and other marginal groups who cannot choose to be indigenous. The first is best summed up, as 'some indigenous people are more indigenous than others'. San groups in Namibia, for instance, have become a permanent underclass of agricultural workers, unable to articulate the same claims to indigeneity as San groups in neighboring Botswana (Sylvain, 2002). In Tanzania, Barabaig NGOs leaders complain that Maasai NGOs dominate the Tanzanian indigenous peoples' movement (Igoe, 2000, in press). Maasai opposition to the evictions from the Mkomazi Game Reserve excluded and alienated other local groups that had been in the area longer than the Maasai (Kiwasila, 1997). In Colorado, over 600,000 tourists a year flock to the Mesa Verde to visit the ruins of the ancient Anasazi peoples, who were the ancestors of contemporary Hopi groups. What most do not know, and will never learn at the visitor center, is that the park was excised from the reservation of the Ute Mountain Ute, who are not related to the ancient Anasazi and benefit very little from the area's booming tourist economy (Burnham, 2000; Igoe, 2004a).

Next, indigenous people are not always the most marginal people displaced and impoverished by protected areas. This situation is especially complicated in developing countries, where non-indigenous peoples are as likely to be impoverished as indigenous ones, and where the line between indigenous and non-indigenous is most likely to be influenced by the perceptions of western conservationists, human rights activists, and eco-cultural tourists. Nugent's (1994, pp. 17–18) account of conservation in Amazonia captures this dilemma:

> In its attempts to make the world over in its own image, Europe's portrayals of society at the fringes have frequently betrayed a kind of stereo tunnel vision: in one eye is presented that which typifies the legacy of civilization, the other observes primitivism. Out of focus, if not out of view, is the netherworld, that vast region of social and historical marginality where images are less pristine and for which more explanation is required than can be summed up in a flattering archetype. [These] out of focus Amazonians ... appear when needed as guides, they are present when laundry needs to be done; they drive cabs and serve up beer, but they are almost incidental, populating the transitional zone between the airport and the Amazonian Indian theme park.

Social scientists often overlook these groups as peoples who have 'chosen to assimilate'. The problem with this perspective is that being assimilated into poverty only means that you are poor with nothing to distinguish yourself in the eyes of outsiders who may bring resources to your communities. Studies from Indonesia (Li, 2000), South Africa (Kuper, 2003), and Tanzania (Igoe, 2000) illustrate that people descended from displaced groups frequently make up significant minorities of the rural populations in developing countries. They are also frequently the most marginal and least ethnically distinct. Nevertheless, their relationships to the environment have profound implications for conservation.

This brief review indicates that the convergence between global indigenism and global conservation is murky, complex and intricate. Both conflicts and collaboration between conservationists and indigenous communities began for the most part in specific landscapes with specific histories. However, the complexities of these encounters, and the frictions they have produced, have been obscured by reified ideals of 'pristine wilderness' and 'noble savages' in the context of transnational bureaucracies geared towards fundraising and the production of standardized interventions. Two examples include step-by-step instructions for moving from a traditional national park to an indigenous protected area (Borrini-Feyerabend et al., 2004) as well as for working with local people to design and implement a conservation landscape (WWF, 2004).

This discursive simplification of the world makes these kinds of interventions appear feasible. Ironically, however, it also obscures the kinds of frictions they are likely to encounter in the give and take of implementation, collaboration, negotiation, and stakeholder mobilization.

Conclusion: Re-entry Friction

As Nugent (1994) points out, the ideal of 'space ship earth', that we are all part of a global community tied to the same terrestrial life support system, is ultimately an elaborate way of saying that we all breathe the same air. It leaves out of focus the fact that not all passengers on 'space ship earth' are traveling on the same class of ticket. In the event of catastrophe, the ones traveling steerage are the most likely to perish and suffer the most in the process.

This has become a sticky point at transnational conservation fora, where heated debates revolve around the question of whether conservation has a special responsibility to people who have been displaced and dispossessed by the same global historical processes that have grievously harmed our global environment. In this relatively frictionless environment, the heat of these debates is relatively minor. They can invoke competing configurations of universal ideals, while selectively invoking specific local experiences to support their position. As it turns out, however, the world is complex enough to provide examples to support just about any argument, providing that it is presented in an environment that is frictionless enough to provide for an adequate amount of spin.

Unfortunately, as Tsing notes, a wheel suspended in the air may spin very well but it is not going anywhere. Supporting particular paradigms or policies by ignoring the realities for which they cannot effectively account may grease the wheels of bureaucratic machines, but it does not change the fact that effective conservation and indigenous liberation must ultimately occur in local circumstances. Conservation professionals often refer to this place as 'where the rubber hits the road', a term Tsing also invokes in *Frictions*. While most bureaucrats and applied scientists I know would be averse to reading such a theoretical monograph, they intuitively recognize one of its central points: the outcomes of a policy or intervention will ultimately be shaped by the 'sticky materiality of practical encounters'—by the friction of the rubber on the road.

Understanding the types of frictions that are likely to send conservation interventions in one direction or another is therefore essential for understanding the types of outcomes that are likely to occur. It will help us to understand, for instance, why Brazilian indigenous leaders entered into alliances with transnational conservation organizations to block hydroelectric plants, while Tanzanian indigenous leaders, and transnational conservation organizations operating in Tanzania, eschewed similar alliances to block large-scale agricultural enterprises—why the WWF supports people living in parks in Latin America but not East Africa—why Maasai leaders describe themselves as 'enemies of conservation'[9]—the abundance of eco-tourism opportunities for indigenous communities in Central America and South-East Asia and their near absence in East Africa and South Dakota—the Ute Mountain tribe's success in establishing a tribal park and the Oglala Sioux tribe's inability to do so—why transfrontier conservation works well in Southern Africa and Mesoamerica, but not in East Africa or the United States (see Igoe, 2004a, Chapter 5, 2004b).

It is impossible to predict specific outcomes, as one might in a physics experiment, where variables like momentum, trajectory, and friction can be controlled. And yet these outcomes are not random either. They have patterns that are recognizable, and which can be attributed to certain variables that are present in some situations and absent in others. It is possible, therefore, to say under which types of conditions certain outcomes are likely to occur.

For instance, alliances between conservationists and indigenous communities are more likely where indigenous peoples have legal authority over natural resources; where they have been allowed to live inside protected areas; where indigenous leaders have good accountability to their constituency; and where indigenous peoples initiated the relationship with conservationists rather than vice versa. In situations where the conditions are the opposite antagonisms are more likely to prevail (Igoe, 2004b).

While understanding these kinds of historically and geographically contingent variables is less appealing than standardized formulas for implementing conservation, it will allow conservationists to determine whether or not specific indigenous communities are likely to be inclined to work with them. By the same token it would allow them to ask whether local people may have historical grievances against conservation that will need to be addressed before alliances with such communities might become a possibility.

It is also important to be cognizant of the ways in which competing, and sometimes collaborating, forces and interests might bump encounters between conservationists and indigenous communities along other trajectories. The vast financial resources of corporations, for instance, have tempted both indigenous leaders and conservationists. Both indigenous and environmental activisms have become increasingly oriented to transnational bureaucracies. In such a context it is possible to believe that 'sound science' in the context of well-funded bureaucracies represents the salvation of our planet's environmental future. It is also possible to ignore processes of social and political marginalization that are not easily explained by 'flattering archetypes'.

Such arrangements make it possible to believe that the biosphere or an indigenous community can be saved simply by writing a check. The belief that only distant and exotic things are worth saving externalizes both problems and solutions. Most fundamentally, it spares people the discomfort of examining the environmental and social impacts of their most mundane activities. It conceals on a day-to-day basis the types of problems that are closest at hand.

The depth of this tendency in American society was starkly revealed in the recent aftermath of Hurricane Katrina. In this case the friction was far from metaphorical. The intense physical impact of the storm rendered abruptly visible the plight of poor Americans who normally inhabit Nugent's netherworld, whose struggle and suffering are too mundane to merit much interest or attention under normal circumstances. Media and politicians were quick to distance the event, repeatedly describing New Orleans as 'Third World', a place beyond normal American points of reference. This discursive distancing was impossible to ignore as I watched events unfold from Tanzania. 'This is how the American media always portrays us', my Tanzanian colleagues repeatedly commented. 'We never thought it would portray Americans in such a fashion.'

The 'Third Worlding' of the American poor may portend a willful 'othering' of people and the environment that defies even physical proximity. On the other hand, there is some evidence that it has prompted Americans to begin reflecting on their own social and environmental impacts. It remains to be seen if a critical mass can make the connections between oil dependency, poverty, the War on Terror, global warming, failures of government, and a general decline in their quality of their lives—let alone is they can find the political will to channel it into tangible actions like the creation of regional economies, integrated agriculture, and the development of alternative fuels.

As one anonymous reviewer pointed out, localized engagements with the environment are likely to be more complex and fraught with conflict than the kinds of transnational engagements described in this article. As they are more likely to be fraught with frictions, this is irrefutably true. An ethic that recognizes one's own connections to, and impacts upon, the environment will therefore be essential to the social maturity necessary to make such a society. In this respect we stand to learn a great deal from the frictions that have occurred in the global convergence of indigenism and environmentalism—most immediately the ways in which a vertically integrated world distorts the most basic relationships of humans to each other and the natural world.

Notes

1   In 2000, the World Conservation Union established a working group on indigenous and local communities, equity and protected areas. The most recent World Parks Congress, convened in Durban (2003) was attended by 120 indigenous representatives (Brosius, 2001; Terborgh, 2004). Indigenous peoples and issues were again conspicuously present at the World Conservation Congress, convened in Bangkok (2004).
2   This term was coined by representatives of the Sierra Club, upset by decisions of the Ute Mountain Tribal Council to build irrigation schemes on their portion of the Animas and Las Platas Rivers.
3   After extensive research in Asia, Africa, and Latin America, journalist Mark Dowie discovered that indigenous peoples around the world have been displaced by conservation. Although western conservationists frequently dismiss hostility toward conservation as irrationally 'negative conservation attitudes', there is nothing irrational about formulating opinions or position based on previous experience. See Igoe, 2004b.

4 Chapin's article can be found online at http://www.un-ngls.org/cso/cso6/worldwatch%20inst%20-%20NGOs%20and%20IPs.pdf. Responses can be found at http://www.worldwatch.org/pubs/mag/2005/181/contents/and http://www.worldwatch.org/pubs/mag/2005/182/online/1/.
5 For a full discussion of the history of the origins of large conservation organizations see MacKenzie, 1988; Bonner, 1993; Neumann, 1998; Spence, 1999; Adams, 2004. For a full discussion of the Global Indigenous Peoples Movement see Niezen, 2003.
6 Enforcement rangers I interviewed identified drugs as one of their greatest enforcement challenges. The Ranger Fraternal Order of Police maintains a list of the ten most dangerous parks in the US (http://www.rangerfop.com/danger03.htm). It also appears that parks are becoming connected to the spread of extractive industries. I recently was hired as a consultant to assess a development project in Tanzania, which claims that it will protect biodiversity with large-scale rice farms using genetically modified seeds.
7 Prior to this period, these organizations depended primarily on foundation money and individual contributions to cover their operating costs.
8 According to Wetlands International—http://www.wetlands.org/reports/dbdirectory.cfm?site_id=108.
9 This term comes from a speech by Maasai leader Martin Saning'o at the World Conservation Congress.

References

Adams, W. (2004) *Against Extinction* (London: Earthscan).
Alcorn, J. (1993) Indigenous peoples and conservation, *Conservation Biology*, 7(2), pp. 424–426.
Allen, H. (1981) Against waking the Rainbow Serpent, *Arena*, 59(2), pp. 25–42.
Bonner, R. (1993) *At the Hand of Man* (New York: Knopf Publishers).
Borrini-Feyerabend, G., Pimbert, M., Farvar, M., Kothari, A. & Renard, Y. (2004) *Sharing Power* (Tehran: IIED), http://www.iucn.org/themes/ceesp/Publications/sharingpower.htm#citation.
Brechin, S., Wilhusen, P. & Benjamin, C. (2003) Crafting conservation globally and locally, in Brechin, S. et al. (eds) *Contested Nature* (Binghamton, NY: State University of New York Press).
Brockington, D., Igoe, J. & Schmidt-Soltau, K. (in press) Conservation, human rights and poverty reduction, *Conservation Biology*.
Brosius, P. (2001) Local knowledges, global claims, in Grim, J. & Sullivan, L. (eds) *Indigenous Traditions and Ecology* (Cambridge, MA: Harvard University Press).
Bruner, A., Gullison, G., Rice, R. & da Fonseca, G. (2001) The effectiveness of parks in protecting tropical biodiversity, *Science*, 291, pp. 125–128.
Burnham, P. (2000) *Indian Country, God's Country* (Washington, DC: Island Press).
Catton, C. (1997) *Inhabited Wilderness* (Albuquerque, NM: University of New Mexico Press).
Chambers, R. (1984) *Rural Development: Putting the Last First* (New York: Longman).
Chapin, M. (2000) *Defending Kuna Yala* (Washington, DC: USAID).
Chapin, M. (2004) A challenge to conservationists, *World Watch*, November/December, pp. 17–31.
Colchester, M. (2002) Indigenous rights and the collective conscious, *Anthropology Today*, 18, pp. 1–3.
Conklin, B. & Graham, L. (1995) The shifting middle ground: Amazonian Indians and ecopolitics, *American Anthropologist*, 97(4), pp. 695–710.
Cronon, W. (1996) The trouble with wilderness, in Cronon, W. (ed.) *Uncommon Ground* (New York: Norton).
Dasmann, R. (1976) National parks, nature conservation and future primitive, *The Ecologist*, 6, pp. 164–167.
Dunn, K. (2003) National parks and human security in East Africa, in *Beyond the Arch Community Conservation in Greater Yellowstone and East Africa* (Mammoth Springs, WY: US National Parks Service).
Escobar, A. (1995) *Encountering Development* (Princeton, NJ: Princeton University Press).
Escobar, A. (1996) Construction nature: elements for a post-structuralist political ecology, *Futures*, 28(4), pp. 325–343.
Ferguson, J. (1990) *The Anti-Politics Machine* (Cambridge: Cambridge University Press).
Goldman, M. (2003) Partitioned nature, privileged knowledge, *Development and Change*, 34(5), pp. 833–862.
Hirtz, F. (2003) It takes modern means to be traditional, *Development and Change*, 34(5), pp. 887–914.
Hodgson, D. (2002) Precarious alliances: the cultural politics and structural predicaments of the indigenous rights movement in Tanzania, *American Anthropologist*, 104(4), pp. 1086–1096.
Igoe, J. (2000) Ethnicity, civil society, and the Tanzanian pastoral NGO movement, Ph.D. Dissertation, Boston University.
Igoe, J. (2003) Scaling up civil society, *Development and Change*, 34(5), pp. 863–886.

Igoe, J. (2004a) *Conservation and Globalization: A Study of National Parks and Indigenous Communities from East Africa to South Dakota* (Riverside, CA: Wadsworth).

Igoe, J. (2004b) History, culture, and conservation: in search of more informed guesses about whether community-based conservation has a chance to work, *Policy Matters*, 13, pp. 162–173.

Igoe, J. (in press) Becoming indigenous peoples: difference, inequality, and the globalisation of East African identity politics, *African Affairs*.

Kiwasila, H. (1997) Not just a Maasai Garden of Eden, *The Observer*, 27 July.

Kuper, A. (2003) The return of the native, *Current Anthropology*, 44, pp. 389–402.

Lawrence, D. (2000) *Kakadu: The Making of a National Park* (Melbourne: Melbourne University Press).

Leakey, R. (2003) Science, sentiment, and advocacy (an interview), *Yellowstone Science*, 10(3), pp. 8–12.

Li, T. (2000) Articulating indigenous identity in Indonesia: resource politics and the tribal slot, *Comparative Studies in Society and History*, 42(1), pp. 149–179.

Mackenzie, J. (1988) *The Empire of Nature* (Manchester: Manchester University Press).

Maren, M. (1997) *The Road to Hell* (New York: The Free Press).

McShane, T. (2003) The devil in the detail of biodiversity conservation, *Conservation Biology*, 17(1), pp. 1–3.

Muehlebach, A. (2001) 'Making place' at the United Nations: indigenous cultural politics at the U.N. Working Group on Indigenous Populations, *Cultural Anthropology*, 163, pp. 415–448.

Neumann, R. (1998) *Imposing Wilderness: Struggles over Livelihood and Nature Preservation In Africa* (Berkeley: University of California Press).

Neumann, R. (2005) *Making Political Ecology* (London: Hodder Arnold).

Niezen, R. (2003) *The Origins of Indigenism: Human Rights and the Politics of Identity* (Berkeley, CA: University of California Press).

Nugent, S. (1994) *Big Mouth* (San Francisco, CA: Brown Trout Press).

Redford, K. (1990) The ecologically noble savage, *Orion*, 9, pp. 25–29.

Redford, K. & Sanderson, S. (2000) Extracting humans from nature, *Conservation Biology*, 14(5), pp. 1362–1364.

Redford, K. & Stearman, A. (1993) Forest-dwelling native Amazonians and the conservation of biodiversity, *Conservation Biology*, 7, pp. 248–255.

Redford, K., Coppolillo, P., Sanderson, E., Da Fonseca, G., Dinerstein, E., Groves, C., Mace, G., Maginnis, S., Mittermeier, R., Noss, R., Olson, D., Robinson, J., Vedder, A. & Wright, M. (2003) Mapping the conservation landscape, *Conservation Biology*, 17(1), pp. 116–131.

Robins, S. (2003) Response to Kuper's Return of the Native, *Current Anthropology*, 44, pp. 398–399.

Roe, D., Hutton, J., Elliot, J., Saruchera, M. & Chitepo, K. (2003) In pursuit of pro-poor conservation—changing narratives. or more?, *Policy Matters*, 12, pp. 87–91.

Sanders, D. (1980) *Background Information on the World Council of Indigenous Peoples*, Fourth World Documentation Project, Lethbridge, AB.

Sanderson, S. (2002) The future of conservation, *Foreign Affairs*, 81(5), pp. 162–173.

Sanderson, S. (2004) Conservation in an era of poverty, *Yellowstone Science*, 12(1), pp. 5–12.

Spence, M. (1999) *Dispossessing the Wilderness* (Oxford: Oxford University Press).

Stephens, J. & Ottaway, D. (2003) Non-profit land bank amasses billions, *Washington Post*, 4 May.

Stepp, R. (2005) Documenting Garifuna traditional ecological knowledge for park co-management in southern Belize, *Meetings of the Society for Applied Anthropology*, Santa Fe.

Stepp, R. Cervone, S., Castaneda, H., Lasseter, A., Stock, G. & Gichon, Y. (2004) Development of a GIS for biocultural diversity, *Policy Matters*, 34, pp. 256–266.

Sylvain, R. (2002) Land, water, and truth: San identity and global indigenism, *American Anthropologist*, 104(4), pp. 1074–1085.

Tapia, C. (2005) Neoliberalism, security agendas, and parks with people: implications for community-based conservation in Columbia, *Meetings of the Society for Applied Anthropology*, Santa Fe.

Tendler, J. (1975) *Inside Foreign Aid* (Baltimore, MD: John Hopkins University Press).

Terborgh, J. (2004) Reflections of a scientist on the World Parks Congress: science and society at the World Parks Congress, *Conservation Biology* 19(1), pp. 619–620.

Turner, T. (1993) The role of indigenous peoples in the environmental crisis: the example of the Kayapo in the Brazilian Amazon, *Perspective in Biology and Medicine*, 36(3), pp. 526–545.

WWF (1997) *Indigenous and Traditional Peoples of the World and Ecoregion-Based Conservation: an Integrated Approach to Conserving the World's Biological and Cultural Diversity* (Gland, Switzerland: WWF International).

WWF (2004) *From the Vision to the Ground: A Guide to Implementing Ecoregion conservation in Priority Areas* (Washington, DC: WWF–US Conservation Science Program).

Jim Igoe is an assistant professor of anthropology at the University of Colorado at Denver, where he teaches conservation, development, identity and power. He has conducted extensive field research on conflicts between parks and neighbouring communities in Tanzania and the American West. He is the author of *Conservation and Globalization: A Study of National Parks and Indigenous Communities from East Africa to South Dakota* (Wadsworth, 2004). He has also co-edited (with Tim Kelsall) a volume called *Between a Rock and a Hard Place: African NGOs, Donors, and the State* (Carolina Academic Press, 2005). Jim is a senior fellow of the Environmental Leadership Program and a member of the IUCN Commission on Conservation, Ecology, Economics, and Social Policy. He is currently a visiting lecturer at the College of African Wildlife Management in Mweka, Tanzania, under a Fulbright Visiting Scholar Grant from the US State Department.

The Lingering Environmental Impact of Repressive Governance: The Environmental Legacy of the Apartheid Era for the New South Africa

PHIA STEYN

Introduction

The first *State of the Environment Report*, published by the Department of Environmental Affairs and Tourism in November 1999, paints a sombre picture about the health of the South African environment. The Report points out that while South Africa has the third largest plant and animal biodiversity in the world, the country has the highest extinction rate of plant and animal species on the globe. By 1999, 3,435 plant species, 102 bird species, 72 reptile species, 12 amphibian species, 142 butterfly species and 90 mammal species were listed as threatened in the South African Red Data Books. In addition it reported abnormally high air pollution levels in some parts of the country, the generation of too much waste to be disposed of in a proper and safe manner, the disposal of hazardous waste untreated, widespread soil erosion and high levels of water pollution, to name but a few (Department of Environmental Affairs and Tourism, 1999; *Die Volksblad*, 28 October 1999, p. 9).

The unhealthy state of the South African environment came as no surprise to those actively involved in environment-related activities in the country, especially those concerned with documenting the deterioration of the environment over a prolonged period. The truth is, as elsewhere in the world, the South African environment had slowly degraded over the past few decades and many of the present-day environmental problems have roots that go back many years and especially to the apartheid era. The historical link between contemporary environmental problems and the environmental, economic and political policies of the apartheid government has ensured that the environmental impact of apartheid lingered on long after the establishment of a multiracial, democratic South Africa in 1994. The 1999 *State of the Environment Report* offers plenty of proof in this regard.

This article aims at exploring the environmental legacy of the apartheid era for the so-called New South Africa by focusing on the some of the main environmental impacts of apartheid-era policies, and governmental environmental management in the new South Africa. An in-depth analysis of all the relevant areas in which apartheid policies impacted negatively on the South African environment and of environment-related changes in the new South Africa is beyond the scope of this article. Rather, the article will focus on the main issues and will in particular aim to identify areas in which there has been continuity in the environmental policies and practices pursued by both the old and the new regimes, and also to identify important changes that occurred and progress that has been made by the post-apartheid government in terms of environmental management.

Environment in Apartheid South Africa

The apartheid era in South Africa dates back to 1948 when the National Party (NP) came to power under the leadership of Dr D. F. Malan. The NP had offered voters their policy of apartheid as opposed to existing segregationist policies of the United Party to address what was perceived by the white electorate as the 'native problem'. As the decolonization process in the European colonial empires gained momentum in the 1950s and 1960s so did international opposition to the NP's apartheid policy and the country's continued governance over Namibia. Consequently, the country was increasingly isolated on international political, economic, cultural and sporting levels from the 1960s onwards, including expulsion from the Commonwealth (1961), the International Olympic Committee (1964) and the General Assembly of the United Nations (1974).

International isolation had important repercussions for the development of governmental environmental management in the country especially given the fact that it started at a time when governments around the world started to pay constructive attention to environmental issues on both international and national political levels. South Africa, for example, did not participate in the preparatory processes for the 1972 United Nations Conference on the Human Environment (Stockholm, June 1972), and made almost no contribution to the debates at the conference beyond protesting at the condemnation of apartheid in the Declaration on the Human Environment (Principle 1) and opposing a total ban on commercial whaling (as the then third largest whaling nation in the world). In addition, South Africa was not invited to become a member of the Governing Council of the United Nations Environment Programme

(UNEP) in 1973 and played no active part in UNEP before 1994 (United Nations, 1972; *The Star*, 10 June 1972, p. 3; Rautenbach, 1973; Wiley, 1986).

An important consequence of the exclusion of South Africa from global environmental initiatives was the fact that the government failed to stay in touch with important changes that occurred both on an international level, and within national environmental governance in other countries. On an international level, the government's inability to identify major paradigm shifts in the management of the natural environment became evident when it started to promote the aims of the *World Conservation Strategy* (IUCN et al., 1980) in 1987 (Republic of South Africa, 1988). By that time, however, the Strategy had become outdated and had been replaced by the influential Brundtland report, *Our Common Future* (1987), as the most important document on the natural environment and the management thereof. The South African government thus opted for an environmental strategy (the *WCS*) in 1987 that was outdated, while the rest of the world, in response to *Our Common Future*, began to take the first tentative steps towards preparing for the implementation of sustainable development policies.

The inability to identify the shift towards sustainable development was greatly influenced by increased attempts to isolate the country internationally in the 1980s, especially after the disastrous 'Rubicon' speech of State President P. W. Botha in August 1985. What little standing the country still had in international environmental circles was shattered in 1987 when acquisitions were aired publicly for the first time in which the South African Defence Force was implicated in an ivory and rhinoceros horn smuggling ring.[1] These factors ensured that South Africa was not invited to participate in the preparatory processes for the 1992 United Nations Conference on Environment and Development (UNCED, Rio de Janeiro, June 1992) and was further denied official representation at the actual event. UNCED also emphasized the lack of legitimacy of the apartheid government on international levels in that it invited official delegations from the African National Congress and the Pan-Africanist Congress to the official proceedings, which delegations were also granted the opportunity to address the conference as a whole. The absence of governmental participation in the UNCED process ensured that the South African government failed to grasp both the future importance of sustainable development and the essence of this developmental model. The fact that South Africa's country report submitted to UNCED failed to integrate environmental and development issues reflects the limited understanding within environment-related governmental structures of sustainable development, and this remained the case until the first democratic elections of April 1994 brought the African National Congress to power (Van der Merwe, 1992; Republic of South Africa, 1992; Wynberg, 1993).

Domestically, isolation coupled with strong governmental reaction to the anti-apartheid movement ensured that the government resisted all attempts by the environmental non-governmental organization (ENGO) sector to politicize the South African environmental movement. Up until the establishment of Earthlife Africa in 1988, the South African environmental movement was characterized by its apolitical and conservation-focused nature in which very good relations between the vast majority of the ENGOs and the government were in the order of the day (Cock, 1991; Steyn and Wessels, 2000). The apolitical nature of the South African environmental movement prior to 1988 ensured that the government was slow to follow global trends in environment-related managerial and legal developments on a national level. A dedicated Department for Environment Affairs, for example, was only established in 1984 after several attempts to pair environmental issues with other state departments failed. The most notorious and damaging pairing was also the very first, which occurred in 1973 when the government placed environmental issues within the Department of Planning. The newly named Department of Planning and the Environment lasted until 1979 and, given the key role the Department played in apartheid planning and zoning, ensured that environmental issues came to be associated closely by the anti-apartheid movement with the implementation of apartheid policies (Rautenbach, 1972; Steyn, 2001).

Not only did the South African government failed to establish a strong, centralized governmental department for environmental issues, but it also failed to pass broad-ranging environmental legislation. While environmental issues were regulated by an impressive list of acts that either directly or indirectly related to the environment, and which ensured that almost all state departments were involved with environmental legislation in some way or another, broad-ranging environmental legislation was considered unnecessary until the 1980s. After a feeble attempt at this in the form of the 1982 Environment Conservation Act (no. 100), the first proper piece of general environmental legislation passed in the country only followed in 1989 with the passing of the Environment Conservation Act (no. 73). This act constituted a major milestone in the development of South African environmental law in that it provided, for the first time, for the effective protection and controlled utilization of the South African environment. It also allowed for greater powers for the Minister of Environment Affairs to oppose developments and resource exploitation that could possibly harm the human and natural environments. Unfortunately, neither of the two environment affairs ministers that served up until 1994 in the apartheid cabinet used these expanded powers, nor did they take the important step of making environmental impact assessments compulsory (Rabie and Erasmus, 1983; Glazewski, 1991; Rabie and Fuggle, 1992; Rabie, 1994).

The resistance from both the government and the ENGO sector to politicize the South African environment during the apartheid era weakened the effectiveness of ENGOs, which, in general, opted to cooperate with the government rather than oppose it in matters that radically affected the natural environment. Consequently, the non-governmental sector of the South African environmental movement continued to focus predominantly on the conservation of fauna and flora, and of particular areas that were fenced in to ensure the continuation of their existence. These protected areas became symbols of responsible stewardship of the natural environment for the South African government, the National Parks Board, the provincial nature conservancies, a number of ENGOs and a large segment of the white people in the country. However, the management of these areas as separate entities that allowed little interference from outside ensured that conservation measures remained divorced from the everyday life of the public in general. It was thus very difficult—almost impossible—to establish an environmental perspective in which humans were seen as being totally dependent on a healthy natural environment in South Africa, and to promote an environmental agenda that included pertinent issues such as pollution control, the unhealthy state of black townships, environmental degradation in the homelands, and the environmental dangers of uncontrolled economic development.

The profoundly detrimental environmental impact that apartheid had on the human and natural environments of all people of colour in South Africa also made it very difficult for these communities to support the dominant environmental agenda in the country. In addition, the government showed very little understanding of the environmental hardship that people of colour had to endure on a daily basis. Indeed, until the Soweto uprisings of 1976 the government showed no empathy with the environmental concerns of the majority of the country's population. Those environment-related initiatives implemented from 1977 onwards in urban black townships, however, should not be taken as genuine attempts to improve the human and natural environments of some black communities. Rather these initiatives represent attempts by an apartheid government that was increasingly coming under siege to appease restless black communities bordering white cities and towns in the country.

Apartheid's environmental toll was tremendous on both homelands and on the black townships bordering the edges of white communities. The homeland system in particular hastened environmental degradation in the Republic through the overpopulation of these areas. By 1980 an estimated 10.5 million black people lived in the homelands that comprised less that 13 per cent of South Africa's total land surface. This in turn meant that the average population density in the homelands was 66 people per km^2. The overcrowding of the homelands had a marked influence on the natural environment and directly led to widespread soil erosion. By 1980 in the Ciskei alone 46% of the land was moderately or severely eroded. With an average of two hectares of land per family, and a general lack of capital for essential farming inputs and conservation measures, land in the homelands deteriorated to the point where it could no longer sustain the people who lived on it. Overpopulation coupled with a general lack of electricity and widespread poverty led to the overexploitation of wood fuel resources within the homelands. By 1980 four of the ten homelands were consuming more wood than their land produced each year, and it was projected that if the annual consumption patterns of between 200 kg and 800 kg per capita per year continued, the homelands would be stripped of all natural woodland by 2020. By the end of the 1980s, the forests in QwaQwa, situated in the eastern parts of the Free State province, about 300 km north-east of provincial capital city of Bloemfontein, had disappeared completely.

Homelands, in general, experienced rapid urbanization with people migrating to urban areas in search of better work opportunities. In most cases there was little infrastructure available to accommodate new arrivals, resulting in widespread squatting along the fringes of the urban centres in the homelands. Though the urban areas were better developed, both rural and urban areas in the homelands experienced a lack of infrastructural development and by 1990 only 46% of people had access to clean water while only 13% had access to adequate sanitation. The lack of essential services impacted on the health of the people, with mortality by the fifth year being around 50% in the homelands by 1990. Ironically, though overcrowded, the homelands experienced a shortage in labour. The system of migrant workers that existed in the South African economy meant that black men and women in their prime economically productive years, spent the majority of their time outside their homelands working in 'white' South Africa. Labour shortages in practice meant that the development of the homelands was neglected while black men and women of working age helped the South African economy to develop (Van der Berg, 1985; Timberlake, 1988; Durning, 1990; Cooper, 1992; Wisner, 1995).

The policy of separate development also found expression in an urban policy that reserved certain areas for certain population groups. The status of black people as 'visitors' to 'white' South Africa meant that little planning and development went into the black townships bordering white communities, especially because black people were in principle not allowed to settle permanently in these areas prior to the 1980s. The resulting racial division in the provision of housing, services and infrastructure ensured a lack of drinking water, waste removal and sanitation services, proper housing and electricity which combined to make townships a hazard for both human health and the natural environment. By 1994, for example, 6.76 million people in the townships had no access to adequate sewage and sanitation systems, while about 2 million of these people still relied on the bucket system for toilets. Around 20% of the people had minimal access to water, with an average of two to three households sharing a water tap in many of the townships bordering the larger cities. Township dwellers in rural South Africa were in general not that fortunate. In the Mhala District in Gazankulu, a water tap was shared on average by 760 people. Lack of proper town planning in black townships resulted in massive housing shortages in these areas, and it is estimated that by 1993 between 5 and 7.7 million people were living in informal housing (i.e. shacks) (Durning, 1990; Cooper, 1992; Smuts, 1995; Wisner, 1995; McDonald, 1998).

A general lack of electricity in the township areas played havoc with the natural environment through abnormally high levels of visible air pollution. Open fires and coal stoves fuelled by either coal or wood provided not only energy to prepare food, but also heated the small dwellings in the townships, and led to high levels of sulphur dioxide (SO_2) and particulate matter at ground level. According to Cooper (1992, p. 4), by 1992 township emissions represented 3% of South Africa's national SO_2 emissions and 24% of all particulates emitted in the country. While relatively insignificant on a national level, coal-related emissions have proved to be an environmental hazard on a local level in the townships for residents and medical reports show that children residing in Soweto, for example, suffered more asthma and chest colds than children elsewhere in the country. This is due to the high levels of Soweto's particulate air pollution, which exceeds World Health Organization limits for at least a quarter of each year, and then by as much as 100%. Coal was used in South African townships during the apartheid era primarily because the electrification of townships was not considered a government priority. And, even where electrification did take place, coal stoves continued to play an essential part in township life because of their versatility. In Soweto, for example, by 1992 about 22% of newly electrified households in townships also continued to use their coal stoves (Durning, 1990; Cooper, 1992; Clarke, 2002).

High levels of air pollution were not confined to black townships. With coal providing around 82% of the country's total energy, the former Eastern Transvaal Highveld (the Ermeloo-Witbank region), in which 80% of all electricity is generated, was subjected to the highest levels of air pollution in the country throughout the year. The 20 coal-fired power stations in the region emitted on average 32.25 tonnes SO_2/km^2, even higher than the 30 tonnes SO_2/km^2 emitted on average in the former German Democratic Republic which was infamous for its abnormally high levels of air pollution (Tyson et al., 1988; Clarke, 1991).

Pollution problems were not confined to the electricity generation industry. Indeed, by the late 1980s a number of well-publicized cases of industrial pollution made headlines across the country. These included the dumping of toxins in the Vaal River by the SASOL I plant at Sasolburg in 1988, the leaking of poisonous chemicals into the Selati River (which runs through the Kruger National Park) by a phosphate company in 1988, the regular polluting of the Olifants and Crocodile Rivers by toxic heavy metals, phosphate and nitrogen, the caustic soda spill of the Atomic Energy Corporation into the Moganwe Spruit close to the Hartbeespoort Dam in 1991, Sappi's Ngodwana Paper Mill Spill in September 1989 and the mercury pollution at the Thor Chemicals plant at Cato Ridge (*The Weekly Mail*, 29 September–5 October 1989, p. 5; Koch et al., 1990; Anon, 1991; *Business Day*, 21 November 1991, p. 5; Van Eeden, 1991). These and other cases of industrial pollution became symbolic of the relatively high levels of industrial environmental neglect and the weak reaction of government to cases of industrial pollution. Sappi, for example, was fined only ZAR 600 for its Ngodwana Paper Mill spill despite the fact that this spill devastated the ecosystems of the Elands and Crocodile Rivers, and killed more than 22 fish species and other forms of animal life in a stretch of river downstream from the mill.

By 1989 the economic crisis that had set in back in 1973 with the Oil Crisis and the corresponding Arab oil embargo and which was exacerbated by economic and technological sanctions, left very little room for the apartheid government to clamp down on industrial pollution. The need to earn foreign currency through the few permitted exports along with the direct involvement of the state in some of the most polluting of industries (e.g. both Iscor and Escom) ensured that the government seldom reacted to even blatant cases of industrial environmental neglect. In addition, by the end of the 1980s the apartheid government had pursued a policy of uncontrolled economic development that excluded any consideration for the environment and the limitations thereof for many decades. International isolation, economic and technological sanctions and the economic crisis merely ensured that this policy remained unchanged at a time when there were real efforts globally to start addressing the environmental problems associated with uncontrolled economic development. Over time this policy had a tremendous impact on the South African human and natural environments through the overexploitation of resources, the slack enforcement of environmental laws, widespread pollution and the establishment of an economic ethic that excluded environmental consideration in the name of survival. The economic ethic lingered on long after the end of apartheid and still continues to derail the successful implementation of sustainable development policies in the new South Africa—only now in the name of poverty reduction.

Environmental Protection versus Poverty Reduction in the New South Africa

The April 1994 elections brought an end to the apartheid era in South Africa and brought the African National Congress (ANC), headed by Nelson Mandela, to power. Prior to its election victory, the ANC had shown great sensitivity towards environmental issues in its policy documents issued between 1990 and 1994. Already in 1992 the ANC committed itself in its policy document *Ready to Govern* to the improvement of the living and working conditions of black people in the country in order to realize its goal of establishing a just and equitable society in South Africa. This was followed by the inclusion of the environment as one of the ten basic needs in the pre-election Reconstruction and Development Policy (RDP). The RDP declared that poverty and environmental degradation were closely related and that improvement in living conditions and access to services and land would all contribute to reducing the negative human pressures on the natural environment in the country. Consequently, the pre-election RDP document promoted the inclusion of environmental considerations in all decision-making processes. Unfortunately the ANC left its pro-environment position behind shortly after coming to power and the RDP White Paper, published in September 1994, omitted the chapter on environment that was included in the pre-election document (ANC, 1992, 1994).

Due to the inequalities created under the apartheid system the key objective of the RDP and many other governmental initiatives was poverty reduction. Consequently, employment creation became a central aspect of the new economic policy, the Growth, Employment and Redistribution strategy (GEAR), published in June 1996, because the ANC government believe that providing people with jobs are the best way to reduce poverty levels in the country. It is argued that this in turn would counter poverty-related environmental problems, which in theory will greatly aid the establishment of sustainable communities around the country. GEAR made no reference to the need to accommodate environmental considerations in central economic and social planning. Indeed, GEAR placed great emphasis on the reduction of state spending, investment incentives, privatization, the expansion of heavy industries and an increase in the rate of natural resource exploitation in order to stimulate economic growth; areas that constituted a major source of environmental degradation in apartheid South Africa. Consequently the ANC initially continued with apartheid-era policies that promoted economic development with little consideration of the environmental impact thereof (Fuggle and Rabie, 1999; Le Quesne, 2000).

Instead of incorporating the environment into mainstream economic and social planning, as is expected under sustainable development, the ANC created a separate forum where all stakeholders could meet to discuss environment-related issues. Despite being removed from the central planning processes, the Consultative National Environmental Policy Process (CONNEPP), launched in 1995, was crucial because it was tasked with the radical overhaul of environment-related legislation (as part of a bigger process to rid the country of apartheid legislation). Many new pieces of environmental legislation resulted from the CONNEPP process, most important of which were the National Water Act (no. 36 of 1998) and the National Environmental Management Act (no. 107 of 1998). Environmental impact assessments also finally became compulsory in 1997, and it is hoped that the much loathed provision in the regulation of air pollution that still allows for best practical means as opposed to polluter pays will finally be abolished in 2005. An important legal development for all South African citizens was the inclusion of an environmental right into the Bill of Rights adopted with the new constitution in 1996. In terms of this Bill all South Africans have the right to a clean and healthy environment and to have the environment protected for current and future generations (Fuggle and Rabie, 1999; Le Quesne, 2000; Department of Environmental Affairs and Tourism, 2005).

Despite many successful initiatives that ensured that 85% of households in South Africa now have access to clean water and 63% have access to sanitation, the ANC government has struggled to come to terms with the environmental legacy of the apartheid era. In terms of environmental management, the ANC inherited a governmental structure that is deeply fragmented, with environment-related functions being shared by almost all government departments. The fact that the environment was assigned a functional area of concurrent national and provincial legislature and administrative competence by the 1996 Constitution further ensured that environmental management not only remained fragmented on a national level between governmental departments, but is now also fragmented in its provincial application. While the ANC did strengthen the role of the Department of Environmental Affairs and Tourism, it is still a long way from the strong, centralized governmental department so greatly needed for the successful protection of the South African environment. And, as in the apartheid era, government departments tasked with the promotion of economic and industrial development are still actively involved in the implementation of environmental legislation that effectively curtails development processes. The conflict of interest that results from this dual role that state departments such as Trade and Industry, and Minerals and Energy have has not been properly addressed in the new South Africa (Fuggle and Rabie, 1999; Steyn, 2001; The Presidency, 2003; Rossouw and Wiseman, 2004).

In addition, the ANC also inherited the industrial pollution problems of the past and initially showed very little enthusiasm for implementing and regulating the brand new environmental legislation passed in the first ANC term. Ironically, in country's submission to the 2002 World Summit on Sustainable Development the government notes that it has urged crude oil refineries to reduce their pollution levels in order to comply with national emission standards. This report also proudly cites four different examples of industry implementing pollution control measures as examples of 'activities changing unsustainable consumption and production patterns' (Republic of South Africa, 2002, p. 11). Unfortunately these are still isolated cases of addressing the very high pollution levels prevalent in the country and much more still needs to be done. The new state structures, however, did allow for greater transparency and while the government initially proved unwilling to take on big business, the new South Africa created the space for its citizens to take on industries that adversely affected their health and livelihood. One of these community-based struggles is the lawsuit against the widespread pollution caused by the manufacturing processes of steel giant Iscor in the Vanderbijl Park district. The inhabitants of Steel Valley, which lies adjacent to the Iscor plant, are currently suing the company for damages to their health and property, caused by the polluting of their groundwater resources, in the Johannesburg High Court. This lawsuit, along with numerous other grievances from Vaal Triangle communities has finally forced the ANC government to address the abnormally high levels of air, water and ground pollution in the region, and it announced in June 2005 that it will start the process of declaring this region the first air pollution 'hot spot' in the country on 1 September 2005, which will force the government and industry for the first time to clean up the Vaal Triangle (Groenewald, 2004; Department of Environmental Affairs and Tourism, 2005; Macleod, 2005).

In an important departure from the apartheid era, the ANC did focus on the promotion of social development with the expansion of housing and basic services at the centre of these policies. However, most of the flagship RDP projects showed very little regard for the immediate environment in many areas such as Bredasdorp and Montagu where floods and heavy rains have inflicted great damage on badly planned RDP houses. Despite criticism from environmental groups of the way in which the government acts upon its social development policy, new directions in global environmental management that placed poverty reduction at the centre of sustainable development by the late 1990s effectively enable the ANC government to continue with its social development programmes without real environmental considerations (Le Quesne, 2000; Steyn, 2002; *Die Burger*, 29 March 2003, p. 1, 7 October 2004, p. 1).

The unsustainable nature of much social and economic development in the new South Africa is in no small part due to the fact that the country is still a long way from developing a national strategy for sustainable development and a national action plan for the implementation of Agenda 21. Hosting the 2002 World Summit on Sustainable Development ironically did not help to speed up the processes. An important contributing factor for the slow progress made in the promotion of sustainable development in the country is the fact that the local government structures, which are responsible for implementing sustainable development processes in the country, have not been included as stakeholders in environmental planning. Consequently, apart from a few metropolitan areas such as Cape Town, Durban and Johannesburg, few local government structures have produced the integrated development plans, which provide the framework for the development role of local governments, required of them in terms of the Municipal Systems Act of 2000 (Republic of South Africa, 2002; Rossouw and Wiseman, 2004).

The ANC had a slow start where the environment is concerned and were hampered in the first two terms by the enormous negative legacy of the apartheid era. Their greatest contributions to environmental issues between 1994 and 2004 were limited to the development of new environmental legislation, the inclusion of all stakeholders in environmental planning and development, the promotion of the equitable distribution of natural resources and access to resources, and the establishment of transfrontier conservation areas. Important pro-environment initiatives included a ban on the free provision of plastic bags (which drastically reduced plastic pollution overnight), the banning of all-terrain vehicles from ecologically sensitive beaches, the clamping down on over-fishing, the introduction of unleaded petrol and the combating of invasive alien plants. True developments in pollution control only started to follow after an amendment to the National Environmental Management Act in 2003 gave the Department of Environmental Affairs and Tourism greater powers to investigate environmental law violations. Consequently, the Directorate of Regulatory Services for the first time obtained the powers of search and seizure, powers which have greatly improved their effectiveness to the point where they are now commonly referred to in the media as the Green Scorpions (after the elite police unit). Maybe with the help of the Green Scorpions the ANC government will prove to be more effective than its predecessors in protecting and promoting the health and well-being of the South

African environment. This is desperately needed if the government wants to realize the environmental rights of the South African citizenry, as expressed in the Bill of Rights (Groenewald, 2004; Nell, 2004; Macleod, 2005).

Conclusion

This article has explored some of the environmental legacies of the apartheid era for the new South Africa. In some respects the transition from the old to the new regime merely meant that someone different was implementing the same or similar environment-related policies in the period after 1994. The ANC government, for example, not only continued with the fragmented approach to governmental environmental management but managed to fragment it even further by assigning provincial and local governments environmental management duties. Likewise, the Department of Environmental Affairs and Tourism has changed very little apart from the people who work there and is still a long way from being the strong, centralized government department so greatly needed for constructive environmental management on a governmental level. The rewriting of the country's environmental laws did signal a great departure from the apartheid era, but the (inherited) unwillingness to implement and properly enforce these laws, especially those related to industry, remains endemic to governmental environmental management in the country. Only in the new South Africa this lack of enforcement is done in the name of poverty reduction while in the apartheid era it was driven by the need to survive economically in a hostile global environment. And, while the country is now once more a respected member of the global political community, the country is still far away from implementing sustainable development policies on a national scale, despite the fact that it hosted the World Summit on Sustainable Development in 2002. It is obvious from various policy documents that there is a greater understanding of the importance of sustainable development within government circles today than at the end of the apartheid period, but this understanding without proper governmental action is meaningless.

Though there is a high level of continuity between the old and the new regimes, there are also important differences in their environmental management practices. Probably the most striking and immediately beneficial to some are the massive regeneration projects launched in black and coloured communities situated in both urban and rural areas. The RDP brought houses, sanitation, safe water, electricity and services to millions of formerly disadvantaged South Africans thereby radically improving the natural and human environments in which these communities live. The involvement of all the stakeholders in environmental management, with the exception of the all-important local government structures, has also ensured that environmental management processes became more transparent. Also the involvement of local communities in environmental management contributes a great deal to countering established notions that successful conservation efforts result from limited human interference. In some ways the ANC is bringing South Africans closer to nature by acknowledging the importance of nature in the survival of many rural communities, and by allowing these communities to actively participate in initiatives that impact on their natural and human environments.

Note

1 Jan Giliomee Private Document Collection (JGPDC, Stellenbosch, South Africa), Habitat Council: C. van Note, Statement on US enforcement of the Convention on International Trade in Endangered Species, 14 July 1988, pp. 10–12.

References

ANC (1992) *Ready to Govern: An Introduction to the ANC's Policy Guidelines* (Johannesburg: ANC).
ANC (1994) *The Reconstruction and Development Programme* (Johannesburg: Umyanyano Publications).
Anon. (1991) Pollution critical in SA as perennial rivers run dry, *Chamber of Mines Journal*, 33(4), pp. 5, 11.
Clarke, J. (1991) *Back to Earth: South Africa's Environmental Challenges* (Johannesburg: Southern Book Publishers).
Clarke, J. (2002) *Coming Back to Earth: South Africa's Changing Environment* (Johannesburg: Jacana).
Cock, J. (1991) Going green at the grassroots: the environment as a political issue, in Cock, J. & Koch, E. (eds) *Going Green: People, Politics and the Environment in Southern Africa* (Cape Town: Oxford University Press).
Cooper, C. (1992) The environment and the poor, *South African Institute of Race Relations Fast Facts*, 10.
Department of Environmental Affairs and Tourism (1999) *State of the Environment: South Africa 1999. An Overview* (Pretoria: DEA&T).
Department of Environmental Affairs and Tourism (2005) Clean air Imbizo: Vaal triangle to be SA's first pollution hot spot. Media Release, 6 June. Available from: http://www.deat.gov.za/NewsMedia/MedStat/2005Jun6/06062005_2.htm (accessed 8 June 2005).
Durning, A. B. (1990) *Apartheid's Environmental Toll*, Worldwatch Paper 95 (Washington, DC: Worldwatch Institute).
Fuggle, R. F. & Rabie, M. A. (1999) Environmental management in South Africa: postscript 1999, in Fuggle, R. F. & Rabie, M. A. (eds) *Environmental Management in South Africa* (Cape Town: Juta & Co. Ltd).
Glazewski, J. I. (1991) Current and future directions in South African environmental law, *Strategic Review for Southern Africa*, 13(1), pp. 12–35.
Groenewald, Y. (2004) Last gasp for mouldy act, *Earthyear*, 5.
IUCN, UNEP & WWF (1980) *World Conservation Strategy: Living Resource Conservation for Sustainable Development* (Gland: IUCN).
Koch, E., Cooper, D. & Coetzee, H. (1990) *Water, Waste and Wildlife: The Politics of Ecology in South Africa* (Johannesburg: Penguin Books).
Le Quesne, T. (2000) The divorce of environmental and economic policy under the first ANC government, 1994–1999, *The South African Journal of Environmental Law and Policy*, 7(1), pp. 1–20.
Macleod, F. (2005) Gutsy dirt busters, *Mail & Guardian Online*, 26 May. Available from: http://www.mg.co.za/articlePage.aspx?articleid=241737&area=/insight/insight_national/ (accessed 19 June 2005).
McDonald, D. A. (1998) Three steps forward, two steps back: ideology and urban ecology in South Africa, *Review of African Political Economy*, 75, pp. 73–88.
Nell, M. (2004) Greening the parties, *Earthyear*, 2.
Rabie, M. A. (1994) The Environment Conservation Act and its implementation, *The South African Journal of Environmental Law and Policy*, 1(1), pp. 113–125.
Rabie, M. A. & Erasmus, M. G. (1983) Environmental law, in Fuggle, R. F. & Rabie, M. A. (eds) *Environmental Concerns in South Africa: Technical and Legal Perspectives* (Cape Town: Juta & Co.).
Rabie, M. A. & Fuggle, R. F. (1992) The rise of environmental concern, in Fuggle, R. F. & Rabie, M. A. (eds) *Environmental Management in South Africa* (Cape Town: Juta & Co.).
Rautenbach, P. S. (1972) Toespraak oor Omgewingsbewaring voor die Vereniging vir die Beskerming van die Omgewing, Pretoria, 18 October 1972, *Society for the Protection of the Environment Newsletter*, 2(4), p. 12.
Rautenbach, P. S. (1973) The International Status of Environmental Conservation, in Department of Planning and the Environment. *Proceedings of the International Symposium on Planning for Environmental Conservation 4–6.9.1973* (Pretoria: DPE).
Republic of South Africa (1988) *Annual Report of the Department of Environment Affairs, 1987-1988*, RP 114/1988 (Pretoria: The Government Printer).
Republic of South Africa (1992) *Building the Foundation for Sustainable Development in South Africa. National Report to the United Nations Conference on Environment and Development (UNCED) to be held in Rio de Janeiro, June 1992* (Pretoria: DEA&T).
Republic of South Africa (2002) *Johannesburg Summit 2002. South Africa: Country Profile* (New York: UN).
Rossouw, N. & Wiseman, K. (2004) Learning from the implementation of environmental public policy instruments after the first ten years of democracy in South Africa, *Impact Assessment and Project Appraisal*, 22(2), pp. 131–140.
Smuts, B. (1995) Green lessons of apartheid, *African Wildlife*, 49(2), pp. 6–12.
Steyn, P. (2001) Environmental management in South Africa: twenty years of governmental response to the global challenge, 1972–1992, *Historia*, 46(1), pp. 25–53.
Steyn, P. (2002) Global environmental management: an exploration of the world summit on sustainable development, *Journal for Contemporary History*, 27(3), pp. 1–13.

Steyn, P. & Wessels, A. (2000) The emergence of new environmentalism in South Africa, 1972–1992, *South African Historical Journal*, 42, pp. 210–231.
The Presidency (2003) *Towards a Ten Year Review: Synthesis Report on Implementation of Government Programmes*. Discussion document, Policy Co-ordination and Advisory Service. Pretoria: Government Communication and Information Service.
Timberlake, L. (1988) *Africa in Crisis: The Causes, the Cures of Environmental Bankruptcy*, new edn (London: Earthscan).
Tyson, P. D., Kruger, F. J. & Louw, C. W. (1988) *Atmospheric Pollution and its Implications in the Eastern Transvaal Highveld*, South African National Scientific Programmes report 150 (Pretoria: CSIR).
United Nations (1972) *Report of the United Nations Conference on the Human Environment Stockholm, 5–16 June 1972* (New York: UN).
Van der Berg, S. (1985) An overview of development in the homelands, in Giliomee, H. & Schlemmer, L. (eds) *Up Against the Fences: Poverty, Passes and Privilege in South Africa* (Cape Town: David Philip).
Van der Merwe, I. (1992) The summit of '92, *Conserva*, 7(5), pp. 4–5.
Van Eeden, M. (1991) Besoedelde Rivier Wek Kommer, *Prisma*, 6(3), p. 36.
Wiley, J. (1986) *Suid-Afrika se Rol en Betrokkenheid by Internasionale Omgewingsbewaring*, C. R. Swart Lecture no. 19 (Bloemfontein: University of the Orange Free State).
Wisner, B. (1995) The reconstruction of environmental rights in urban South Africa, *Human Ecology*, 23(2), pp. 259–284.
Wynberg, R. P. (1993) Exploring the Earth Summit. Findings of the Rio United Nations Conference on Environment and Development: Implications for South Africa. M.Phil. Dissertation, University of Cape Town.

Phia Steyn teaches African environmental history in the Department of History at the University of Stirling. Her research interests are twofold, namely the environmental impact of multinational oil production in ethnic minority territories in the African and Latin American tropics, and an environmental interpretation of the apartheid South Africa. She is currently doing research for an environmental history of apartheid South Africa (1948–1994).

From Stockholm to Kyoto and Beyond: A Review of the Globalization of Global Warming Policy and North–South Relations

BJÖRN-OLA LINNÉR AND MERLE JACOB

Introduction

One of the persistent trends of major international environmental negotiations beginning at the United Nations Conference on Environment and Development (UNCED), Stockholm 1972 and continuing through to Rio and the Johannesburg summit has been the emergence of irreconcilable differences between the North and South. Current negotiations within the United Nations Framework Convention on Climate Change (UNFCCC) suggest that North–South economic inequality will also play a significant role in the efforts to reach a multilateral agreement on how to proceed after the period of commitment within the Kyoto Protocol ends in 2012.

The task of this paper is to provide a historical overview of how North–South relations have impacted on the framing of the problem of global warming and the consequences for creating and implementing viable solutions. The paper is divided into four sections, including the present which will be devoted to outlining the structure and introducing the argument to be elaborated later. The second section will feature a summary historical overview of the global warming debate. In the third section we will identify and analyse some of the major areas of disagreement that divide North and South. We have chosen to focus on three themes: the mitigation versus adaptation quandary, technology transfer and knowledge inequities; and finally the role of multilateralism in global climate policy. The fourth and final section of the paper is a summary examination of possible implications for the South of the proposed emissions trading schemes.

We will use political economy as our analytical lens for examining the material at hand and, more specifically, the core propositions found in the world systems and dependency (WSD) approaches for a number of reasons. One is convenience: through the use of an analytical framework one can select a small number of significant observations to illustrate a broader point in a way that a strict chronological account would not allow. Another is to ascertain whether employing an alternative analytical frame to the dominant regimes framework (Vögler, 1995) will shed new light on the problem at hand. A third is that the WSD approach is among those scientific perspectives that allow one to understand the theoretical reasoning behind the arguments that have hitherto influenced the political positions of Southern states. While few WSD analyses take up the global environmental problematique or aspects thereof, political economic approaches generally and world systems in particular are becoming increasingly popular frames for tackling the analysis of the global environmental problematique. Roberts et al. (2003) examined the issue of carbon dioxide emissions from a WS perspective while Görg and Brand (2000) have analysed the problem of biodiversity in global perspective (see also Çoban, 2004).

WSD is not a coherent theoretical perspective but a tradition with a number of diverging views that find a common source of inspiration in the work of Ferdinand Braudel and Raul Prebisch and others in the 1960s. Despite the heterogeneity of the perspective, the following number of postulates may be said to be command consensus among proponents:

(i) The current World economy took on its defining features in Europe between 1500 and 1650 (Frank and Gills, 1993);
(ii) Among these features are a stable tri-part international stratification system of core, semi-periphery, and periphery through which individual countries may move (up or down), but which itself has not changed;
(iii) The ability of countries to achieve upward mobility is constrained by their trade relations with the world economy and their geopolitical role and power, which together condition their structural location within the hierarchy (see, e.g., Evans et al., 1985; Gereffi and Wyman, 1990); and
(iv) This structural location—their world-system 'position'—plays an important role in shaping their class structure and internal political battles.

The dynamics of core-periphery relations would according to WSD determine how the international relations of the global environmental problematique develop and the range of possibilities available to given nation states. Our main thesis in this paper is that the logic of centre–periphery relations as outlined in WSD both explains the positions of different countries on the issue of global warming and contributes to the absence of trust that characterizes the negotiations between North and South.

Global Warming and North–South Relations: Historical Overview

The problem of climate change was first placed on the international political agenda at the Stockholm conference on the Human Environment (1972). A number of preparatory reports had pointed to the problem of adverse human impact on the climate. The official documents from the preparatory process recognized that 'the Earth's temperature may rise as a result of the increased atmospheric content in carbon dioxide due to future consumption of fossil fuel' (UN, 1972a, para. 42). A two centigrade increase of the global average surface temperature over a period of centuries would cause melting of the polar ice caps, rising sea levels and corresponding loss of land areas. On the other hand, the Earth could experience global cooling caused by particle emissions. More research was called for to determine the effects of increase of carbon dioxide in the atmosphere. Even so, in addition to natural climatic variations the official background document to the conference concluded 'we now realize that man's activities may also add a powerful destabilizing factor to the interplay of the natural forces that determine the climate' (UN, 1972a, para. 44).

The action plan of the Stockholm meeting advised a general precautionary approach on climate and governments were recommended to 'be mindful of activities in which there is an appreciable risk of effects on climate' and to '[c]arefully evaluate the likelihood and magnitude of climatic effects' of planned activities and to fully consult states that could effected (UN, 1972b, rec. 70).

The end of the 1970s witnessed an intensification of focus on climate and greenhouse gases (GHGs) and the 1980s might be dubbed the decade of climate meetings. The kick-off event for this was the First World Climate Conference which was organized by the World Meteorological Organization (WMO), the United Nations Environment Programme (UNEP), and the International Council of Scientific Unions (ICSU). The conference concluded that climate change was a serious problem that called for political planning to counter its consequences for social and economic development (WMO, 1979). In the wake of the first world climate conference came a series of other intergovernmental meetings on the same topic.

The Villach workshop on climate change is perhaps the best known of these meetings since it was at Villach that decades of research was crystallized into well publicized warnings about an anthropogenically induced climate change due to rising concentrations of CO_2 and other GHGs (World Climate Program, 1985). Two follow-up conferences in 1987 provided additional sources of support for an international convention and WMO was able to conclude that it was time to investigate further the 'need for law of the atmosphere as a global commons' (WMO, 1988). These meetings are commonly referred to as an important background to the climate convention (Jäger and Ferguson, 1991; Franz, 1997; Samhat, 1998; Bodansky, 2001).

The increased political attention devoted to anthropogenically induced climate change in the 1980s was the result of a confluence of events in which science was one factor. Other contributing factors included growing public concern for the environment and unprecedented media coverage of environmental events. A third contributing factor was the preparations for the UN Conference on Environment and Development (UNCED). The last was also prompted by the dismal situation reported by UNEP in its ten year review of the events after the Stockholm conference. UNEP concluded that the situation was gloomy in virtually all areas at issue (UNEP, 1982). This failure was among other things attributed to the structure of the global economy. It was argued that 'worsening of environmental problems in developing countries arising from the present international economic order which has slowed down their development and the protection of the environment' (Holdgate, 1982).

The following year (1983), the World Commission on Environment and Development was formed and charged with the task of proposing long term environmental strategies for achieving sustainable development by the year 2000 and beyond. Critical to this task was 'to help define shared perceptions of long term environmental issues' (WCED, 1987, p. ix). *Our Common Future* covered virtually all international environmental concerns of its time and ranked climate change as one of the more serious threats for global sustainable development.

In addition to the commonly referred scientific climate meetings held in the North, the UN resolution in 1989 preceding the decision for a framework convention listed a large number of other meetings which also formed a basis for the General Assembly's decision (UN, 1989a). Several of these meetings expressed concern about the effects of global warming on poorer countries and called for a framework convention (Commonwealth Heads of Government Meeting, 1989; Conference of Non Aligned Heads of State, 1989). Other declarations referred to in the UN General Assembly resolution, such as the 1989 Caracas Declaration adopted at the special ministerial meeting of the Group of 77 (G-77), did not explicitly mention climate but underscored the dependent relationship between environment protection and the development process (G-77, 1989). The UNGA decision also referred to declarations from developing country meetings, stressing the serious consequences of sea-level rise for low-lying coastal and island states (e.g. South Pacific Forum, 1989). In a UN resolution passed the same day as the decision to launch a climate convention, the General Assembly urged the international community to provide effective and timely support to these countries so they could adapt to these threats (UN, 1989b).

The Road to the Convention

Given the above, one might contend that the road was well paved for formation of the Intergovernmental Panel on Climate Change (IPCC) by WMO and UNEP. Two years later this body published its First Assessment Report which confirmed the scientific basis for concern for human induced climate change and called for a global treaty to address the problem (IPCC, Working Group III et al., 1991). This report had a substantive political influence as it provided an important basis for negotiations on the 1992 Convention (quoted in Bodansky, 2001, p. 28). In the same year, the General Assembly underscored '[c]onservation of climate as part of the common heritage of mankind'. The resolution concluded that climate change had to be dealt with in a 'global framework'. Referring to other recent resolutions and reports such as *Our Common Future* it stressed that 'changes in climate have an impact on development' (UN, 1988).

The UN resolution deciding on a conference on environment and development to some extent reflects these concerns. It emphasized that one of the rationale for the decision was that the 'largest part of the current emission of pollutants into the environment originates in developed countries, and recognizing therefore that those countries have the main responsibility for combating such pollution' (UN, 1989c). The climate convention was a part of the Rio package. The UN stipulated that this was to be ready for signature at the Rio conference.

A month before the Rio Earth Summit, the UNFCCC was adopted at the United Nations Headquarters in New York and was opened for signature at the conference. It entered into force almost two years later in March 1994. To date it has been ratified by 188 countries. The ultimate objective of the convention is to stabilize human induced greenhouse gas emissions at safe levels. Since it is a framework convention, these levels were not specified, but were to be negotiated afterwards. This objective continues, however, with conditions which have been very important in the polemics surrounding the Kyoto Protocol. 'Such a level should be achieved within a time-frame sufficient to allow ecosystems to adapt naturally to climate change, to ensure that food production is not threatened and to enable economic development to proceed in a sustainable manner' (UN, 1992, art. 2).

The convention distinguishes between two groups. Annex 1 countries are the industrialized countries which have historically predominantly contributed to GHGs in the atmosphere (the OECD, Russia and several other Central and Eastern European countries). Under the convention, these 'are committed to the non-legally binding aim of returning their greenhouse gas emissions to 1990 levels by the year 2000' (UN, 1992). Non-Annex 1 Parties are mainly the developing countries. They are to report in general terms on their actions to address climate change and adapt to its effects. Almost all countries, except some of the oil producing states, agreed in principle with the objectives of the convention. The differences in opinion centred on more detailed goals and obligations. Three issues divided the opinions: 1) target and timetables, 2) financial and technology transfer, 3) implementation mechanisms.

The European Community and the Alliance of Small Island States (AOSIS) argued for explicit and concrete targets and timetables for limiting emissions from industrialized countries. The US and the oil-producing states dismissed such commitments. Many developing countries supported the idea with the proviso that it would apply to industrialized countries. A second controversial issue was the financial assistance and technology transfer. Industrialized countries wished to use the Global Environment Facility (GEF)[1] for this end, while developing countries pressed for the establishment of a new fund. Countries such as India also requested additional financial resources from industrialized countries to assist developing countries to implement the convention. Third, the OECD countries generally favoured the introduction of strong institutional arrangements to oversee implementation with recurrent meetings of the parties to the convention. It included a scientific advisory body, a body to assist implementation, detailed reporting requirements, as well as established procedure to handle non-compliance. Developing countries feared that such strong institutional regulation might violate national sovereignty and advocated a more voluntary framework convention (UN, 1992). In particular Article 4.7 of the convention was instrumental in bridging the conflicting positions of North and South in the negotiations, which was important to make the Group of 77 more inclined to agree to the convention (B. Kjellén, interview by author, 2005).

The extent to which developing country parties will effectively implement their commitments under the convention will depend on the effective implementation by developed country parties of their commitments under the convention related to financial resources and transfer of technology and will take fully into account that economic and social development and poverty eradication are the first and overriding priorities of the developing country parties (UN, 1992). In the end the convention reflects a careful balance between these positions. Many issues were also referred to the coming Conference of the Parties (COP).

The Struggle for Commitments

When the time came for more thorough decisions, two major conflicts erupted. The EU and the USA came to blows over emission reductions and North and South engaged in another clash over developing countries' participation in agreements. The North pushed for manifest targets also for developing countries, whereas Southern countries pointed to the historical responsibility of the industrialized countries. A few months before Kyoto, the US Senate unanimously decided that the US should not accept a treaty that would not require all countries, including developing, to commit to emission reduction (Byrd and Hagel, 1997). In the negotiations leading up to the Kyoto Protocol there was also strong pressure from the United States for flexible arrangements to meet the targets of the protocol. After intense negotiations three instruments were defined: Joint Implementation, Emissions Trading and Clean Development Mechanism (CDM).

Prior to the Kyoto meeting, Brazil proposed that responsibilities to mitigate GHGs should be based on each country's historic contribution to the earth's mean surface temperature increase, rather than present emissions. This would give developing countries some time for economic development before taking on emissions reductions targets. Annex I parties that did not comply were to make a contribution to a fund for each effective emissions unit above its emissions ceiling. The CDM originated from this proposal. In contrast to Brazil's proposal it shifts the focus to mitigation projects undertaken by developing countries. The CDM is intended to contribute to the ultimate objective of the UNFCCC with a two-tier solution: (i) transfer of cleaner technology to developing countries which will reduce emissions and (ii) certified emissions reductions by Annex 1 parties (UNFCCC, 1997, 1998).

In the Kyoto Protocol, which entered into force in February 2005, Annex I parties committed themselves to reduce their overall emissions of six GHGs by at least 5% below 1990 levels in the first commitment period between 2008 and 2012. Specific targets varied between the countries. The Kyoto Protocol left many of the operational details for coming COPs and subsidiary bodies to work out during further negotiations. The protocol was criticized by the South for not having sufficiently recognized the need for economic and social development in non-industrialized countries. In addition, it was argued that it downplayed adaptation issues, which were of immediate concern for the vulnerable poor countries (Bhandari et al., 1999). Despite the efforts to achieve compromise represented by the carefully crafted course set by the convention and the Kyoto Protocol, a number of important tensions remain. In the next section of this paper we intend to outline two issues of this type.

Critical North–South Tensions and Global Warming

Technology Transfer

The problem of global warming is seen by developing countries as one which has been created by Northern countries who in turn have benefited from the activities that have led to environmental damage. This perspective not only links global environmental change to development in the North but to the prospect of future development in the South. It is also a view that may be argued to have some support in the Brundtland report. Depending on how one reads the debate on global warming and the various conventions, resolutions and agreements passed, one could conceivably argue that this position is widely accepted and enshrined in several of the proposed arrangements, e.g. the GEF and IPCC's recommendations that developing countries should be given assistance and compensated. This view has even been recognized in Article 4.8 of the United Nations Framework Convention on Climate Change.

Although some aspects of the discussion suggest that there might be winners and losers in climate change, the dominant approach that has characterized the negotiations has been to avoid framing the global warming issue in terms of winners and losers. The two most common reasons advanced for this are that: (i) absolute winners and losers in climate change are difficult to establish because what is defined as a win or a loss is ultimately dependent on level of aggregation or scale, and (ii) mitigating warming of the climate will lead to net benefits for society as a whole so there is little point in establishing individual winners and losers since losses are acceptable because the net benefit for the whole is greater (Nordhaus, 1991). This line of reasoning frames the problem of global warming in biophysical terms and avoids any discussion of social and political determinants or consequences of the issue. Thus GHG emissions from fossil fuel use in developed countries is treated as the same as emissions from agricultural activities in developing countries (Agarwal and Narain, 1991; Shue, 1993). The South's position issues from a political economic framing of global warming similar to that of WS in that it argues that global warming cannot be framed in purely biophysical terms since some countries benefited socially and politically from generating environmental damage. Further, the proposed solutions imply a greater burden for the South.

Since the Stockholm conference in 1972, it has been increasingly apparent that development cannot continue to be defined in terms of high growth and high consumption that was synonymous with the trajectory followed by OECD and other industrialized nations. Global sustainable development depends on, among other things, the ability of Southern nations to outline and follow development visions based on low impact lifestyles. The ability of the South to achieve this is in turn dependent on it having access to environmentally efficient technology at affordable prices. This implies that in adopting policies to mitigate global warming, the South can be expected to incur both political and economic costs. Political costs in terms of being able to justify to the populace why the affluent lifestyles that have hitherto been promised as a possible future are no longer attainable and the high upfront economic costs of pursuing an alternative technological trajectory.

Even within the biophysical frame it is acknowledged that some Southern nations, such as those located in low lying coastal areas, will be particularly disadvantaged by global warming. Southern states have taken the line that the above arguments come together to imply that they should be awarded compensation and at the very least assistance to overcome the additional challenges that adopting policies for mitigating and/or adapting to global warming would present to them.

According to the WSD perspective, state behaviour is strongly determined by history and position in the world system. Reasoning from this, it may be argued that core states will, despite the fact that the issue clearly warrants a departure from the norm, have difficulty in adopting a new frame. Further, even if they were to do so, it would hardly produce much effect since only a radical restructuring of the system itself can bring about significant change. This logic not only explains the behaviour of the core (Northern) states vis-à-vis their peripheral (Southern) counterparts but also the fact that little attention has been given to the problem of disadvantaged peripheries in the North itself.

Knowledge Disparities

More important than, but related to the problems associated with technology and future development possibilities is the problem of the disparities between the North and South with respect to knowledge production and absorption in relation to global warming. Since the UN Conference on Science and Technology for Development in 1979 it has been well understood that the majority of Third World countries do not possess the necessary scientific infrastructure or capacity (personnel, capital) to support their development aspirations. This has consequences for the ability of Third World countries to negotiate successfully on issues ranging from trade to environment. The area of global warming is a particularly strong case of this general problem for two closely related reasons.

One is that the preparations for the negotiations depend on investments in expensive equipment and highly skilled scientific labour (Demerrit, 2001). Prioritizing this expense in the face of other needs in the South is neither politically justifiable nor desirable. Similar arguments can be made by some Northern countries as well so this position is not unassailable. The other is that the science and politics of climate change are inextricably interlinked. Science drives and has driven the national and international politics of climate change and expectations of policy relevance shape the scientific agenda in terms of methods, questions posed, standards of proof and other epistemological aspects of scientific practice. Even the game between climate sceptics and the environmental lobby involves a bewildering series of interpretations and reinterpretations of data, charges of political partisanship and emphasis on the indeterminacy of scientific knowledge as a basis for political action. The South has also been engaging in this game despite its limited scientific capacity. The result has been that it is now a recognized problem in the negotiations that countries routinely question scientific arguments because they distrust the source.

The South's distrust of 'the science of global warming' is in part rooted in vulnerability arising from its inability to rely on its own scientific resources. Another reason for distrust is that science tends to favour the biophysical framing of climate change rather than the political economic lens that the South would prefer to use to understand climate change and its policy consequences. The reductionism inherent to scientific practice as well as the fact that Northern scientists dominate the climate change science community all converge on favouring a biophysical approach that ignores the social and political implications of proposed actions. It is important to bear in mind, however, that these very features of scientific practice were instrumental in getting the problem of climate change on the political agenda in the first place.

Another less acknowledged but equally important point of division has to do with the differences in national policy cultures generally and more specifically variations in national preferences for constructing the science–policy interface. Nations often differ in the way that they construct the demarcation between scientific expertise and political authority. This means that in some instances policymakers may lose legitimacy if they appear to be allowing scientists to be 'calling the shots'. This also holds true for Northern states; some of the misunderstanding between European Union and the United States on global warming may in part be attributed to differences in how these countries view the role of scientific expertise in decision making.[2]

Diverging Interests and Common Expectations: G77 and Global Warming

In discussions about North–South relations on problems such as global warming, the South is often seen as and represents itself as a homogeneous group. This homogeneity is a deliberate political construction which is as much sustained by the real vulnerability developing countries feel vis-à-vis their wealthier counterparts in negotiations as by the fact that it is the divergences among Northern countries that often take centre-stage. Nowhere is this more evident than with the issue of global warming. The position of developing countries may be briefly described as one which argues for a multilateral response to global environmental problems. Developing countries further argue that the industrialized countries have a historic responsibility as they are the predominant source of pollution and should therefore shoulder the burden of the costs of global environmental conservation. This burden includes compensation to developing countries for additional expenses incurred in promoting environmental conservation.

Despite the persistence of the traditional groupings in international negotiations such as the G77, the US and some other OECD countries as one group and the EU as a third group, the problem of global warming has created a number of new interest coalitions which threaten the solidarity of the traditional groups. One of these is the differences between the interests of the AOSIS and the OPEC countries, another is the role of the larger Third World states such as India, China, Brazil and Argentina whose interests in issues like technology transfer and debt relief have grown in complexity since the initial formation of the G-77 group.

The much vaunted peace dividend from the end of the Cold War has come to developing countries chiefly in the form of the decoupling of economic development from political ideology. This means that liberal economic globalization is as much alive in the South as it is in the North. Within Third World countries many of the intellectual elite now challenge the narrative of development as a Western myth intended to perpetuate underdevelopment while the political elite struggle on the international stage for the right to pursue this very myth. In practical terms, many developing countries are turning to each other in bilateral agreements to get access to knowledge and assistance that they traditionally sought in North–South negotiations. India, China and Brazil in particular are now and will increasingly in the future become exporters of technology to other Third World countries.

The continued existence of the G-77 group as a political entity in the face of these tensions may be explained theoretically by the WSD argument that although individual countries may change their relative positions in the system, the system dynamic remains unaltered. More practically, the G-77's persistence may be explained by a number of other factors. One is a shared understanding among developing countries of global environmental negotiations as a starting point for negotiations over the unequal consumption of resources rather than for the protection of the environment from the excesses of industrial capitalism. The other is that both the weaker and the stronger nations need the group for leverage on issues such as global warming. A third is that the failure of the G-77 to break into smaller groups with stronger ties may have to do with the interaction between the G-77 as a group and the North. To the extent that the Northern countries themselves find it convenient to treat the South as an amorphous whole whose constituent parts exist independently only when it may be convenient for the exercise of power then the G-77 will need to persist as G-77.

One potential test case in this respect is climate change, since developing countries on aggregate are expected to increase their GHGs emissions as they pursue industrial development. These increasing emissions it is believed will provide them with a bargaining chip vis-à-vis developing counties that are pressing for global commitments of mitigating GHG emissions (Miller, 1995). Climate change will hurt some of the developing countries more than others for a variety of reasons. This makes the bargaining chip hypothesis only partially valid for developing countries. Some may strengthen their negotiating positions, whereas others have too much at stake to attain a favourable bargaining situation. The emergence of this scenario is dependent on the willingness of the international community to actually take responsibility for the global commons from rhetoric to reality.

Emissions Trading: A Way Out of the Impasse?

In the post-2012 period, developing country GHG emissions are expected to exceed industrialized countries' emissions some time between 2010 and 2012 according to IPCC model projections (IPCC 2001). This for many observers implies that large-scale reduction of GHG emissions has to include participation of non-Annex 1 countries, in spite of development concerns and the North's historic responsibilities. This particular line of argument is seen as one of the more difficult points of negotiation. It may be that a stronger emphasis on synergies between sustainable development and climate change policy is one way out of this impasse.

At present the linkage between climate policy and sustainable development rests almost exclusively on the market based CDM operating on a primarily local project level. The purpose of CDM as it was defined in the Kyoto Protocol was to help direct foreign corporate investment to facilitate sustainable development. What is meant by sustainable development is basically up to national definitions. However, at the same time it is in the present round of UNFCCC confined to a local phenomena and realized by foreign corporate investment (Grubb, 1999, p. xxxix). It remains to be seen whether the trust in the CDM is warranted given the historical legacy of failure.

In the Kyoto Protocol and subsequent COPs sustainable development is predominantly associated with CDM, and as such it is predominantly confined to local issues. However, climate change policy is intimately linked to sustainable development dimensions of global resource and material flows. By creating a platform for a potential global emissions market, the Kyoto Protocol is merging the present liberal economic globalization with climate change policy. According to Grubb, CDM 'gives the Kyoto Protocol commitments the global investment scope which the United States and most other JUSCANNZ[3] countries had been desperately seeking, and explicitly enshrines the role of the private sector (Grubb, 1999, p. 136). Some actors in the global South argue that technological transfer and the monetary flows connected with CDM and Joint Implementation will follow the line of most foreign investment and go to the larger economies of developing countries, and leave Least Developed Countries on the margin (Najam et al., 2003). Since the poorer countries do not produce high enough quantities of emissions for effective projects that will render good return in emission credits, they run the risk of being left out in the investment calculations (Gupta, 1997; Anand, 2004).

The emissions trading schemes seem to follow the logic of the global warming issue as a whole in so far as it challenges the traditional grouping of developing countries as one negotiating bloc. One potential way forward may be for countries to adjust their negotiation strategy to the evolution of their particular interests. The G-77 formation has been very good at delivering rhetorical victories for the South such as the concept of sustainable development and arguments for the historical debt of the North to the global commons. The translation of these rhetorical gains into real advantages for the South and ultimately for the future of the global commons may rest in sacrificing the comfort of the solidarity of the G-77 at the altar of conservation goals of the South. This approach may also be advantageous in view of the fact that discussions about large scale arrangements for technology transfer are no longer relevant in the context of nation state discussions. Northern countries do not own these resources and the increasing globalization of capital has meant that, on their own territory, many Northern states are as powerless as their Southern counterparts in the face of business decisions to transfer resources from one context to another.

Conclusion

International negotiations on climate change follow the general pattern of all major international environmental negotiations since Stockholm 1972. Issues such as technology transfer and the differential scientific capacities of Southern and Northern countries continue to be major points of disagreement between the North and the South. Likewise, traditional political bloc groups such as G-77 appear to continue even in the face of real differences in interests with respect to outcomes of the international negotiations. In the light of this, the world system and dependency postulate that without radical restructuring of the global economy little change may be expected in nation state behaviour which continues to be a relevant frame for understanding international negotiations on the environment.

Nevertheless, climate change negotiations have brought to the fore a number of new and interesting insights which promise hope for the future. One is that despite continued contestation, the Kyoto Protocol has managed to come into force. Another is that all major actors acknowledge the need to reconcile environmental protection and development concerns of the South, at least rhetorically. A third is the fact that the challenge to the role of scientific knowledge in policy inherent in the different objections raised both by Third World countries and the USA. On one hand, this battle may be dismissed as political efforts to stall proceedings for as long as possible, on the other a number of important lessons about the interaction of science and policy may be gleaned from this ongoing discussion. For example, the insight that differences in the role assigned to science in different policy systems will ultimately affect policymakers' willingness to accept scientific findings in international settings. While the problem of scientific uncertainty has received much attention to this date, the other part of this issue, which is how to reconcile different views on the role of scientific expertise in the policy process, requires further study.

Acknowledgement

This article draws on research funded by MISTRA's Climate Policy Research Programme (CLIPORE).

Notes

1 The GEF is a multi-billion-dollar facility set up in the early 1990s to assist developing countries with the costs of environmental protection. The GEF is administered by the World Bank and this institution is charged with seeing to it that development projects are consistent with the goals of sustainable development. The GEF is not without its critics or problems, the most obvious of which is that many countries did not honour their pledges to the institution. A second is that developing countries argued that GEF assistance was biased towards problems which the North defined as pressing e.g. climate change and overlooked local environmental problems.
2 Recently, the National Academy of Science released its report stating that 'There is now strong evidence that significant global warming is occurring'. The Bush Administration has however issued its own reading of these results which denies this evidence. See the *Observer International*, 19 June 2005 and *Climate Change Science: An Analysis of Some Key Questions* (Washington: National Academy of Science, 2005).
3 JUSCANNZ is an acronym for the alliance of Japan, the USA, Switzerland, Canada, Australia, Norway and New Zealand, which was active as a group during the Kyoto Protocol negotiations.

References

Agarwal, A. & Narain, S. (1991) *Global Warming in an Unequal World* (New Delhi: Centre for Science and the Environment).
Anand, R. (2004) *International Environmental Justice: A North–South Dimension* (Aldershot: Ashgate).
Bhandari, P., Gupta, S., Pachauri, R.K., Srikanth, S. & Srivastava, L. (1999) *Climate of Concern: Bridging the Divide* (New Delhi: Tata Energy Research Institute).
Bodansky, D. (2001) The history of the global climate change regime, in Sprinz, D. F. & Luterbacher, U. (eds) *International Relations and Global Climate Change* (Cambridge, MA: MIT Press), pp. 45–76.
Byrd, R. C. & Hagel, C. (1997). A resolution expressing the sense of the Senate regarding the conditions for the United States becoming a signatory to any international agreement on greenhouse gas emissions under the United Nations Framework Convention on Climate Change, 105th CONGRESS, 1st Session, S. RES. 98, 12 June 1997.

Çoban, A. (2004) Caught between state-sovereign rights and property rights: regulating biodiversity, *Review of International Political Economy*, 11(4), pp. 736–762.
Commonwealth Head of Government Meeting (1989) Langkawi Declaration on the Environment signed on October 21st, 1989 in conjunction with the Commonwealth Head of Government Meeting on 18–24 October 1989 in Langkawi, Malaysia, http://www.jas.sains.my/jas/Masm/cermin+test.htm (accessed 6 June 2005).
Conference of Non-Aligned Heads of State (1989) *Ninth Conference of Heads of State of the Non-Aligned States*, 9/EC/Doc. 8/Rev. 3, 7 September.
Demeritt, D. (2001) The construction of global warming and the politics of science, *Annals of the Association of American Geographers*, 91(2), pp. 307–337.
Evans, P.B., Rueschemeyer, D.& Skocpol, T. (eds) (1985) *Bringing the State Back In* (New York: Cambridge University Press).
Frank, G. A. & Gills, B. (1993) *The World Systems: Five Hundred Years or Five Thousand?* (London: Routledge).
Franz, W. E. (1997) *The Development of an International Agenda for Climate Change: Connecting Science to Policy*, Environment and Natural Resources Program Discussion Paper, E-97-07, Kennedy School of Government, Harvard University.
G-77 (1989) Caracas Declaration of the Ministers of Foreign Affairs of the Group of 77 on the Occasion of the Twenty-Fifth Anniversary of the Group, http://www.g77.org/Docs/Caracas%20Declaration.html (accessed 1 June 2005).
Gereffi, G. & Wyman, D. L. (1990) *Manufacturing Miracles: Paths of Industrialization in Latin America and East Asia* (Princeton, NJ: Princeton University Press).
Grubb, M. (1999). *The Kyoto Protocol: A Guide and Assessment* (London: Royal Institute of International Affairs, Energy and Environmental Programme, Earthscan).
Gupta, J. (1997) *The Climate Change Convention and Developing Countries: From Conflict to Consensus?* (Dordrecht & London: Kluwer Academic).
Görg, C. & Brand, U. (2000) Global environmental politics and competition between nation-states: on the regulation of biological diversity, *Review of International Political Economy*, 7(3), pp. 371–398.
Holdgate, M. W. (ed.) (1982) *The World Environment 1972–1982: A Report* (Dublin: United Nations Environment Programme, Tycooly International).
IPCC (2001) *Climate Change 2001 IPCC Third Assessment Report* (Geneva: Intergovernmental Panel on Climate Change).
IPCC, WMO and UNDP (1991). *Climate Change: The IPCC Response Strategies* (Washington, DC: Island Press).
Jäger, J. & Ferguson, H. L. (1991) *Climate Change: Science, Impacts and Policy: Proceedings of the Second World Climate Conference* (Cambridge: Cambridge University Press).
Miller, M. A. L. (1995) *The Third World in Global Environmental Politics* (Buckingham: Open University Press).
Nordhaus, W. D. (1991) To slow or not to slow: the economics of the greenhouse effect, *The Economic Journal*, 101, pp. 920–937.
Najam, A., Huq, S. & Sokonae, Y. (2003) Climate negotiations beyond Kyoto: developing countries concerns and interests, *Climate Policy*, 3(3), pp. 221–231.
Roberts, J. T., Grimes, P. E. & Manale, J. L. (2003) Social roots of global environmental change: a world-systems analysis of carbon dioxide emissions, *Journal of World-Systems Research*, IX(2), pp. 277–315.
Samhat, N. H. (1998) A genealogy of climate change: deterritorializing space, respatializing international community, *Online Journal of Peace and Conflict Resolution*, 1(4), http://www.trinstitute.org/ojpcr/1_4 (accessed 12 May 2005).
Shue, H. (1993) Subsistence emissions and luxury emissions, *Law and Policy*, 15, pp. 39–59.
South Pacific Forum (1989) Final Communiqué of the Twentieth South Pacific Forum, held at Tarawa (Kiribati) 10–11 July, reprinted in UN Document A/44/463.
UN (1972a) Conference on the Human Environment: Identification and control of pollutants of broad international significance. A/Conf.48/8, 7 January.
UN (1972b) United Nations Conference on the Human Environment Action Plan for the Human Environment.
UN (1988) Protection of global climate for present and future generations of mankind, A/RES/43/53, 6 December.
UN (1989a) Protection of global climate for present and future generations of mankind, A/RES/44/207, 22 December.
UN (1989b). Possible adverse effects of sea-level rise on islands and coastal areas, particularly low-lying coastal areas, A/RES/44/206, 22 December.
UN (1989c) United Nations Conference on Environment and Development, A/RES/44/208, 22 December.
UN (1992) United Nations Framework Convention on Climate Change.
UNEP (1982) The Environment in 1982: Retrospect and Prospect, Nairobi, UNEP/GC(SSC)/2.
UNFCCC (1997) Proposed Elements of a Protocol to the United Nations Framework Convention on Climate Change, Presented by Brazil in Response to the Berlin Mandate, FCCC/AGBM/1997/MISC 1/ADD.3.

UNFCCC (1998) Report of the Conference of the Parties on its Third Session, Held At Kyoto. From 1 To 11 December 1997, FCCC/CP/1997/7/Add.1, 18 March.
Vogler, J. (1995) *The Global Commons: Environmental and Technological Governance*, 2nd edition (John Wiley and Sons).
WMO (1979) Proceedings of the World Climate Conference: a conference of experts on climate and mankind, Geneva, 12–23 February 1979 (Geneva: WMO).
WMO (1988) Developing Policies for Responding to Climatic Change: A Summary of the Discussions and Recommendations of the Workshops Held in Villach (28 September–2 October 1987) and Bellagio (9–13 November 1987) under the Auspices of the Beijer Institute, Stockholm, Geneva, World Meteorological Organization.
World Climate Program (1985) Report of the International Conference on the assessment of the Role of Carbon Dioxide and of Other Green House Gases in Climate Variations and Associated Impacts, Villach, Austria, 9–12 Ocotober.
World Commission on Environment and Development (WCED) (1987) *Our Common Future* (Oxford: Oxford University Press).

Björn-Ola Linnér is associate professor at the Department of Water and Environmental Studies and the Swedish Institute for Climate Science and Policy Research, Linköping University. His research focuses on post-war international cooperation and policy making on climate change, sustainable development and global food security. He is the author of, among others, *The Return of Malthus: Environmentalism and Post-war Population-Resource Crises* (White Horse Press, 2003).

Merle Jacob is guest professor at the Swedish Institute for Climate Science and Policy Research, Linköping University and Professor at the Research Policy Institute, Lund University. His research interests are research policy and the interaction between science and policy.

State of Denial: The United States and the Politics of Global Warming

KEVIN C. ARMITAGE

> I've been involved in a number of fields where there's a lay opinion and a scientific opinion. And in most cases, it's the lay community that is more exercised, more anxious... But, in the climate case, the experts—the people who work with the climate models every day, the people who do ice cores—they are *more* concerned. They're going out of their way to say, 'Wake up! This is not a good thing to be doing.'
>
> (Theoretical physicist Robert Socolow, quoted in Kolbert, 2005, p. 55)

Introduction

On 28 July 2003, Oklahoma Republican Senator James Inhofe took to the floor of the United States senate to denounce concern over global climate change as a preposterous betrayal of reason. 'Put simply', asserted Inhofe, chairman of the powerful Committee on Environment and Public Works, 'man-induced global [climate change] is an article of religious faith.' Warming to his subject, the senator railed that the 'debate over global warming is predicated on fear, rather than science'. Astonishingly, Inhofe concluded that global warming is 'the greatest hoax ever perpetrated on the American people' (Inhofe, 2003). Despite explicitly endorsing scientific research as a basis for informed public policy, in a recent update of his 2003 speech

Senator Inhofe cited novelist Michael Crichton's recent anti-environment thriller, *State of Fear* (Crichton, 2004) both as a source of scientific information—he called it 'the real story about global warming'—and as an accurate depiction of the environmental community, whose worry over global warming he ridiculed as 'hysterical'.

How is it that a powerful member of the United States government can so blatantly misrepresent scientific research and its policy implications without becoming a laughingstock? Inhofe is hardly alone; he represents the position of the current presidential administration and of millions of citizens of the United States. Yet a recent review of the 928 peer-reviewed scientific articles on climate change published between 1993 and 2003 found not a single example of research that contradicted the consensus scientific view that human activity, primarily the burning of fossil fuels, is changing the global climate (Oreskes, 2004). Indeed, the scientific consensus is simply overwhelming. Donald Kennedy, chief editor of *Science*, wrote in the 30 March 2001 issue: 'By now the scientific consensus on global warming is so strong that it leaves little room for the defensive assertions... Consensus as strong as the one that has developed around this topic is rare in science' (Kennedy, 2001).

Despite this fact, global warming 'skeptics' assert that central tenants of the science of global warming are unsettled. Their strategy of claiming that climate science is inconclusive and thus more research rather than mitigating policy is the prudent response to the accumulated data has worked very well. This tactic is especially important for residents of the United States who constitute only 4% of the world's population but emit one-quarter of the world's CO_2—about 40,000 pounds per US citizen each year, more than China, India and Japan combined (*The Independent*, 13 June 2005).

To understand the interplay of power politics and the science of global warming in the United States, one must note that concerns over climate change emerged at the same time as a fierce right-wing backlash against environmentalism. Yet environmentalism remains popular among the American public. Indeed, according to a May 2005 survey published by the Pew Research Center for People and Policy, 77% of those polled believe the country 'should do whatever it takes to protect the environment', while 63% subscribe to that view 'strongly' (Pew Research Center, 2005). The political enemies of environmentalism such as Senator Inhofe thus attack the evidentiary basis that underpins environmentalism, rather than its values and goals. What follows, then, is an abbreviated history of global climate change and popular environmental consciousness in the United States, with an emphasis on how right-wing anti-environmentalists use the authority of the scientific process while simultaneously undermining its findings to thwart constructive action on this most pressing issue.

The 1970s: Environmentalism and Global Cooling

The first Earth Day, celebrated on 22 April 1970 in communities across the United States, drew more than 20 million people to its global environmental concerns (Guha, 2000, p. 80). Importantly, Earth Day coincided with definitive recognition of the importance of climate change issues. Two studies from 1970 and 1971, respectively the Study of Critical Environmental Problems (SCEP) and the Study on Man's Impact on Climate (SMIC), stressed the ecological importance of increasing concentrations of atmospheric CO_2. Such studies prompted a comprehensive gathering of climate experts from 14 nations in Stockholm in 1971. This was the first major conference focused entirely on the 'Study of Man's Impact on Climate' (Weart, 2003, p. 71). Though no consensus as to likely effects of climate change yet existed, all the participants agreed serious and threatening change was possible.

Just as consciousness of the potential importance of climate change was beginning to rise in the late-1970s, environmentalism in the United States faced a profound backlash. Though events such as Earth Day were crafted to avoid political affiliation, environmentalism, with its critique of industrial modernity, skepticism of capitalist economics, and calls for government intervention in economic activity, was often seen as part of the political left. Environmental initiatives threatened core components of right-wing ideology such as the primacy of individual liberty, the absolute rights of private property, free enterprise and laissez-faire government. Right-wing think-tanks and media outlets thus began a relentless public relations campaign that attacked environmentalism as alarmist or worse. In conjunction with right-wing politics, the fossil fuel industry, wishing to avoid regulation, taxation and negative publicity, used pro-industry research and catchy advertisements to persuade the public that climate change was simply not a concern (Weart, 2003, p. 105).

Adding to contemporary skepticism about the significance of global warming was the debate over cooling. There was in fact a slight planetary cooling trend from the 1940s through the 1970s. Some scientists working in the then-emerging field of climate science argued that particulate matter from coal burning might be causing this cooling trend while others cited the use of industrial and agricultural aerosols. Many scientists, of course, maintained that warming was the problem. The public had every right to be confused about the issue. Weart (2003, p. 115) quotes *Business Week* in 1976 warning its readers that, 'the dominant school maintains that the world is becoming cooler'. One year later the magazine declared CO_2 'may be the world's biggest environmental problem, threatening to raise the world's temperature' with horrific long-term damage. Global warming deniers continue to use this relatively minor 1970s debate to discredit concerns over climate change. Widely syndicated right-wing newspaper columnist (and Princeton Ph.D.) George Will, for example, disputes contemporary concern over climate change with the misleading claim that '30 years ago the fashionable panic was about global cooling' (Will, 2004).

By the mid-1970s, scientists understood that various forcing mechanisms—the ice age cycle; CO_2 warming; aerosol cooling—affected climate in crucial ways, but they were uncertain how any single factor might affect the atmospheric future. This conclusion was supported by a 1975 report from the National Academy of Sciences that summarized the lack of an existing scientific consensus on global climate change. The cooling debate, however, was largely settled during this time, at the International Symposium on Long-Term Climate Fluctuations, sponsored by the World Meteorological Organization (WMO) and held in Norwich, England in the summer of 1975. Research presented at the symposium demonstrated, in the words of William Kellogg, 'that low-lying industrial aerosols, and also smoke particles from slash and burn agricultural practices, absorb sunlight quite strongly and do *not* cause a cooling of the lower atmosphere when they are over land' (Kellogg, 1987, p. 122). In other words, the factors previously thought to cool the troposphere proved not to have such effects, clearing the way for researchers to focus on CO_2 accumulation as the primary factor driving climate change.

In a reflection of the political implications of climate research findings, the Central Intelligence Agency (CIA) of the United States followed the debate over climate change closely. The CIA commissioned a series of reports that argued that climate change in the form of global cooling was 'perhaps the greatest single challenge that America will face in coming years' (Quoted by Ross, 1991, p. 202). The CIA noted that only the United States and Argentina would likely benefit from global cooling, a trend that could return the United States to 'the primacy in world affairs it held in the immediate post World War II era' (Quoted by Ross, 1991, p. 202). Yet the political destabilization stemming from crop failures and other negative consequences of climate change ultimately made global cooling an area of concern from the point of view of the US security apparatus. According to Andrew Ross, such concerns exercised 'sway over such organizations as the World Meteorological Organization and World Weather Watch' (Ross, 1991, pp. 203–204). Cold War *realpolitik* intruded upon objective science, a phenomenon that continues with current geopolitical strategizing about climate change.

The Rise of Global Climate Science

By the late 1970s climate researchers amassed enough evidence about global warming that scientists began to be overtly fearful for the future. These fears materialized in calls for concrete action at the first World Climate Conference. Hosted by the WMO in Geneva in February of 1979, the World Climate Conference was the first to issue a statement calling upon the world community to alleviate the potential worst effects of climate change. Not only did the conference beseech governments to 'foresee and to prevent potential man-made changes in climate that might be adverse to the well-being of humanity' (WMO, 1979, p. 713), it called upon the world to consider the fundamental changes necessary to mitigate the climate change problem:

> It is possible that some effects on a regional and global scale may be detectable before the end of this century and become significant before the middle of the next century. The time scale is similar to that required to redirect, if necessary, the operation of many aspects of the world economy, including agriculture and the production of energy. Since changes in climate may prove to be beneficial in some parts of the world and adverse in others, significant social and technological readjustments may be required. (WMO, 1979, p. 714)

The statement concluded by noting that the international cooperation needed to face such an all-encompassing problem required a peaceful world, one in which open and substantive transnational collaboration was possible. Cooperation was institutionalized in the form of the World Climate Program (WCP), the first internationally coordinated program that investigated the world's climate.

By the mid-1980s an international consensus began to emerge that increasing atmospheric carbon dioxide levels would likely produce increases in global mean temperatures. This consensus was reflected in a conference organized by the WCP at Villach, Austria in October 1985. The conference report summarized 'the most advanced experiments' as demonstrating that 'increases of the global mean surface temperature for a doubling of the atmospheric CO_2 concentration or equivalent, of between 1.5 and 4.5 °C' (WMO, 1986, p. 2). Crucially, the climate scientists gathered at Villach called upon governments to take action: 'While some warming of the climate now appears inevitable due to past actions, the rate and degree of future warming could be profoundly affected by governmental policies' (Quoted by Weart, 2003, p. 151). Beginning at Villach, climate researchers took direct steps into the political sphere through advocacy.

The world seemed to get a glimpse of its climate future in 1988. Heat and drought caused severe crop losses in the American Midwest, the worst since the Dust Bowl of the 1930s. The USSR suffered drought, as did China. Unexpected floods ravaged Africa, Brazil, Bangladesh and India. Hurricanes struck the Caribbean, along with a cyclone in New Zealand and a typhoon in the Philippines. These disasters provided compelling background to the political events of 1988, the most dramatic year in the history of the politics of climate change. Colorado Senator Timothy Wirth scheduled hearings on the greenhouse effect for 23 June, the anniversary of the hottest day ever recorded in Washington, DC (Mazur and Lee, 1993, p. 697).

The testimony featured James Hansen, chief climate scientist at NASA's Goddard Institute for Space Studies (GISS) and a national figure with a reputation for prudence. But rather than being overly cautious, Hansen chided his fellow researchers by arguing that 'it is time to stop waffling so much. We should say that the evidence is pretty strong that the greenhouse effect is here' (quoted by Paterson, 1996, p. 33).

Shortly after Hansen gave his testimony to congress, a conference planned at Villach took place in Toronto. Titled 'The Changing Atmosphere: Implications for Global Security', the meeting consisted primarily of scientists, with the hope that consensus could be more readily reached without governmental representatives. The conference report concluded that humans were polluting the atmosphere and should undertake immediate ameliorative measures. Nor did the conference report shy from dramatic warnings: 'humanity is conducting an uncontrolled globally pervasive experiment whose ultimate consequences could be second only to global nuclear war (Toronto Conference, 1988, p. 46). Moreover, the conference report advocated detailed policy proposals, most notably the reduction of greenhouse gas emissions. For the first time, scientists called for targeted reductions, specifically that by 2005 emissions should be 20% below the 1988 level.

Due to the striking events of 1988, global warming received a great deal of media coverage and become a central focus of the environmental community. It also received an apparent outpouring of support by some of the dominant politicians in the United States. Then presidential candidate George H. W. Bush made global warming a vital political issue with a memorable call to action: 'Those who think we're powerless to do anything about the greenhouse effect are forgetting about the White House effect' (quoted by Agrawala and Andresen, 2001, p. 3).

The world community also took notice. Understanding the global nature of the climate change issue, the WMO and other United Nations agencies—particularly United Nations Environmental Program—created in 1988 the Intergovernmental Panel on Climate Change (IPCC). The panel consisted of a hybrid of scientists and government representatives, and sought to assess scientific information related to climate change and to formulate realistic response strategies for management of the issue. The political lobbying on the IPCC was intense, particularly from the oil, coal, and automotive industries, as well as oil dependent nations such as Saudi Arabia (Weart, 2003, pp. 161–162). It was under these hotly politicized conditions that in 1990 the IPCC issued its first report, a painstakingly worded and bureaucratically cautious document that noted the planet was indeed warming, but that definitive science as to the cause of the warming was a decade away.

Right-Wing Politics and Global Warming

As Weart (2003, p. 159) argues, the IPCC embodied the long-term liberal dream of using dispassionate scientific research as a basis for transnational policy. It also aroused liberalism's enemies, such as United States President George H. W. Bush. Though President Bush kept his campaign promise of hosting a conference on global warming, he reversed the strong rhetoric and activist stance that characterized his presidential campaign. Instead the President claimed that scientific uncertainty clouded the issue. He favored more research, the unchanging mantra—along with denial—of most right-wing politicians in the United States. The press at the time noted that the White House sought to emphasize scientific uncertainties and the economic costs of emissions reductions at the expense of political action (*Economist*, 14 April 1990, p. 46). A White House policy memo, inadvertently leaked to the news media, argued that the best way to deal with global warming was 'to raise the many uncertainties' surrounding the issue (*New York Times*, 19 April 1990, p. B4).

Furthermore, the Bush administration flatly rejected the 1990 IPCC report, a maneuver that drove much of the politics at the United Nations Conference on Environment and Development—colloquially, the 'Earth Summit'—held in Rio de Janeiro on 3–14 June 1992. The conference is significant to the history of climate change because it was in Rio that over 150 states signed the Framework Convention on Climate Change (FCCC). Governments negotiated the FCCC quickly so that ratification could coincide with the Earth Summit. The negotiations foundered over the issue of establishing targets and timetables for greenhouse gas emission reductions, with the United States and oil producing states rejecting emissions limits against small island states and the European Community who favored them. The second issue confounding the talks was the economic inequality between industrialized countries and developing ones, and the ensuing call for the industrialized world to bear disproportionate economic costs associated with combating climate change. In a late compromise, the parties agreed to a non-binding call for the return to 1990 emission levels for CO_2 and other greenhouse gases. Though rife with loopholes, the agreement created basic principles to guide policy making and a foundation for further negotiation.

As the world used scientific information to mount a coordinated effort to combat climate change, the right-wing movement in the United States stepped up mobilization efforts to challenge the legitimacy of global warming as a problem. Right-wing think-tanks criticized the evidentiary basis of global warming in sober language that nonetheless hinted at a scientific boondoggle. Typical of the criticism was this charge, leveled by the Competitive Enterprise Institute: 'A decade of focus on global warming and billions of dollars of research funds have still failed to establish that global warming is a significant problem' (quoted by McCright and Dunlap, 2000, p. 511). This supposedly even-handed examination of science typified the response of right-wing critics of global warming in that it claimed support from peer-reviewed scientific literature. Indeed, in a survey of the conservative movement's reaction to global warming, McCright and Dunlap (2000) found that 71% of the documents they sampled attempted to discredit the scientific evidence for global warming. Attacks on the science underpinning our understanding of global warming served the political purpose of narrowing the debate to technical deliberations, which forestalled humanistic and ethical approaches that might have aroused public concern and prompted political change.

Right-wing reaction to global warming is not simply a popular response to a complex issue, but 'a direct function of the exercise of power by an influential countermovement' (McCright and Dunlap, 2000). The wildly affluent carbon-based corporate interests, often working in conjunction with right-wing think-tanks, mounted an intense public relations campaign against the 'politicized science' of global warming. In 1989 a partnership of oil companies created the Global Climate Coalition (GCC). The GCC lobbied extensively against climate change legislation and mounted a large-scale advertising blitz meant to assuage any trepidation the public might have about the climate change issue. They were aided in their efforts by a tiny yet respectable set of scientists who doubted the science of global warming, and who could offer impressive credentials and authority—if not peer-reviewed scholarship—to the idea that concern over climate change was, at best, overblown. The fossil fuel lobby financed many of these prominent global warming deniers (Gelbspan, 1997, 2004).

Despite the protests of climate change deniers, during the 1990s the world scientific community grew increasingly alarmed and increasingly adamant in its demand for political action. Of particular note is the appeal issued in November 1992 by 1,700 leading scientists, including the majority of Nobel laureates, titled *World Scientists' Warning to Humanity*. The document begins by claiming that 'human beings and the natural world are on a collision course' and calls for, among other ameliorative actions, a 'move away from fossil fuels to ... cut greenhouse gas emissions'. Shockingly, this statement received relatively little attention in the United States media. The second IPCC report, released in 1995, seemed to support the World Scientists' warning with its conclusion that, 'The balance of evidence suggests that there is a discernable human influence on global climate.' The scrupulously cautious language reflected the highly politicized environment of the IPCC, but at least the report drew widespread media attention. The right wing in the United States, ever suspicious of cooperative international programs, openly scoffed at the report and the Clinton administration put little effort into the global warming issue.

Against this political hostility, the international community stuck to its negotiation schedule. Most important, the agreements signed in Rio led to the 1997 United Nations Conference on Climate Change held in Kyoto, Japan. Swarms of reporters and representatives of NGOs attended the conference along with nearly 6,000 official delegates. A coalition of world scientists issued another statement, *World Scientists' Call for Action*, which implored political leaders to adopt legally binding commitments to reduce heat-trapping gases significantly below 1990 levels. Yet the conference became entangled in questions over global equity and the power relationships between wealthy and developing countries. The negotiations nearly broke down several times, only to survive due to a dramatic appearance by US Vice President Albert Gore. On the last day of negotiations, Gore flew to Kyoto and pushed through a compromise in which industrialized countries would reduce their aggregate emissions by 5.2% below 1990 levels by 2012, but developing countries would be exempt from targeted emission reductions until the next round of negotiations. But even before the Kyoto meeting, the United States Senate voted 95–0 to reject any treaty that failed to require emissions reductions in developing countries. Consequently, the Clinton administration—which put little political muscle behind the climate change issue—never submitted the treaty for ratification. Not only did this omit the world's largest producer of greenhouse gases from reducing emissions, but it also gave other countries the excuse to continue their own unsustainable practices.

The failures of Kyoto were put into stark relief by the most recent (2001) IPCC report. Despite intense lobbying from industry, the report concluded that the world was rapidly warming. Strong evidence demonstrated that 'most of the observed warming over the last 50 years is likely to have been due to the increase in greenhouse gas concentrations' (IPCC, 2001). Indeed, the report worried that humanity might triple preindustrial atmospheric CO_2 levels, which could lead to a disastrous 5.8 °C increase in the global mean temperature.

Despite this worldwide scientific consensus regarding climate change, in March 2001 the administration of George W. Bush rejected any significant reduction of CO_2 emissions by the United States and publicly renounced the Kyoto protocols. The US rejection of Kyoto confirmed a larger pattern of unilateralism by the Bush administration that also included sharp differences with its traditional European Union ally over such issues as the creation of the International Criminal Court, the ban on antipersonnel land mines, and the biodiversity treaty (Mathews, 2001). Bush administration unilateralism presents particular problems for international environmental policy that by definition necessitates a multilateral commitment to global governance.

Yet, as was the case with global cooling, the United States security apparatus is deeply concerned over the potential consequences of global warming. In a classified report that was leaked to the Knight-Ridder newspaper chain, the Department of Defense's Office of Net Assessment, an internal think-tank, speculated that the worst-case global climate change scenario 'would challenge United States National Security in ways that should be considered immediately' (*Knight-Ridder*, 24 February 2004). Dryly entitled 'An Abrupt Climate Change Scenario and Its Implications for U.S. National Security', the report cites 'plausible' consequences of climate change that include famine in Europe and nuclear showdowns over control of the world's dwindling fresh water supply. The document suggests that climate change over the next 20 years might result in a global catastrophe costing tens of millions of lives due to war and natural disaster. The catastrophe could include 'eastern European countries, struggling to feed their populations with a falling supply of food, water and energy, eyeing Russia, whose population is already in decline, for access to its grains, minerals and energy supply. Or, picture Japan, suffering from flooding along its coastal cities and contamination of its fresh water supply, eyeing Russia's Sakhalin Island oil and gas reserves as an energy source.... Envision Pakistan, India, and China—all armed with nuclear weapons—skirmishing at their borders over refugees, access to shared rivers, and arable land' (*Knight-Ridder*, 24 February 2004).

The Pentagon report was a reaction to one of the most unsettling findings of scientists in recent decades: drastic climate change can occur in only a few years. Before the 1950s, scientists generally thought of climate change as an extremely slow process understandable only through a geological, not human, time scale. Yet the idea that people could change the climate combined with new scientific data—particularly from studies of ancient ice that revealed a new history of planetary climate change—to irrevocably alter the old view. In 2002, the National Academy of Sciences concluded that abrupt climate change is possible: 'Recent evidence shows that major and widespread climate changes have occurred with startling speed ... [G]reenhouse warming and other human alterations of the earth system may increase the possibility of large, abrupt, and unwelcome regional or global climatic events' (NAS, 2002; quoted by Speth, 2004, p. 60). This frightening possibility prompted the 2004 Hollywood special effects blockbuster, *The Day After Tomorrow*.

Yet even the political framing of global climate change as a security concern, as opposed to an environmental or human rights issue, failed to prompt action by the Bush administration. As late as December 2002 the Bush administration was still citing the 'numerous uncertainties' that supposedly remained about 'global warming's cause and effect' and thus called for more research on the issue (*Washington Post*, 4 December 2002, p. A8). Not surprisingly, confusion over the issue saturated the general public. A 1997 Gallup survey found that only 42% of the public believed that scientists mostly agree that global warming is a real threat; the public was just as likely (44%) to say that scientists were divided on the issue. Polls and focus groups from the late 1990s demonstrated that people did not connect global warming to their daily lives, were vague about its cause and effects, or simply viewed the problem apocalyptically, as an insoluble dilemma (Weart, 2003, p. 189). One important study found that concern over global warming diminished significantly between 1989 and 1997 (Immerwahr, 1999). At the time when science confirmed the existence of global warming, the public in the United States grew less sure of its reality. Clearly, the intense media presence of right-wing global warming deniers has had a profound effect. Indeed, a memo from American Petroleum Institute leaked to the *New York Times* stated that, 'Victory will be achieved when ... recognition of uncertainty becomes part of the "conventional wisdom"' (Mooney, 2005).

This confusion about the scientific consensus regarding global warming and available options to mitigate its effects derived not only from right-wing counter-mobilizations that challenged the existence of global warming, but from the respectable, mainstream media. In a curious twist of professional ethics, the very notion of balanced reporting contributes to public confusion concerning the climate change issue. As shown in a carefully researched study by Boykoff and

Boykoff, in order to achieve 'balanced' reporting, the 'prestige' newspapers in the United States—specifically the *New York Times*, *Washington Post*, *Los Angeles Times* and the *Wall Street Journal*—all offered roughly equal space to peer-reviewed science and those who claim global warming is not scientifically credible. In this way a superficial adherence to 'balance'—that is, reporting 'both sides' of a debate—distorted evidence and the overall understanding of the issue. Though many in the media accurately reported the story, overall the media provided 'balanced coverage of a very unbalanced issue' (Boykoff and Boykoff, 2004, p. 133). Hence, 'when it comes to coverage of global warming, balanced reporting can actually be a form of informational bias' (Boykoff and Boykoff, 2004, p. 126). In this respect, then, the journalistic norm of evenhandedness helped create a false impression about a lack of scientific consensus on global warming. Balanced coverage is not always accurate coverage.

This kind of false journalistic balance unwittingly supported right-wing propaganda. In a strategy memo obtained by the Environmental Working Group, famed right-wing pollster and media consultant Frank Luntz advised the Republican Party how to handle its unpopular environmental positions, including its rejection of the Kyoto Protocol. Luntz advised Republican politicians to underscore 'your commitment to sound science'. Luntz suggested that politicians emphasize how 'the scientific debate' about global warming 'remains open'. According to Luntz, 'there is still a window of opportunity to challenge the science' and thus not commit to regulations (Environmental Working Group, 2003). In this manner those who reject global warming could appear reasonable and evenhanded in their call for more research. Confused by competing claims, citizens of the United States continue to wait for 'definitive' science.

The climate of confusion and despair among the public helps explain why the United States government has been so reluctant to face the climate change issue in a substantive manner. This refusal has continued even after a surprising Bush administration about-face regarding the existence of global warming. To the astonishment of many political observers and greenhouse activists, in August of 2004 the George W. Bush administration released—albeit quietly—a report that unequivocally stated that CO_2 emissions were the most plausible explanation for observed greenhouse warming. Frustratingly, the report did not signal a change in policy; George W. Bush still rejected the Kyoto Protocol. John H. Marburger, science advisor to the Bush administration, asserted that the report had 'no implications for policy'. 'There is no discordance' claimed Marburger, 'between this report and the president's position on climate' (*Washington Post*, 27 August 2004).

Both public awareness and climate policy in the United States thus remain years behind the rest of the world; climate change was barely even mentioned during the 2004 presidential campaign. In early June 2005 the *New York Times* confirmed the continuing strategy of global warming denial on the part of the Bush administration—despite its earlier acknowledgement of the problem. In his press briefing of 8 June 2005, White House Press Secretary Scott McClellan falsely claimed that the National Academies of Science holds that there are 'considerable uncertainties' regarding the science of climate change. At other times, the Bush administration has simply doctored evidence. One shocking disclosure found that the chief of staff for the White House Council of Environmental Quality, Philip A. Cooney, a former oil industry lobbyist with no scientific training, altered and adjusted descriptions of climate research in government climate reports. The *New York Times* reported that the changes 'tend[ed] to produce an air of doubt about findings that most climate experts say are robust' (*New York Times*, 8 June 2005). In many instances, the changes appeared in the final reports. Cooney resigned following the revelations, only to be hired the next day by ExxonMobil.

Shamefully, it appears that the Bush administration is globalizing its strategy of attacking the scientific data that demonstrates global warming. Shortly before the July 2005 meeting of the Group of Eight leaders in Gleneagles, Scotland, the national science academies of 11 countries released a forceful statement urging world governments to take immediate action to curb gas emissions tied to global warming (Joint Science Academies, 2005). Yet, as revealed by *The Observer* (19 June 2005), the Bush administration worked diligently in its preparation for the summit to 'undermine completely the science of climate change'. The Bush administration continued to deny that global warming existed and watered down G8 plans to combat climate change by altering the 'Gleneagles Plan of Action' to cast doubt on the science of global warming. Subsequent terrorist bombings on the London subway system diverted media attention away from the climate change problem, and the summit failed to substantially address the climate change issue.

Global warming deniers must doctor the evidence because significant new science that demonstrates the seriousness of climate change appears nearly every week. One particularly compelling analysis proved that oceans are warming considerably, a finding that demonstrates a 'stunning' correlation between ocean temperatures and atmospheric pollution (*Independent/UK*, 19 February 2005). Just two months later, a study headed by James Hansen found that the earth is absorbing much more heat than it is releasing, a validation of computer projections of global warming. Hansen described the results as a 'smoking gun' that verifies global warming (*Associated Press*, 29 April 2005). But such 'smoking guns' are largely one-day news stories removed from the context of scientific consensus over climate change and have thus yet to affect the US public or climate policy.

The right wing continues its successful propaganda campaign to dispute climate science, and the current presidential administration, despite warnings from its own scientists, gives no indication of honestly grappling with the policy implications of global warming. Until the public receives consistent and honest information regarding the overwhelming scientific consensus about climate change, it appears all to likely that the world's largest producer of greenhouse gases will continue its disastrous policies.

Notes

1   This article relies upon Spencer Weart's work, *The Discovery of Global Warming* (Harvard, 2003). Those interested in further exploration of the history of climate change research should read Weart's book, then move on to the extensive website he maintains. It is also titled 'The Discovery of Global Warming' and can be accessed at http://www.aip.org/history/climate.

References

Agrawala, S. & Andresen S. (2001) U.S. Climate Policy: Evolution and Future Prospects, *Energy and Environment* (Summer, 2001), pp. 117–137.
Boykoff, M. T. & Boykoff, J. M. (2004) Balance as bias: global warming and the US prestige press, *Global Environmental Change*, 14, pp. 125–136.
Crichton, M. (2004) *State of Fear* (New York: HarperCollins Publishers).
Environmental Working Group (2003) *Briefing: Luntz Memo on the Environment*. Online at: http://www.ewg.org/briefings/luntzmemo/.
Gelbspan, R. (1997) *The Heat is On: The High Stakes Battle over Earth's Threatened Climate* (New York: Addison-Wesley Publishing Company).
Gelbspan, R. (2004) *Boiling Point: How Politicians, Big Oil and Coal, Journalists, and Activists Are Fueling the Climate Crisis—and What We Can Do to Avert Disaster* (New York: Basic Books).

Guha, R. (2000) *Environmentalism: A Global History* (New York: Longman).
Immerwahr, J. (1999) *Waiting for a Signal: Public Attitudes toward Global Warming, the Environment and Geophysical Research* (New York: Public Agenda). Online at: http://www.agu.org/sci_soc/attitude_study.html.
Inhofe, J. (2003) The Science of Climate Change, Senate Floor Statement by US Senator James M. Inhofe (R-Okla) Chairman, Committee on Environment and Public Works, 28 July. Online at http://inhofe.senate.gov/floorspeeches.htm.
IPCC (2001) *Climate Change 2001: The Scientific Basis. Contribution of Working Group I to the Third Assessment Report of the IPCC*, ed. Houghton, J. T. et al. (Cambridge: Cambridge University Press). Online at www.ipcc.ch/pub/reports.htm.
Joint Science Academies (2005) Joint science academies' statement: Global response to climate change. Online at http://www.nationalacademies.org/morenews/20050607.html.
Kellogg, W. W. (1987) Mankind's impact on climate: the evolution of an awareness, *Climate Change*, 10, pp. 113–136.
Kennedy, D. (2001) An unfortunate U-turn on carbon, *Science*, 291, 30 March, p. 5513.
Kolbert, E. (2005) The climate of man—III, *The New Yorker*, 9 May.
Mathews, J. T. (2001) Estranged Partners, *Foreign Policy*, 127 (November/December), pp. 48–53.
Mazur, A. & Lee, J. (1993) Sounding the global alarm: environmental issues in the US national news, *Social Studies of Science*, 23, pp. 681–720.
McCright, A. M. & Dunlap, R. E. (2000) Challenging global warming as a social problem: an analysis of the conservative movement's counter claims, *Social Problems* 47(4), pp. 499–522.
Mooney, C. (2005) Some like it hot, *Mother Jones*, May/June.
Oreskes, N. (2004) The scientific consensus on climate change, *Science*, 3 December.
Paterson, M. (1996) *Global Warming and Global Politics* (London: Routledge).
Pew Research Center for People and the Press (2005) Beyond red vs. blue. Online at: http://people-press.org/reports/display.php3?PageID=948.
Ross, A. (1991) *Strange Weather: Culture, Science, and Technology in the Age of Limits* (New York: Verso).
Speth, J. G. (2004) *Red Sky at Morning: Americans and the Crisis of the Global Environment* (New Haven, CT & London: Yale University Press).
Toronto Conference (1988) The changing atmosphere: implications for global security, in Abrahamson (ed.) *The Challenge of Global Warming* (Washington, DC: Island Press).
Weart, S. R. (2003) *The Discovery of Global Warming* (Cambridge, MA: Harvard University Press).
Will, G. (2004) Crichton's villains are environmental hysterics, *Chicago Sun-Times*, 23 December.
WMO (1979) *Proceedings of the World Climate Conference*, Geneva, 12–13 February, World Meteorological Organization Report No. 53, Geneva, Switzerland.
WMO (1986) *Report of the International Conference on the Assessment of the Role of Carbon Dioxide and of other Greenhouse Gases in Climate Variations and Associated Impacts, Villach, Austria, 9–15 October 1985*, WMO Publication no. 661 (Geneva: World Meteorological Organization).
World Scientists' Call for Action (1997) Online at: http://www.ucsusa.org/ucs/about/page.cfm?pageID=1007.
World Scientists' Warning to Humanity (1992) Online at: http://www.ucsusa.org/ucs/about/page.cfm?pageID=1009.

Kevin C. Armitage is Visiting Assistant Professor in the Department of History and Program in American Studies at Miami University in Oxford, OH. He is the author of several essays and the forthcoming book on progressive conservation, *Knowing Nature: Nature Study and American Life, 1873–1923*.

The Globalization of Local Air Pollution

PETER BRIMBLECOMBE

It has become commonplace to remark that air pollution does not respect national boundaries. Accounts of acid rain or forest fire smoke serve to remind us of the need to address air pollution problems in an international context. Often pollutants that originate at a local scale are experienced at a regional or global level. Despite this awareness of the transport of local air pollution across great distances, the way in which local air pollution connects with changing emission, control methodologies and policy at a global scale are not always appreciated.

This paper will trace the increases in urban air pollution, which were characteristic of the twentieth century. However, it has not simply been a case of cities becoming polluted. Urban air pollution has increasingly taken on similar forms such that cities, which once experienced quite different types of pollution, have gradually converged to exhibit a remarkably universal atmospheric environment. Much of this similarity arises because air pollution everywhere increasingly derives from liquid fuels, mostly used in automobiles, mediated by atmospheric photochemistry. The homogeneous nature of air pollution should not be taken as reflecting a static situation, as the last century saw a wide range of novel pollutants and novel problems emerge.

In parallel there has been a convergence of health standards, formed from a generally agreed understanding of the effects of air pollution. This has led to a consistency in legislative concern and the public and political desire for improved air quality. The global nature of local air pollution has further meant that strategies for controlling it have become broadly similar everywhere. Monitoring networks and the way in which air pollution is reported to the public are increasingly derived using the same methodology. Emerging air pollution problems such as dust and forest fire smoke are not restricted to just one country and are widely experienced, most especially in tropics. Novel fuels such as biodiesel may become more widely used. Our indoor air is also polluted by consumer products, which derive from a homogeneous international marketplace. This homogeneity is consistent with lifestyles that are increasingly similar in urban environments worldwide.

Related to all this is the question of how the processes of the globalization and convergence are proceeding and result in all aspects of air pollution being international or global rather than reflecting peculiarly local characteristics.

Historical Origins of Local Air Pollution

In the past, and this can mean 500 or 100 years ago, the air pollution of cities took on an individual character. London made a transition to coal in the thirteenth century and this distinguished its atmosphere from that of the rest of that distant world. Combustion derived pollution was elsewhere derived from wood, but even here there were possibilities that it would be mixed in with the activities of local artisans. Thus these proto-industries added metallic elements and organic materials to wood smoke emissions. More regional aspects of geography also intervene. Thus cities of the Asia-Pacific coasts experienced the springtime dust loadings far back in time that mixed in with the purely urban pollution. In the last 100–200 years local air pollutants in South-East Asia were mixed with the smoke of forest fires driven either by the clearance activities of spice growing in the Indonesian Archipelago or the expansion of rubber plantations (Brimblecombe, 2005). In marine settings, sea-salt is an ever present aerosol that combines with pollutants from human activities.

This local character of early pollution led to local regulation. In medieval London special laws developed that referred to the emissions from specific trades, limeburners, blacksmiths and armourers (Brimblecombe, 1987). Early modern Europe developed a wealth of local regulatory arrangements (e.g. Fournel, 1805; Diederiks and Jeurgens, 1990). Mieck (1990) has argued that these numerous pollution decrees from the Middle Ages are essentially a response to single sources of what he terms *pollution artisanale* as distinct from the later and broader *pollution industrielle*, that characterized an industrializing world. In England early regulations became antiquated enough to inhibit progress in the nineteenth century (Bowler and Brimblecombe, 2000) because such localized *ad hoc* responses failed to allow a coherent approach to the regulation of emerging air pollution problems. A local approach to air pollution began to change with legislation such as the Alkali Acts (1863) in Britain which created a national agency, the Alkali

Inspectorate, to control pollution. Nationwide administration was strengthened under the Public Health Act (1885), which gave national guidance to the way smoke abatement should be handled by local government (Brimblecombe and Bowler, 1990). The globalization of regulatory action was also embedded in imperialism. The expanding industry of late nineteenth century India meant both British experts and British regulations were transferred to the colonies (Anderson, 1997; Brimblecombe, 2003b).

This increasing sense of the global nature of the problem was also reflected in an interest in what lessons might be learnt from experiences abroad. Germany's growing expertise (Schramm, 1990) attracted Victorian UK interest (e.g. Booth and Kershaw, 1904). Perhaps more broadly a real sense of impending globalization came with the British Foreign Office analysis: *Laws in Force in certain Countries in regard to the Emission of Smoke from Chimne* (HMSO, 1905).

Air Pollution of the Twentieth Century

By 1900 there was a sense of convergence. This was essentially driven by the increased energy consumption of cities that was generated by using fossil fuels (mostly coal) needed to provide a high density fuel for furnaces and steam engines. The steam revolution meant industry everywhere began to adopt common practices. By the early twentieth century in Europe and North America and to some extent the large cities of the colonies, urban air pollution was dominated by smoke and sulphur dioxide from coal burning.

Before the twentieth century, the notion that air pollution was a local phenomenon was reflected in the way pollution was described. London was called 'The Big Smoke' and Edinburgh was known as 'Auld Reekie'. Victorian Londoners called their pollution 'London Particular' or the fogs 'Pea Soupers'. In Glasgow, the public health official, Des Voeux, chose the word 'smog' to describe the pollution by combining the words smoke and fog. Today the word has completely globalized to the extent that it no longer refers to fogs at all and popularly refers to all air pollutants.

The twentieth century was to be dominated by problems associated with the automobile. Alice Hamilton (1869–1970) of Harvard University studied lead metabolism in the human body and was dismayed when Standard Oil began to put lead into gasoline in the 1920s (Uekoetter, 2003). Carbon monoxide was also studied, which led to an understanding of its effect on the oxygen-carrying capacity blood.

Volatile automotive fuels gave rise to a much more profound effect, which was first observed in Los Angeles. Here the dispersed structure of the city and failure of the public transport system meant the automobile was widely used. The booming economy, sea-breezes, a coastal mountain range and long hours of sunlight contributed to what soon became known as 'Los Angeles smog' during the Second World War.

The smog in Los Angeles did not come directly from the exhaust pipe as pollutants such as carbon monoxide and lead. Rather it was formed in the atmosphere. In this way Los Angeles smog was secondary rather than primary pollution. Haagen-Smit, a biochemist, realized that the smog was ozone produced from reactions of fuel vapour in the intense sunlight. Understanding these processes in the 1950s created the modern discipline of atmospheric chemistry, but the discovery had impacts well beyond scientific debate. The reactions in the atmosphere were relevant in the political domain as they constrained the management of air pollution in the late twentieth century. In particular, it made regulation more difficult because the pollution became separated from the sources of pollutants and was mediated by atmospheric chemistry.

In terms of our perception, the pollution was no longer visibly linked with a single source as it was in the days of the smoky factory chimney.

The peculiar nature of Los Angeles smog in the 1950s served to give it a local character. Despite the complexities of its origin, there were experiences that could be shared, but scientists called the new smog 'photochemical pollution', recognizing that such chemistry was universal and would not be restricted to Los Angeles. All that was required was the widespread use of volatile fuels, and sunlight. In the mid-1970s some bright dry summers saw high photochemical ozone concentrations in the UK and across Europe (Cox et al., 1975). The Los Angeles photochemical smog was globalized.

While Los Angeles smog was recognized by the 1950s, the type of pollution that characterized London for 700 years still remained. London had not managed to solve its air pollution problems in the first half of the twentieth century, although it had been fortunate in having few of the bad fogs that had characterized the Victorian era (Bernstein, 1975). The run of good luck ended with the Great Smog of 1952. The fog began on 5 December. Pollution accumulated under an inversion less than 100 m deep and within 12 hours a large number of people showed symptoms of respiratory illness. A week after the fog the Minister of Health revealed an increase to 4,703 compared with 1,852 the same period of the previous year, although the final number may have been three times larger than this (Brimblecombe, 2002).

This led to the UK Clean Air Act (1956) which tackled domestic smoke in addition to factory smoke through the creation of smokeless zones in cities. This meant people could not use coal in their homes, an affront to personal freedom which worried politicians of the time, who recognized that an improved environment may restrict our individual choice (Brimblecombe, 2002). Despite an enduring impression that the Clean Air Act was responsible for the profound improvement in London's air quality, recent appraisals have been more thoughtful, attributing reductions to burning cleaner fuels, especially the use of gas; tall stacks on power stations, and their relocation outside cities; and the decline of heavy industry (Brimblecombe, 1987, 2002; QUARG, 1992).

The specific actions under the Clean Air Act were detailed in memoranda on industrial premises, smoke control areas and chimney heights. This is reminiscent of the current European Directive 96/62 Air Quality Monitoring and Management where functional detail is embodied in daughter directives and position papers. It is now typical to find the important scientific detail that justifies legislation to be found in detailed supplementary documentation such as *Criteria Documents* in the US or *Position Papers* in the EU. In this way the development of the Clean Air Act has had important effects on the way legislation was framed in other countries and the US and EU, and exemplified approaches are increasingly widely adopted.

The classic air pollution problems of coal burning cities have gradually gone. Some cities in Turkey or China continued to burn coal in large quantities at the end of the twentieth century, but this has been increasingly replaced by gas in domestic and smaller scale industries. The old air pollution problems seem to have almost disappeared, but have been replaced by other more modern problems. Broadly the success with the control of the pollutants from coal has come about because the gross impact was from the primary pollutants. Emission control works very effectively with primary pollutants. A similar story can be told for these pollutants from the automobile. Removing lead from fuels reduced emissions, while an effectively operating catalytic converter reduces carbon monoxide emissions. However, this approach does not work so effectively for secondary pollutants. Here the sources and the resultant air pollution are mediated by atmospheric chemistry. Through the 1980s it became clear that the US Clean Air Act 1970 had not attained its goals. This became so serious that the act was amended and reinvigorated in 1990, with much improved results.

One important issue with secondary pollutants is that regulation must control air chemistry, rather than focusing simply on the emissions. This means that the clear relationships between emitted pollutants and the resultant air pollution break down and involve us in more complex strategies of air quality management in our cities. Air quality management involves assessment of emissions and modelling the chemistry along with decisions about how to reduce the pollutant emissions to achieve the most effective results (Elsom, 1992). There is often a good deal of flexibility in where emissions might be reduced to achieve the desired improvement in air quality, so social considerations can also be accounted for. However, air quality management is undeniably sophisticated and involves a high level of technical input. It is this kind of expertise that sometimes raises an element of concern among politicians and decision makers, especially when results of the modelling seem counter-intuitive. At times, lowering the pollutant emissions can actually raise the concentrations of the photochemical pollutants.

Globalizing International Standards

Despite the complexity, the fact that photochemical smog has now become globally so widespread has meant that control strategies have also become universalized. Increasingly, air quality management is seen as the appropriate strategy in approaching modern air pollution problems from cities such as Los Angeles or Mexico City with high petroleum use in automobiles. In the twenty-first century it seems that most cities experience air pollution that is increasingly derived in this way.

Along with the strategies for controlling air pollution, the standards we hope to attain have become more international or globalized. Initially individual countries set their own air pollution standards, though basing it on an international toxicological literature. However, in the 1980s the World Health Organization (WHO) published its *Air Quality Guidelines for Europe*, which had an influence that extended well beyond Europe. Its influence has been reinforced with more recent guidelines, making the WHO an important agent in unifying our approach to regulation. The documentation of the US Environmental Protection Agency was also influential. Recently the WHO guidelines have been revised, promising to have continuing influence. The EU, the UK and other states have done their own research and provide more recent updates. However, they are increasingly convergent. The same experts frequently serve on the panels that analyse data and lay out the reasoning behind air quality standards have tended to emerge everywhere.

Numerous international organizations foster the development of agreements regarding air pollution. Although often involving transboundary pollutant problems they nevertheless influence thinking on a more local scale. The most notable may be the continuing *Convention on Long-range Transboundary Air Pollution* which grew out of concerns over sulphur emissions in the 1960s. It led to the Convention being established in 1979. In 1964 the International Union of Air Pollution Prevention and Environmental Protection Associations was founded to represent environmental protection specialists across the private, public and voluntary sectors and continues to give unity the practical aspects of managing air pollution. Scientists group themselves in bodies such as the Commission on Atmospheric Chemistry and Global Pollution which was created in the late 1980s to confront concerns over rapid changes observed in the Earth's atmosphere. In Europe a two phase programme EUROTRAC (Transport and Chemical Transformation of Environmentally Relevant Trace Constituents in the Troposphere over Europe) ran from 1986 to 2002 with many projects relevant to air pollution on all scales. These groups give an enormous and effective sense of cohesion that has created internationally accepted protocols in managing air pollution.

In some ways one might argue that it is reasonable that health standards be international or global. After all people are the same everywhere, so surely the toxicology should be similar. However, it may well be that climatic conditions, especially temperature, could make people more or less sensitive to pollutants. There are also local behavioural issues, perhaps even diet and health status, that alter our response to air pollutants. Thus it remains necessary for governments to consider the national character of exposure when adapting international standards to the local situation. This is very likely to be important when we go beyond human health and consider, for example, agricultural or vegetation impacts. In addition, despite the convergence of pollution, most specifically in cities there are still local air pollutants that need special attention in terms of their health impact. Two very notable regional pollutants are the Aeolian dust of the Pacific Rim and the forest fires of South-East Asia.

Twenty-First Century Air Pollutants

In the twenty-first century, although emissions of the classic primary pollutants have often declined substantially, there is a wider range of pollutants of concern. Legislation has increasingly had to describe them in some detail. In Europe the development of the Directive on Air Quality Monitoring and Management presented a standardized list of pollutants to be covered by the daughter directives. National interests in specific pollutants were, in the end, limited in favour of broad regional agreements. Thus neither fluoride (of interest to France) nor 1,3 butadiene (of interest to Britain) were included.

One can argue over whether air pollution is getting better or worse, but there can be few doubts that it has changed dramatically. Often one pollution problem was solved, only to have a new one created, making the twentieth century one of huge transitions. The century started with primary smoke and sulphur dioxide from stationary sources using solid fuels. By the end of the century the atmosphere of most major cities were concerned about secondary photochemical air pollutants, where the volatile precursors and nitrogen oxides came from liquid fuels used in mobile sources. The transitions may continue. The importance of the diesel engine, particularly in Europe, has led to increasing amounts of fine diesel soot particles in urban atmospheres. This has become a particular worry now that we understand the key role fine particles play in the health effects of air pollutants. The special concern over suspended fine particulate material in the atmosphere arose from the work of Dockery et al. (1993) that showed a relation between daily mortality and the presence of fine particles. Thus diesel use emerged as a concern. The need to reduce greenhouse emissions has raised interest in the use of biofuels in automobiles; now a key element of European Union policy. However, there are fears that biofuels will give rise to higher nitrogen oxide emissions.

It is not only novel sources that might have to be considered as changes. Sulphur dioxide is now at such low concentrations in most cities that its effects are decoupled from those of particulate matter. Even in China, where fossil fuel use has grown to meet the requirements of vast industrial expansion, urban sulphur dioxide is increasingly kept in check. The older view, that sulphur dioxide and smoke interacted to affect health over long averaging times, has gone. This has been replaced by a concern over the exposure to short bursts (10–15 minutes) of sulphur dioxide, such that the vast improvements in Europe have still left us with a significant correlation between sulphur dioxide and health effects (Ayers, 1998).

At the end of the twentieth century there was a general view that air pollution in cities of the developed world, at least in the gross sense, was getting better and that in cities of the developing world it was getting worse. There are some obvious reasons for such a generalization, most especially the enormous expansion of industry and motor traffic that has come as a part of the growth of cities in the developing world. It is also true that the regulatory process and the focus on enforcement has been weak at times. However, this generalization ignores the global availability of control technologies and strategies for air pollution control. It is possible that the rapid transitions in pollutant emissions that have occurred here will have parallels in an equally rapid development of regulatory processes. This is not automatic, but there are signs that the governments of developing countries are showing a willingness to adopt more effective air pollution control measures. Thus, the concentrations of major air pollutants such as sulphur dioxide and particulates are very high in Beijing, yet the urban government is now able to show some evidence of improvement.

Thus far our discussion of air pollution has neglected pollution indoors. However, outdoor air does not necessarily reflect the exposure of individuals. Surveys in California, indicate that people spend 87% of their time indoors, 7% in enclosed transit and 6% outdoors. The time spent indoors increases among vulnerable groups such as the old, young and unwell. In addition some gender differences remain in some countries whereby women are more likely to spend more time in domestic settings and often polluted parts of the house (Boy et al., 2002), such as the kitchen. Here the levels of air pollution are often highest. Poorer people are vulnerable as they have a more limited choice of fuel or find it difficult to achieve adequate ventilation. Kerosene and gas contribute a less mutagenic PAH fraction than coal, firewood and cigarette smoke (Adonis and Gil, 2001).

There are a number of factors that have caused indoor air spaces to be more vulnerable to pollution in recent times. Energy conservation in cold countries imposes requirement for lower amounts of heating and has led to lower air exchange rates. Thus indoor concentrations are expected to be higher under very cold conditions when the exchange rates are low and the heating requirement is highest. The use of novel materials in the construction and furnishing of new buildings has introduced a range of compounds into the indoor environment. These have typically been organic compounds from simple carbonyls such as formaldehyde through to more complex compounds that originate from glues, paints and polymers. Carpets have been an especially problematic among a range of materials that 'outgas' (Brimblecombe and Cashmore, 2004).

There is also an issue of perception. The home is typically perceived as an essentially safe and unpolluted environment in comparison with the urban world outside it. Furthermore, governments have often found indoor air a problem to deal with, partially because it provokes the issue of personal freedom and the potential of numerous transactions in a regulatory sense. However, beyond this its regulation frequently crosses departmental boundaries, which makes administration especially difficult. It so often demands attention from a combination of departments of environment, housing, health, worker safety and even cultural heritage.

Although indoor air pollution might initially seen far from global in nature, we have to recognize that it is generated by processes that are often very similar. This is not to neglect the peculiarly regional characteristics exemplified by mosquito coils in the tropics, and some localized fuels, such as dung, or incense is widely used in some communities. However, many aspects of the indoor environment are becoming similar, because materials, solvents, coatings, fabrics that act as sources are produced for a global market.

Converging Lifestyles and Converging Pollution

Our lifestyles have a strong influence on air pollution. We have seen that urbanization and the choice of fuels is very important. In contemporary society the choice of interiors, domestic fuels and consumer products also increasingly influence the state of the air we breathe. As there is a convergence in our lifestyles, so pollution has become globally more homogeneous. It has proved simple to regulate the emissions from industry or to relocate it into rural areas as a way of reducing pollution. Controlling private emissions from cooking, heating or vehicle ownership has always been more difficult as it involves many transactions and inevitably curtails some aspect of individual freedom.

There are even more intricate effects of our changing lifestyle. The hot summer of 2003 saw a large number of excess deaths among the elderly people in France. Some blamed this on the heat while others blamed it on the pollutant ozone. It is not clear what the relative roles played by these external forces were, but there was widespread dismay at the social structure within France that exacerbated the effects. There is an increasing tendency for old people to live alone rather than in an extended family, and a desire for lengthy summer holidays both among families and the health professionals. This meant that in the urban centres, where elderly people suffered, there was little support for them in a nation that had gone on holiday. It is easy to dismiss this simplistic scenario as too journalistic to be credible, but it reminds us of a reality common throughout the world—our social structures are changing. The old and the vulnerable are frequently outside the structures we are left with, which can seriously exacerbate the health effects of air pollution.

Just as it was a challenge in the 1950s over the choice of coal as a fuel in British homes today freedom of choice is often at odds with policies regarding air pollution emissions. The dominance of the car as a source means that air pollution generation is now in the hands of the general public, most particularly the motorist. Engineers and administrators have often opted for technical fixes to this problem, including better fuels, engines or catalytic converters. However, sociological fixes are potentially more effective. It might be easier to solve air pollution problems in cities if their citizens did not wish to drive their cars so much. Traditionally it has been argued that such re-education, though perhaps effective, is too slow for the required pace of change.

Nevertheless we can see these types of social controls being implemented. In recent years Mayor Ken Livingstone introduced congestion charges in London. These were designed to control the vehicles entering the city, but have the potential to reduce air pollution (Beevers and Carslaw, 2005). There is much interest in this process everywhere, as few doubt the need to control automotive pollutants. There is little doubt, as in London, such restrictions will confront considerable public opposition (e.g. the recent defeat of a proposed scheme in Edinburgh, Scotland) Even those broadly in favour of pollution reduction find the impositions of such schemes objectionable and can raise numerous arguments against them: e.g. they are costly; they affect the poor more than the wealthy, the public transport system will not cope, etc. But the implementation and modest success of London's scheme has not been missed by policy makers around the world.

However, social fixes may not be as slow acting as has previously been imagined. Some industries manage to change public behaviour very rapidly. Fashions change quickly. Enormous campaigns create enthusiasm for new cars, but rarely aim at creating a parallel enthusiasm for public transport, in cities where it is poorly used. Indoor heating accounts for about a third of the UK carbon emission, but between 1970 and 2000 the average temperature in centrally heated homes increased from 14.5°C to 18.1°C. People now wear fewer clothes indoors in winter, yet if the fashion industry persuaded us to wear warmer clothes indoors a 1°C decrease in indoor temperatures could give a 2% reduction in UK carbon emissions.

Lifestyles have changed. The way in which we smoke, drink, clean and cook all influence indoor air pollution. New relationships with work, and most particularly the gender balance and in future the age of the working population affect our exposure to pollutants, especially those in the home and kitchen. Some indoor air pollution problems, such as sick building syndrome, raise important sociological issues. Health issues in sick buildings sometimes seem to affect the disenfranchised users of the interior air spaces most severely (Pommer et al., 2004). We can expect changes here as the social dynamic changes within buildings of the future.

Politicians, the Public, Science and Government

Air pollution is not a chemical or meteorological process that can be separated from its social or political context. The twentieth century saw the complexities of atmospheric science apparent in the political thinking. Climate change, El Nino, the ozone hole, acid rain and most recently global dimming have all sparked wide debate. This has encompassed politicians, activists and the wider public.

Over the last 50 years environmental activists have been an important part of the politics of air pollution. Their thinking may have originated with rather localized groups in the Victorian era, who had interests in sanitation, gardens or birds, but it was transformed to a global concern within organizations such as Friends of the Earth and more recently with a special focus on globalization by ATTAC. Here there is a desire to create an international movement for democratic control of financial markets and their institutions and to escape from the notions of a hierarchical structures or a geographical centre. Although not focused on environment specifically we can see the way in which globalization can be reinterpreted by public interest groups.

Mid-century thinking was much influenced by visions of catastrophe that had its origins in notions of religious apocalypse, perhaps science fiction (Brimblecombe, 2004) and ecological models (McCormack, 1989). By the late 1960s many writers were interpreting droughts, food shortage, pesticides, pollution, and population growth as portents of global doom. These notions can be widely found in many popular books of the time such as Ehrlich's *The Population Bomb* (1968), Alvin Toffler's *Future Shock* (1970), Gordon Rattray Taylor's *The Doomsday Book* (1972), and *Limits to Growth* (1972) At a more local level these are included in works such as Brian McConnell's *Britain in the Year 2000* (1970) and Edward Goldsmith's *Can Britain Survive?* (1971).

Although the decades that followed saw more focus on specific issues, the continuing link between the environment and peace and the underlying importance of global catastrophe remained. Such visions received special emphasis with the increasing understanding of the importance of rising carbon dioxide concentrations and global warming. The environmental movement aimed to raise awareness of the importance of these global changes and promoted lifestyles that seemed more ecologically sensitive (Porritt and Winner, 1988).

The wide array of environmental threats and the subtle nature of their origin often left the public confused. Politicians found the scientific debate that surrounded these issues equally confusing. Nevertheless the environment was increasingly seen as an important part of the education system, but public concern has not always been matched by public understanding. However, a general sense of a continued threat to the environment remains and reinforced by an ease of access to graphic information through the media and more recently the internet. The importance of involving the public in political decision making is a particular characteristic of recent decades. Initially public participation was stressed by environmental activists, but ultimately it has been incorporated into the broader political thinking.

This concern has meant that contemporary air pollution management frequently embodies the desire to report air pollution concentrations to the public. The data has often been received with little enthusiasm and lots of mistrust (Bickerstaff and Walker, 2001). Some of this arises simply in the same way as we do not trust any government statistic or forecast. However, we need to consider that air pollution data is complex and refers to a range of chemicals most people have not heard of, expressed in concentration units that are unfamiliar. The public often feel that air pollution data is an attempt to blind them with science. The increasing desire to report air pollution data at all has convinced many people that things must be getting worse.

As the social landscape has changed, so has the administrative. The huge professionalization so evident during the Victorian period has ensured an increasing importance of expertise in government and the regulation of environmental issues (Brimblecombe, 2003a). Expertise is now an expectation of administrators within government, such that we increasingly find those working to improve air quality are well trained in the technical background required for air pollution control. Training has thus become globalized, with a small group of core text books, often in English, being especially well known.

Despite a growing level of technical expertise, the interface between science and policy is not particularly comfortable for politicians. The complexity of modern air chemistry is still difficult for politicians to grasp as it goes well beyond what could be immediately expected as part of general scientific knowledge. This is especially problematic given the increasing importance of secondary air pollution problems where the pollutants can easily become detached from their sources. Nevertheless few politicians would risk claiming that they take no cognizance of scientific advice. Ultimately, they may fail to understand it or choose to ignore it. The reasons why politicians ignore the advice of their analysts can stem from their different roles and personalities. Policy makers are expected to be decisive so they like advice that has universal applicability and is efficient. Absolutisms and clear and definitive answers that ignore uncertainty are preferred. By contrast scientists often feel misgivings about offering opinions completely free of doubt and are locked into the notions of probable explanations.

Politics traditionally moves slowly, and air pollution issues are frequently debated over very long periods of time before there is action. The Clean Air Act 1956 was the result of four years' work after the London Smog of 1952, but it had a legislative history that went back into the nineteenth century (Ashby and Anderson, 1981). The creation of the required clean air zones, after this Act, was often slow even where there was a desire to create them. Fortunately, in the modern world even the legislative process seems to be speeding up. The provisions of the EC Directive Air Quality Monitoring and Management in 1996 had to include the newly emerging science of fine particulate matter (often from diesels) that developed in the early 1990s. This work was so new that successive drafts and papers had to continually change the way particulate matter was referred to as: 'suspended particulate matter' (EC Council Directive 96/62/EC, 27 September 1996), 'fine suspended particulate matter' (EC Open procedure 96/C 41/13) and 'PM10 and PM2.5' (EC Proposed Directive COM(97) 8 August 1997).

Rapid decision making is important in situations in times of change, especially where new pollutants emerge. In terms of local air pollution, the increase in diesel particles above is a good example. Rapid decisions can be hampered because the novelty of the issue makes it difficult to grasp in the early stages. At first the subtle issue of particles that were fine enough to reach the alveoli deep in the lung were hard understand. The fact that they were called

PM2.5 rather than something striking such as 'killer particles' diminished their relevance to politicians and the public alike. Problems need to seem an immediate and obvious threat, which has meant that the important emerging problems of secondary organic pollutants, dust and forest fire smoke can easily evaporate from political agendas and democratic structures have problems coping with long-term (and perhaps geographically distant) issues such as global warming which take place over many decades. Climate change and sea level rise are notable century-long processes driven by carbon dioxide emissions that will far outlast individual political careers. It is also noticeable that health issues feature prominently in political decision making, while broader issues of the environment, aesthetics or cultural landscapes are more difficult to bring to the top of political agendas.

Environmental movements have suffered from similar tensions between local and global issues. They have often tried to engage with the public through the notion: 'think globally act locally'. This is captivating, but it does not always alleviate the tensions between local campaigners and those with more strategic interests. Some of the most effective campaigns have often been those that have addressed very specific local issues, such as plans for factories, the location of local waste tips, or the routing of new roads.

Recently the global change debate has been aided by interest in a win–win or no-regrets relationship with local air pollution problems. Air pollution models can be used together with energy system models to study the impacts of climate change mitigation strategies on air pollution (Syri et al., 2002). Concomitant local emission reductions may improve human health, reduce corrosion of materials, and reduce damage to vegetation partly through less acid rain and of lower concentrations of tropospheric ozone. Thus co-benefits mean that the economic gains that accrue are greater than those attributable to greenhouse gas reduction alone. This can be seen as part of the widening importance of carbon-neutral policies as 'best practice' at urban level. This link between local improvements and efforts to achieve goals that are more distant in time and space can make them politically more palatable.

Conclusions

This paper has stressed the global nature of air pollution, even that which originates at a local level. It sees a convergence of many elements of the air pollution problem as we enter the twenty-first century. The formation, control and perception of air pollutants has become increasingly similar across the world. Our transport, agriculture, material wealth, social structure and attitudes to work and gender have many similarities that they lacked in the past. The individual ownership of automobiles has widened responsibility for air pollution. This has helped ensure it has increasingly common features.

Air pollution that emerged in the twentieth century is more complex than that which dominated cities in the past. It no longer necessarily derives from single and obvious sources such as the smoky factory chimney. It is often invisible and more importantly its source may be far from obvious. In the case of photochemical smog it derives from a wide range of sources and is transformed by the action of sunlight and air chemistry into a new and resistant form of air pollution. Solving modern air pollution problems can involve detailed study, analysis and modelling, so seeming removed from the satisfyingly direct approaches of the past. The lack of apparent connections and the emergence of new and more subtle pollution problems are often hard for politicians and policy makers to bring before the public. It must at times seem politically expedient to ignore them, especially where they are distant in time and space.

Understandings of pollution at a regional and global level and on long time scales demand international agreements. Although we can hardly regret the passing of the old localized forms of air pollution, there is a danger that *globalization of local air pollution* may ultimately weaken the power of local concerns. It favours the actions of distant bureaucracies out of tune with local situations. Local pollution may still have important distinctions that are worth identifying. Even major environmental groups can have difficulty operating at very local levels. Nevertheless in the age of the internet the experiences of very small pressure groups can rapidly spread. There are advantages in considering indigenous knowledge and appreciating local experience of air pollution in improving air quality. Local perceptions are often satisfyingly intuitive and contrast with global views of air pollution that demand trust in remote administrative structures.

It is said that pollution can be regarded as 'matter out of place'—this takes on a new meaning when we think in the global context.

References

Adonis, M. & Gil, L. (2001) Indoor air pollution in a zone of extreme poverty of metropolitan Santiago, Chile, *Indoor and Built Environment*, 10(3–4), pp. 138–146.
Anderson, M. R. (1997) The conquest of smoke: legislation and pollution in colonial Calcutta, in Arnold, D. & Guha, R. (eds) *Nature, Culture and Imperialism* (Oxford: Oxford University Press).
Ashby, E. & Anderson, M. (1981) *The Politics of Clean Air* (Oxford: Clarendon).
Ayers, J. G. (1998) Health effects of gaseous air pollutants, pp. 1–20 in Hester, R. E. & Harrison, R. M. (eds) *Air Pollution and Health* (London: The Royal Society of Chemistry).
Beevers, S. D. & Carslaw, D. C. (2005) The impact of congestion charging on vehicle emissions in London, *Atmospheric Environment*, 39(1), pp. 1–5.
Bernstein, H. T. (1975) The mysterious disappearance of Edwardian London fog, 1(1), pp. 189–206.
Bickerstaff, K. & Walker, G. (2001) Public understandings of air pollution: the 'localisation' of environmental risk, *Global Environmental Change—Human and Policy Dimensions*, 11, pp. 133–145.
Booth, W. H. & Kershaw, J. B. C. (1904) *Smoke Prevention and Fuel Economy-based on the German work of E. Schmatolla* (London: A. Constable & Co.).
Bowler, C. & Brimblecombe, P. (2000) Control of air pollution in Manchester prior to the Public Health Act, 1875, *Environment and History*, 6, pp. 71–98.
Boy, E., Bruce, N. & Delgado, H. (2002) Birth weight and exposure to kitchen wood smoke during pregnancy in rural Guatemala, *Environmental Health Perspectives*, 110(1), pp. 109–114.
Brimblecombe, P. (1987) *The Big Smoke* (London, Methuen).
Brimblecombe, P. (2002) The great London smog and its immediate aftermath, pp. 182–195 in Williamson, T. (ed.) *London Smog 50th Anniversary* (Brighton: NSCA).
Brimblecombe, P. (2003a) Emergence of the sanitary inspector in Victorian Britain, *The Journal of the Royal Society for the Promotion of Health*, 123, pp. 182–195.
Brimblecombe, P. (2003b) Origins of smoke inspection in Britain (circa 1900), *Applied Environmental Science and Public Health*, 1, pp. 55–62.
Brimblecombe, P. (2004) Die Apokalypse im Nebel. Der Londoner Smog im späten 19. Jahrhundert, in Uekoetter, F. & Hohensee, J. (eds) *Wird Kassandra heiser? Beitraege zu einer Geschichte der 'falschen Öko-Alarme'* (Stuttgart: Steiner).
Brimblecombe, P. (2005) History of early forest fire smoke in S.E. Asia, pp. 385–396 in Sem, G. J. et al. (eds) *History and Reviews of Aerosol Science* (Mt. Laurel, NJ: American Association for Aerosol Research).
Brimblecombe, P. & Bowler, C. (1990) Air pollution in York 1850–1900, pp. 182–195 in Brimblecombe P. & Pfister, C. (eds) *The Silent Countdown* (Heidelberg: Springer-Verlag).
Brimblecombe, P. & Cashmore, M. (2004) Indoor air pollution, *Journal de Physique*, 6, pp. 209–221.
Cox, R. A., Eggleton, E. J., Derwent, R. G., Lovelock, J. E. & Pack, D. H. (1975) Long-range transport of photochemical ozone in north-western Europe, *Nature*, 218, pp. 118–221.
Diederiks, H. & Jeurgens, C. (1990) Environmental policy in 19th century Leiden, pp. 167–181 in Brimblecombe, P. & Pfister, C. (eds) *The Silent Countdown* (Berlin: Springer-Verlag).

Dockery, D. W., Pope, C. A., Xu, X. P., Spengler, J. D., Ware, J. H., Fay, M. E., Ferris, B. G. & Speizer, F. E. (1993) An association between air-pollution and mortality in 6 United-States cities, *New England Journal of Medicine*, 329, pp. 1753–1759.

Elsom, D. M. (1992) *Atmospheric Pollution* (Oxford: Blackwell).

Fournel, F. (1805) *Traite du Voisinage* (Paris: Ganery, Rondonneau & Dufresne).

HMSO (1905) *Laws in Force in certain Countries in regard to the Emission of Smoke from Chimneys* (London: HMSO).

McCormack, J. (1989) *The Global Environmental Movement* (London: Belhaven Press).

Mieck, I. (1990) Reflections on a typology of historical pollution: complementary conceptions, pp. 73–80 in Brimblecombe, P. & Pfister, C. (eds) *The Silent Countdown* (Berlin: Springer-Verlag).

Pommer, L., Fick, J., Sundell, J., Nilsson, C., Sjostrom, M., Stenberg, B. & Andersson, B. (2004) Class separation of buildings with high and low prevalence of SBS by principal component analysis, *Indoor Air*, 14(1), pp. 16–23.

Porritt, J. & Winner, D. (1988) *The Coming of the Greens* (London: Fontana).

QUARG (1992) *Urban Air Quality in the United Kingdom* (Bradford: Department of the Environment).

Schramm, E. (1990) Experts in the smelter smoke debate, pp. 196–209 in Brimblecombe, P. & Pfister, C. (eds) *The Silent Countdown* (Heidelberg: Springer-Verlag).

Syri, S., Karvosenoja, N., Lehtila, A., Laurila, T., Lindfors, V. & Tuovinen, J. P. (2002) Modeling the impacts of the Finnish Climate Strategy on air pollution, *Atmospheric Environment*, 36(19), pp. 3059–3069.

Uekoetter, F. (2004) The merits of the precautionary principle, pp. 119–153 in De Puis, M. (ed) *Smoke and Mirrors* (New York: University of New York Press).

Peter Brimblecombe is Professor in Atmospheric Chemistry at the School of Environmental Sciences, University of East Anglia. He is also Senior Executive Editor of *Atmospheric Environment* and on the boards of *Chemosphere, Idojaras, Journal of Cultural Heritage and Environment International*. His research work on solubility of atmospheric gases, thermodynamics of atmospheric electrolytes, air pollutant damage to materials, and the history of air pollution is widely published in academic books and journals.

FORUM: GLENEAGLES, KYOTO AND GLOBAL WARMING

The Gleneagles G8 Summit and Climate Change: A Lack of Leadership

JAN OOSTHOEK

> While uncertainties remain in our understanding of climate science, we know enough to act now to put ourselves on a path to slow and, as the science justifies, stop and then reverse the growth of greenhouse gasses...
>
> Around 2 billion people lack modern energy services. We need to work with our partners to increase access to energy...
>
> The World Bank will take a leadership role in creating an new framework for clean energy and development, including investment and financing.
> *The Gleneagles Communiqué*, G8 Meeting 2005, Scotland

When the G8 leaders met in Scotland in July 2005 one of the issues at the top of the agenda was global warming. More than a year before the summit, Tony Blair summarized well the importance of the issue when he described it as 'long-term the single most important issue we face as a global community' (The Climate Group, 2004). Even the Pentagon has suggested that 'The risk of abrupt climate change... should be elevated beyond a scientific debate to a US national security concern' (Schwartz & Randall, 2003, p. 2).

Seen in this light the result of the Gleneagles G8 meeting has been disappointing and can be summarized as 'business as usual'. The urgency of the situation, as recognized in the statements above, was watered down in the final communiqué of the meeting, although it recognized 'that climate change is a long-term and serious challenge' (G8, 2005). In addition it failed to stress that present climate change is very much the product of human activity. Instead, the G8 statement attributes a considerable part of global temperature increase to natural variations. That is very worrying since many climatologists believe that we should be well on our way towards the next glaciation (see Ruddiman, 2005). Nevertheless, the G8 leaders acknowledged that humans probably contribute to some extent to global warming and that for this reason greenhouse gas emissions should be stabilized, just as a precaution. An emphasis has been put on the development of more energy-efficient and new technologies to stabilize emissions. Furthermore, the communiqué puts much emphasis on the economic development of poor countries in order to cope with the effects of global warming: 'As we work on our own adaptation strategies, we will work with the developing countries on building capacity to help them improve their resilience and integrate adaptation goals into sustainable development strategies'. An additional aim set in Gleneagles is to give billions of people in developing countries access to modern energy services. This suggests that economic development is seen as the recipe to deal with the environmental impacts caused by global warming. It looks like a licence for unchecked global economic expansion.

Climate Change Language

Over the past 15 years the climate change language in G8 communiqués has come full circle. In the early 1990s, the then G7 recognized human-related global warming and climate change as a serious problem. They also acknowledged that scientific uncertainty should be 'no excuse to postpone actions'. The prescription for combating global warming and environmental problems in general was economic growth, the free market, and democratic systems to ensure proper accountability. The exchange of scientific data and the development of alternative technologies were also seen as key factors in dealing with global warming (Sandalow, 2005).

Statements to this extent continued until 1997 when the tone of the communiqué of the Denver G8 summit changed dramatically under the influence of the publication of the second assessment of the Intergovernmental Panel on Climate Change (IPCC, 1995). It recognized that human-induced global warming is a reality: 'overwhelming scientific evidence links the build-up of greenhouse gasses in the atmosphere to changes in the global climate system'. The communiqué further stressed that drastic action to reduce greenhouse emissions was needed in the decades to come. High hopes were pinned on the third Conference of the Parties later that year in Kyoto, to come up with a timetable and a plan for drastic action (Sandalow, 2005).

During the 1998 G8 meeting in Birmingham the first cracks appeared in the unity displayed the year before. The group repeated that it recognized global climate change as 'the greatest threat to future prosperity' and it continued that they 'welcomed the recent signature of the [Kyoto] protocol by some of us and confirm the intention of the rest of us to sign it in the next year' (Sandalow, 2005). Although the US initially signed up to the Kyoto Protocol, it indicated in 2001 that it would not ratify the agreement. This means that the US is not bound to meet its agreed target to reduce greenhouse emissions by 7 per cent by 2012.

Full Circle

In the years following the Birmingham G8 meeting the language with regard to global warming remained neutral and repeated the group's commitment to deal with global warming. In 2003 the protection of biodiversity was added to the environmental agenda and linked to global warming. The following year an action plan for encouraging science and technology for sustainable development was accepted by the G8 (Sandalow, 2005). This almost squeezed out the issue of global warming and greenhouse gas emissions and by doing so it had become a development issue. The G8 came full circle when economic development was reinforced during this year's meeting in Scotland in July, and signalled a return to the emphasis on economic and technological development of the early 1990s.

One of the fundamental obstacles to G8 engagement with global warming is that the most industrialized countries are reliant on that key driver of climate change: fossil fuels, in particular oil. The G8 countries produce just under 50 per cent of global carbon dioxide emissions and are home to most of the world's large oil companies (Blair, 2004). Russia, which has the biggest oil reserves of all G8 countries, depends on its revenues from oil exports for its economic survival. This dependence of the G8 countries on fossil fuels and the attached economic interests makes it hard for them to radically change their ways and become less oil dependent.

However, there is probably a way out of the carbon trap, even with a continued reliance on fossil fuels. The G8 leaders are right about investment in energy-efficient and new technologies but that has to go hand in hand with a clear carbon reduction policy. At the moment the G8 are not committed to set clear targets and to enshrine these in international treaties, which is hard to understand. Treaties with clear targets for the reduction of CFCs in the 1980s proved highly successful and led to a phasing out of this harmful gas within a decade. If that had not happened the ozone layer would have deteriorated even faster and CFCs would have overtaken carbon dioxide as the most important greenhouse gas by the early 1990s (Cicerone, 2000).

Corporate and Local Action

It has been argued that there were good alternatives for CFCs available and that these do not so clearly exist for CO2-producing activities. That argument is weak, however, since new technologies that will reduce carbon dioxide emissions are becoming available. A good example is a technology that combines the capture of carbon dioxide emissions from coal power plants and oil refineries and their subsequent injection into geological formations for long-term storage (Socolow, 2005). More recently the Tennessee Valley Authority announced that it will install in one of its coal fired power plants a bioreactor containing blue-green algae that will remove CO2 from flue gas produced by the plant (Di Justo, 2005). These techniques could significantly contribute to slowing down the rise of atmospheric CO2 concentrations.

That the corporate world and local authorities are prepared to invest in these technologies becomes clear from mounting criticism — by big companies, city councils and regional governments in the US and other industrialized countries — that something has to be done. Recently General Electric announced it will increase investment in the development of cleaner technology to $1.5 billion per annum by 2010.[1] In May the local authorities of more than 140 North American cities promised at a meeting in Seattle that they will cut greenhouse emissions by 7 per cent in order to meet Kyoto targets (Pearce, 2005). These are only a few examples of local and corporate initiatives around the globe which give hope that the problem of greenhouse-gas emission can eventually be brought under control.

Leadership?

As the above discussion clearly illustrates, what is most urgently needed to support long-term investment in carbon-neutral technologies is political leadership, especially by the G8 countries. Furthermore, if the developed countries fail to take action, the political leadership of the developing world will not see the need to take drastic action either. In this scenario economic development can never be the solution to the problem of global warming. The G8 leaders are right about investing in energy efficiency and new technologies as well as poverty eradication, but this is not sufficient. A lot of trouble could be saved if the G8 leaders were to set international standards and legally enforceable limits on greenhouse-gas emissions. Eventually leadership by the most industrialized countries, not least the US, becomes absolutely necessary to reverse global warming. Politicians can no longer simply 'default' on their responsibility.

Note

1   See the Ecomagination website: http://ge.ecomagination.com (accessed 9 October 2005).

References

Blair, T. (2004) A year of huge challenges, *The Economist*, 29 December.
Cicerone, R. J. (2000) Human forcing of climate change: Easing up on the gas pedal, *Proceedings National Academy of Sciences*, 97(19), pp. 10304–10306.
The Climate Group (2004) Speech by Prime Minister Tony Blair, 27 April, http://www.theclimategroup.org/tcg_pmspeech.pdf (accessed 9 October 2005).
Di Justo, P. (2005) Blue-green acres, *Scientific American*, 293(3), pp. 10–11.
IPCC (1995) *Second Assessment Climate Change* (Geneva: IPCC).
Pearce, F. (2005) Cities lead the way to a greener world, *New Scientist*, 186(2502), pp. 8–9.
Ruddiman, W. F. (2005) How did humans first alter global climate?, *Scientific American*, 292(3), pp. 34–41.
Sandalow, D. (2005) *G8 Summit Leaders' Statements Climate Change Language, 1990–2004* (Washington: The Brookings Institution).
Schwartz, P. & Randall, D. (2003) *An Abrupt Climate Change Scenario and Its Implications for United States National Security* (Washington: DOD).
Socolow, R. H. (2005) Can we bury global warming?, *Scientific American*, 293(1), pp. 39–45.

Jan Oosthoek is a Visiting Fellow in the School of Historical Studies at the University of Newcastle upon Tyne. His work encompasses many aspects of environmental and world history, including pollution history, land management, environmental globalizations and environmental policy making. He is at present Vice-president of the European Society for Environmental History.

Views of Kyoto and Beyond: Interviews with Herman Daly and Jonathan Lash

NANCY BAZILCHUK

The Kyoto Protocol, the international agreement that sets binding limits on greenhouse gas emissions, finally came into effect on 16 February 2005, nearly eight years after it was first negotiated and without the participation of the globe's largest greenhouse gas producer, the United States.

While the protocol was envisioned as a first step towards more substantive emissions reductions, few would have predicted how badly the effort has foundered, especially after 2001, when President George W. Bush withdrew the support and involvement of the US. As the nations of the world again convene to look beyond Kyoto, what could be done to make a future agreement better, given the difficulties that the Kyoto Protocol faced?

Jonathan Lash, president of the World Resources Institute, a Washington think-tank, says the world needs a far stronger agreement than what was negotiated in Kyoto if it is ever to get climate change under control — and that requires using somewhat unconventional approaches to involve the US. But Herman E. Daly, a professor at the University of Maryland's School of Public Policy, says the world should forget about negotiating a new Kyoto. Instead, he says, give the power to charge the real price of burning fossil fuels to an unlikely candidate: OPEC.

Both Lash and Daly agree that action is imperative. 'The science is pretty clear,' Lash said. Citing research by Pacala and Socolow (2004), Lash said that avoiding catastrophic climate change 'requires not tinkering at the edges, but significant changes.'

Where Businesses Go, Government Will Follow

In America, where the dollar can speak louder than partisan politics, Lash and his staff at the World Resources Institute think that getting businesses to acknowledge the problem of global climate change will eventually force the US government to take seriously climate change, and return to the international negotiating table. Lash is no stranger to government from the inside, having served from 1993 to 1999 as co-chairman of the President's Council on Sustainable Development, a group of US government, business, labour, civil rights, and environmental leaders that developed recommendations for strategies to promote sustainable development. He has also served as a member of advisory groups to the administrator of the US Environmental Protection Agency and the US Trade Representative.

While President George W. Bush simply does not want to acknowledge that climate change is a problem, Lash says that denial will be more and more difficult to make as companies across the US make business decisions that assume a carbon-limited world.

To this end, WRI has been working with multinational corporations to help them see the business advantages of proactively addressing climate change. The most public success to date was announced in May 2005, when General Electric's CEO, Jeffrey Immelt, held a press conference with Lash to announce a new program called 'Ecomagination', which will significantly expand GE's investments in and sales of climate-friendly technologies and services (Ignatius, 2005). GE has operations in more than 100 countries, with revenues in excess of $150 billion a year.

Immelt pledged to double the company's investments in research and development of cleaner technology by 2010, bringing its annual investment to $1.5 billion — or about what the US government currently allots for the same sort of research. The company has also pledged to double its revenues from the sales of green products and services — from $10 billion in 2004 to at least $20 billion in 2010. At the same time the company says it will reduce its greenhouse gas emissions 1 percent by 2012 as compared to 2004. In the absence of this pledge, the company's projected growth would have led to a 40 percent increase in emissions during the same time period (General Electric, 2005).

When introducing the program, Immelt acknowledged the importance of being proactive to solve environmental problems. But he was also clear about the company's motives: 'We are going to solve tough customer and global problems and make money doing it' (General Electric, 2005).

GE may be the largest company to embrace a company strategy to limit greenhouse gas emissions, but it is by no means alone. A number of other large multinational companies have taken similar steps, including DuPont, IBM, and Alcoa. American cities and numerous state governments have adopted voluntary emissions reductions, and in October 2003 the Chicago Climate Exchange officially opened for trade in greenhouse gases — all in the absence of official involvement from the US government.

'This is a big step' for a company or a government to take, Lash said, 'to realize that climate change is such a big trend and that carbon constraints are absolutely going to shape tomorrow's markets — so that they have to have products that will respond to tomorrow's markets. Think what they could do if we created policy incentives that increase the benefits for them.'

These voluntary actions are laudable, Lash said, but in the end the goal must be to involve the US in future international negotiations. While international cooperation has stalled, China is building the equivalent of 25 new, large coal-fired power plants a year, which means the country will outstrip the US's coal consumption by 2010 and will exceed it by 50 percent by 2030 (International Energy Agency, 1999).

'It is absolutely of the first importance to get the US re-engaged,' Lash said. 'Taking meaningful steps to reduce emissions in an international process simply can't happen if the US isn't participating. It is politically too risky and too difficult to move without the US.'

Forget Kyoto. Think Riyadh

Daly, an economist, says that solving the problem of global climate change requires a radically different approach to economic growth. Fundamental to Daly's paradigm is the transformation of the economy so that the rate of all natural resource consumption is matched to the ability of the ecosystem to absorb the wastes from that use (Daly, 1996, 2005). This approach is grounded in Daly's experience as senior economist in the World Bank's environment department from 1988 to 1994, where he helped develop sustainable development guidelines.

From this viewpoint, Daly says, the price of fossil fuels absolutely must be paired with the costs of discharging wastes, primarily CO_2. The Kyoto Protocol, the world's first timid effort to attempt this, failed miserably because nations could not reach an agreement on the international distribution of CO_2 emission rights.

The solution to this problem may be 'a far reach', he concedes, but is workable: give OPEC the right to collect 'sink rents', or a valuation of the capacity of the atmosphere to absorb the CO_2 from fossil fuels (Daly, 2001). Daly says OPEC could fold the cost into prices at the source, when petroleum is first sold.

Adopting this approach would require increasing OPEC's monopoly power, as it does not now have a monopoly on petroleum or on fossil fuels. Nor does OPEC own the rights to emit pollution to the atmosphere. To address this, Daly says, OPEC would have to accept the role of a global fiduciary, distributing the income from the sink rents to address inequities between the developed and developing countries. If OPEC were to adopt this role, other petroleum producers such as Norway might be willing to join the cartel, which would both increase its monopoly control over petroleum and help in OPEC's fiduciary role (Daly, 2001, p.9).

OPEC already has a mechanism for distributing funds, the OPEC Fund for International Development, which could be expanded to include sink rents. This new income could be dedicated to global sustainable development in poor countries, particularly investments in renewable energy and energy efficiency.

Another benefit of this approach, Daly says, is that it excludes no one, whereas the Kyoto Protocol effectively excluded developing countries because of fairness issues. Excluding developing countries 'undermines the prospects for accomplishing the goal of the treaty, namely limitation of global greenhouse gas emissions to a more sustainable level', he says. With OPEC in charge, 'the South, as well as the North, would have to face the discipline of higher petroleum prices in the name of efficiency, but the South would, in the name of fairness receive a disproportionate share of the sink rents' (Daly, 2001, p. 8).

The resulting increased cost for petroleum would also encourage efficient use of existing resources, but as a downside would encourage the use of non-petroleum fossil fuels like coal, he says. To counteract this trend, nations would have to enact legislation limiting emissions from coal (Daly, 2001, p. 12).

Daly recognizes that the task of distributing money to developing countries represents an ethical responsibility that countries might be unwilling to cede to OPEC, and that OPEC itself may not want. However, 'the obvious alternative to such a global fiduciary authority has already failed', he says. 'The inability to reach an agreement on international distribution of CO_2 emission rights was the rock on which Kyoto foundered' (Daly, 2001, p. 9).

Daly concedes that the ideal would be a true international agreement that covers all fossil fuels, rather than a monopoly-based restriction imposed by a cartel, and only on petroleum. But, he argues, Western countries have clearly shown that they are unwilling to adopt limitations on GDP growth rates that would result from a broad-ranging international limit on greenhouse gas emissions. 'The conceptual clarity and moral resources are simply lacking in the leadership of these countries', he says (Daly, 2001, p. 12).

OPEC may also lack the moral clarity necessary to undertake this role, Daly says, but accepting the task involves an element of self-interest — the responsibility could increase the cartel's legitimacy, enabling it to solidify its power.

If the world is ever to truly develop in a sustainable way, then countries will have to accept ecosystem-based limits, he says.

'Petroleum is the logical place to begin. And OPEC is the major institution in a position to influence the global throughput of petroleum.

'Maybe the whole idea is just a utopian speculation. But given the post-Kyoto state of disarray and the paucity of policy suggestions, I do believe that it is worth initiating a discussion of this possibility' (Daly, 2001, p. 13).

References

Daly, H. E. (1996) *Beyond Growth: The Economics of Sustainable Development* (Boston, MA: Beacon Press).
Daly, H. E. (2001) Sustainable development and OPEC. Invited paper, *OPEC and the Global Energy Balance: Towards a Sustainable Energy Future*, Vienna, Austria. Available from: http://www.hubbertpeak.com/daly/OPECsustdev.pdf [Accessed 4 October 2005].
Daly, H. E. (2005) Economics in a full world, *Scientific American*, 293(3), pp.100–107.
General Electric (2005) *Ecomagination*. Fairfield, CT. Available at http://ge.ecomagination.com/@v = 051205_1515@/index.html (accessed 26 September 2005).
International Energy Agency (1999) *Coal in the Energy Supply of China. Report of the Coal Industry Advisory Board.* Paris: International Energy Agency. Available at http://www.iea.org/textbase/nppdf/free/1990/coalchina99.pdf (accessed 4 October 2005).
Ignatius, D. (2005) Corporate green, *The Washington Post*, May 11, p.A17.
Pacala, S. & Socolow, R. (2004) Stabilization wedges: solving the climate problem for the next 50 years with current technologies. *Science*, 305, pp.968–972.

Nancy Bazilchuk is a lecturer at the Norwegian University of Science and Technology in Trondheim, and a freelance environmental and science journalist. Her publications have appeared in *New Scientist*, *Frontiers in Ecology and the Environment*, and *Conservation in Practice*. She has been a Knight Science Journalism Fellow at the Massachusetts Institute of Technology (1996–1997) and has won a number of American science writing awards, including the AAAS Westinghouse Science Journalism Award.

Fueling Injustice: Globalization, Ecologically Unequal Exchange and Climate Change

J. TIMMONS ROBERTS & BRADLEY C. PARKS

Introduction: Pollutions of Poverty and Wealth

The globalization of economic production fundamentally reshapes how a 'fair' solution to the climate change problem must be forged. Emissions are increasing sharply in developing countries as wealthy nations 'offshore' the energy- and natural resource-intensive stages of production. Meanwhile, case study research and the systematic analysis of thousands of hydrometeorological disasters over the past two decades show that the world's poorest nations are least able to prepare for, handle, and recover from the effects of global climate change (e.g. Roberts and Parks, 2007). In this article, we examine who is putting the world's climate at risk from greenhouse gases, asking four straightforward questions that lead to some very difficult issues: Who is responsible for climate change? What are the different ways of accounting for responsibility and who prefers each? What are the implications of addressing global inequality in responsibility for climate change? How can the globalization of economic production be incorporated into a just climate treaty?

We argue that global warming is all about inequality: in who will suffer its effects most, who is most responsible for the problem, and who is willing and able to address the problem. These compounding inequalities overlay an already polarized North–South debate and enmesh rich and poor countries in an adversarial negotiating environment. As such, it has become exceedingly difficult to broker a mutually acceptable international agreement that would stabilize the climate.

To a naïve observer, resolving the crisis of global climate change might be a matter of rational measurement of the atmosphere, giving equal shares of its capacity for absorbing greenhouse gases to all humans and assigning responsibility to individuals based on what they have put into it. It is, after all, a basic rule of civil justice, Superfund, and kindergarten ethics that those who created a mess should be responsible for cleaning up their share of the mess. Yet internationally, this simple question of who is to blame for the problem leads to a hornet's nest of contentious issues.

Resolving the climate change crisis depends fundamentally upon achieving a mutually acceptable understanding of 'what is fair'. Fairness principles can provide 'focal points' that reduce the costs of negotiating and bargaining, make agreements more palatable to domestic audiences (who frequently possess an indirect veto power over ratification and implementation), and realign the incentives of rich and poor nations to create fewer opportunities for shirking, defection, and other types of opportunistic behavior (Roberts and Parks, 2007; Wiegandt, 2001).

However, norms of fairness are extremely elastic and subject to political manipulation, and fairness focal points rarely emerge spontaneously. In many cases, countries hold genuinely different perceptions of fairness because of their highly disparate positions in the international system. Some poor nations, for example, believe that they are unjustly suffering the consequences of the North's profligate consumption. Others believe that they are entitled to pursue 'cheap' economic growth using fossil fuels and other natural resources at hand, since now-wealthy countries did the same at their early stages of development. Several rich nations, by contrast, argue that a climate agreement excluding developing countries is unfair and meaningless since 'non-Annex I' emissions will increase exponentially over the next few decades.[1] Other rich nations have suggested that if they continue to bear the weight of sustaining global economic growth and international financial stability, it would be both unfair and unrealistic to expect them to make sharp and immediate reductions in their carbon emissions.

Making matters more complicated, oil-exporters argue that in the absence of legal text that provides for their compensation and diversification into less carbon-intensive sectors, they cannot reasonably be expected to participate in any agreement. Small island states take an entirely different view; they believe that a 'fair agreement' would immediately stabilize the climate, forestall the complete destruction of island nations and cultures, and address their basic economic needs and extraordinary vulnerability to climate-related stress and hydrometeorological disasters. Nations in cold locations, with higher heating bills, and countries with large land areas have also argued that their special 'national circumstances'—which predispose them towards higher emissions levels from transportation of goods and people—must be taken into consideration in crafting a fair deal for all nations. Still others argue that a distinction must be drawn between 'survival' and 'luxury' emissions (Agarwal and Narain, 1991; Parikh and Parikh, 2002). In short, we live in a morally ambiguous world where social understandings of fairness are 'configurational', depending on countries' position in the global hierarchy of economic and political structure.

In this article we review a new and relatively under-utilized theory of 'ecologically unequal exchange' and apply it to the case of climate change. We assess whether wealthy nations are 'dematerializing' or 'decarbonizing' by assessing how emissions are skyrocketing in developing nations. We describe four distinct principles that have been proposed to assign responsibility for carbon emissions, discuss their inadequacies, and briefly lay out some 'hybrid' proposals currently under consideration. We suggest combining hybrid proposals with environmental aid packages that help poorer nations transition from carbon-intensive pathways of development to more climate-friendly development trajectories, using remuneration from the so-called 'ecological debt'. In the context of deadlock over a completely inadequate Kyoto Protocol, we argue that fairness principles, climate science, and an understanding of globalization and development must be integrated.

Dematerialization, Ecologically Unequal Trade, and the Ecological Debt

Several authors and politicians have argued that wealthy countries are 'dematerializing' their economies as people become 'postconsumerist', or post-modern, in their consumption patterns. That is, citizens of the global North increasingly value consumption of services and experiences over material products (Adriaanse et al., 1997; Inglehart, 1990; Ruth, 1998). As such, many have argued that economic growth is decoupling from resource consumption. Despite the fact that a declining material intensity of GDP does not necessarily translate into lower levels of *absolute* resource consumption, this 'dematerialization' trend is celebrated as a great environmental victory (Giljum and Eisenmenger, 2004).[2] This is tied to a second and related claim made by World Bank and WTO analysts—that exports from Third World nations are continually being upgraded and are increasing poor nations' prospects for positive economic growth and development (World Bank, 1992; Bhagwati, 2004).[3]

Both of these arguments have come under attack by a group of scholars forging a literature on 'ecologically unequal exchange' (Andersson and Lindroth, 2001; Cabeza-Gutés and Martinez-Alier, 2001; Damian and Graz, 2001; Giljum, 2003, 2004; Giljum and Eisenmenger, 2004; Giljum and Hubacek, 2001; Heil and Selden, 2001; Hornborg, 1998a, 1998b, 2001; Machado *et al.*, 2001; Martinez-Alier, 2003; Muradian and Martinez-Alier, 2001a, 2001b; Muradian and O'Connor, 2001; Muradian *et al.*, 2002; Russi and Muradian, 2003; Sachs, 1999). These scholars suggest that while exports are indeed shifting, trade relations remain extremely unfair because poorer nations export large quantities of under-priced products whose value does not include the environmental (and social) costs of their extraction, processing, or shipping.[4] Rich and poor nations are therefore said to possess different 'biophysical metabolisms' that shape the global distribution of environmental burdens and benefits (Fischer-Kowalski and Amann, 2001). This argument has found empirical support and led to the logical but radical claim that the wealthier nations owe some kind of remuneration (an 'ecological debt') to poorer nations for the environmental damage 'embodied' in their energy- and material-intensive products (Machado *et al.*, 2001; Muradian *et al.*, 2002; Princen *et al.*, 2002).

In late 2001, scholars and activists from the global South met in the African nation of Benin to articulate a position on the so-called 'ecological debt' (a close cousin of the 'ecologically unequal exchange' idea). The argument, as originally developed by Spanish economist Joan Martinez-Alier and the Ecuadorian environmental group Acción Ecológica, is that wealthy nations have been running up a huge debt over centuries of exploiting the raw materials and ecosystems of poor nations (Martinez-Alier, 2003; Simms *et al.*, 2004; Acción Ecológica, 2003). The debt encompasses the historical and modern exploitation of non-Western natural resources and the excessive use of 'environmental space' for dumping waste (e.g. expropriating global atmospheric resources). An extraordinary coalition of environmental, human rights, and development NGOs has lobbied for the ecological debt to either be paid or used as balance to forgive national economic debts (Simms *et al.*, 2004).[5] This idea has traveled around the world very quickly, and garnered the support of the Chinese government and the G-77 at the 2000 South Summit in Havana, Cuba. Many developing countries have also articulated this position during climate negotiations (Roberts and Parks, 2007).

The intellectual heritage of the 'ecological debt' and 'ecologically unequal exchange' literature can be traced back to the 'structuralist school' of the 1940s, 1950s, and 1960s. At that time, Raul Prebisch and his colleagues at the UN's Economic Commission on Latin America (ECLA) found a striking empirical pattern: the export commodity prices of poor nations seemed to consistently fall relative to the prices of items exported by wealthy nations. ECLA argued that this was the result of weak income elasticity of demand for primary products, a massive oversupply of labor, and poor union organization in developing countries. Together these led to stagnant wages, inflation and lower export prices as opposed to rising wages and stable prices achieved in core nations. Structuralists therefore argued that the liberal emphasis on global GDP growth was a highly misleading indicator of international well-being. Some nations were growing, some were stagnating, and others were declining or falling into deep depression. Much of this variation, in their view, could be explained by countries' 'natural' comparative advantages—the value of their resource-based exports and labor oversupply.

The 'ecological debt' and 'ecologically unequal exchange' literature is also rooted in world-systems theory, which postulates that national development cannot be understood in isolation from the global system, where relatively few nations wield great economic and military power (Braudel, 1981; Frank, 1969; Wallerstein, 1972). World-systems theorists argue that nations can move up or down the global hierarchy, but must do so in a world where there are already powerful economic players with developed industrial bases and relatively overwhelming military might that can be used to manipulate political and economic relations. The international division of labor is said to function in the following way: core wealthy nations import raw materials and export high value services and industrial manufactures while controlling powerful financial institutions; poor peripheral nations export their natural resources and supply cheap labor directly to manufacturers; and semi-peripheral middle-income nations lie somewhere in the middle, with some industry, higher-value services, and a partially diversified export structure. While a few nations move up the global hierarchy of wealth and power, the underlying relations of extraction, production and consumption between core and (semi-)peripheral nations remain intact.

The emphasis of world-systems theory on historicism and structuralism helps to explain why many peripheral and semi-peripheral nations are locked into ecologically unsustainable patterns (Roberts and Grimes, 2002; Roberts *et al.*, 2003). World-systems theorists argue that the volatility and periodic collapse of export commodity prices lead poor nations to ramp up the extraction and sale of material goods that they are already selling at a near loss. Giljum (2004, p. 17), for example, argues that:

> [L]ow prices for primary commodities allow industrialized countries of the capitalist core to appropriate high amounts of biophysical resources from the peripheral economies in the South, while maintaining external trade relations balanced in monetary terms. ... [W]hat within the system of prices appears as reciprocal and fair exchange masks a biophysical inequality of exchange in which one of the partners has little choice but to exploit and possibly exhaust his natural resources and utilize his environment as a waste dump, while the other partner may maintain high environmental quality within its own borders.

In his path-breaking 1985 book *Underdeveloping the Amazon*, sociologist Stephen Bunker also theorized extensively on the issue of ecologically unequal exchange. Based on case study research in Brazil, he argued that every time an economy exports its natural resources, an energy and material loss takes place, 'decelerating' the extractive economy and 'accelerating' the productive economy. He also suggested that 'regions whose economic ties to the world system are based almost exclusively on the exchange of extracted commodities, can be characterized as extreme peripheries because of the low proportions of capital and labor incorporated in the total value of their exports and because of the low level of linkages to other economic activities and social organization in the same region' (Bunker, 1985, p. 24). Furthermore, 'accelerated energy flow to the world industrial core permits social complexity which generates political and economic power there and permits the rapid technological changes which transform world market demands. It thus creates the conditions of the core's economic and political dominance over the world system to which the dominant classes of peripheral economies respond with their own accumulation strategies' (Bunker, 1985, p. 24). Therefore, in Bunker's model, the core's productive economy consumes commodities directly and indirectly through manufactures, but also effectively consumes the extractive economy, draining it of its energy and matter and damaging the local ecology, social organization, and infrastructure.[6] In effect, the core relies on the periphery as both a source and sink (for high entrophic by-products and waste).[7]

A number of scholars have recently exposed Bunker's thesis to empirical testing. One particular hypothesis has attracted much more attention than any other: that when nations exchange goods, the market prices of primary products are often undervalued, and in the course of extracting, moving, and processing products for export there is a massive transfer and degradation of materials and energy that goes unrecognized. Using a 'materials flow' accounting methodology, a number of economists have argued that physical numeraires can be used to bring these flows of material and energy back into the equation. The easiest way to do this is to measure the physical weight of import and export flows. However, more sophisticated methodologies are being developed to account for indirect material flows used in the production process, as well as waste and emission flows (Giljum, 2004; Machado et al., 2001; Muradian et al., 2002).

Empirical work using materials flow analysis has led to an important finding: many developing countries traditionally seen as successful, export-oriented economies are suffering huge, unrecorded (economic and ecological) losses (Giljum, 2004; Machado et al., 2001; Muradian et al., 2002). Using time series data on consumption of natural resources, Giljum (2004) finds that Chile's natural resource exports have increased threefold and its use of material inputs has increased by a factor of six over the period 1973–2000. Giljum identifies a clear link between this pattern and huge export drives in the forestry, fishing, mining, and fruit-growing sectors (also see Quiroga, 1994). In a similar study, Muradian and Martinez-Alier (2001b) document the responses of developing countries to declining terms of trade. They find that falling prices correlate with large export drives for primary products. Of the 18 natural resource exports from developing countries they examine, all but two saw their prices fall between the 1970s and 1990s, yet 14 of the 18 exports increased dramatically in volume over the same period in physical terms.

Tracking material and energy flows from extraction to production to final disposal is illuminating not only from an export perspective, but also from an 'import' perspective. The most systematic and comprehensive empirical study employing this latter approach examines the EU-15 region and concludes that, while the EU maintains balanced external trade relations in monetary terms with all other major regions of the world, it runs an enormous trade deficit in physical terms (Bringezu and Schütz, 2001a). Primarily due to the import of fossil fuels, semi-manufactured products, and abiotic raw materials, the EU imports—in physical terms—more than four times what it exports. Yet, 'EU-15 exports have a money value of 4 times that of imports. With regard to trade relations with Southern regions such as Africa and Latin America, one ton of EU exports embodies a money value 10 times higher than one ton of EU imports' (Giljum and Eisenmenger, 2004, p. 84, emphasis added). Thus, from both an import and export perspective, materials flow analysis suggests that core economies are draining ecological capacity from extractive regions by importing resource-intensive products and have shifted environmental burdens to the South through the export of waste (Andersson and Lindroth, 2001).

In this regard, materials flows analysis appears to have debunked earlier claims that we have entered an era of dematerialization. In reality, what appears to be happening is that some core economies are being 'relatively dematerialized' as they export to poor countries, or 'peripheralize', the material-intensive stages of the production process. Domestic production has no doubt become more efficient—where efficiency is defined as the material intensity of one's own production—in the core zones of the world economy. However, nations that increasingly import the material-intensive goods required by their lifestyles are clearly no less materialist and no more sustainable than they were when they bore their own environmental burdens (Fisher-Kowalski and Amman, 2001).[8]

Cutting the Carbon Cake: Four Ways to Share the Burden

Global climate change is a key area in which ecologically unequal exchange appears to be in effect. Statistical research suggests that trading more products increases emissions by poorer nations, while lowering them for wealthier nations (Heil and Selden, 2001; Roberts and Parks, 2007). As such, devising a mutually acceptable agreement to stabilize the climate raises the difficult issue of how to determine who is most responsible for the problem. Four different methods of 'differentiation' have been proposed during the fifteen or so years of climate negotiations, each with crucial assumptions and implications for climate stabilization, social justice, political expediency, and who will bear the greatest burden of change if accepted as the basis for a climate treaty. These are: grandfathering, carbon intensity, contraction and convergence to a global per capita norm, and historical responsibility.

The Kyoto Protocol, as it was negotiated in 1997, was based on grandfathering—that nations should reduce their emissions incrementally from a baseline year. Large emitters, therefore, had their high discharges of greenhouse gasses 'grandfathered' in, with relatively minor adjustments averaging 5.2%, for the foreseeable future. The carbon intensity approach, introduced by the World Resources Institute and favored by the second Bush administration starting in 2002, calls for voluntary changes in efficiency to drive reduction of emissions. In this approach, the goal is to have strong economic growth with as few carbon emissions as possible. Both of these proposals have the effect of departing incrementally from the current status quo without placing radical demands on powerful nations.

On the other side of the spectrum are two proposals that strongly favor developing countries: historical responsibility and per capita contraction and convergence. India, China, and much of the developing world favor a per capita approach in which each person on Earth is given an equal right to the ability of the atmosphere to absorb carbon. Under the per capita proposal, nations whose per capita consumption of fossil fuels is significantly lower than the world average would be given significant room to grow and emit. Most per capita plans would allow them to trade their extra carbon emission credits for the capital they need for development. By comparison, nations with highly fossil energy-intensive economies would face sharp requirements to cut their consumption of fuels.

Brazil also introduced a proposal in 1997 that would take into account the amount of damage done by nations in the past to the atmosphere's ability to absorb more greenhouse gases. This historical responsibility approach puts the onus on nations that put greenhouse gases in the atmosphere in past decades to reduce their emissions quickly, most notably Britain and the United States. Some developing countries have supported this approach and demanded that some indemnification be paid for the so-called 'carbon debt'. We take up each alternative approach here, examining its roots and implications, the principles upon which it is based, and how each has been approached or ignored in global climate negotiations over the past dozen years.

Grandfathering

The treaty that emerged from back-room bargaining at Kyoto in 1997 was based on the concept of grandfathering—that the world's wealthier nations would make efforts to reduce their carbon emissions relative to a baseline year; in this case, 1990.[9] After a series of drawn-out negotiations, individual reductions targets were agreed upon among rich nations, mostly 6–7% below the 1990 baseline by 2010.[10] The approach was decided upon for Kyoto because of its political expediency.

For more than a decade of climate negotiations, similar arguments have been made in response to calls for sharp and immediate cuts in emission levels. Many countries contend that 'national circumstances' and economic hardships affect their ability to make deep and immediate reductions. At Kyoto and the many meetings since, the United States, Russia, and several other high-emissions nations bargained hard for minor changes to the status quo. The US Senate and current US administration have underscored that even a Kyoto-type treaty would unfairly damage the nation's economy and send jobs overseas. On the Senate floor in Fueling Injustice November 2003, dozens of senators argued the McCain–Lieberman Climate Stewardship Act would place painful limits on US economic growth and create terrible suffering among different groups of Americans.

The principle of grandfathering has not been applied to developing countries. However, were it to resurface (as focal points often do, see Goldstein and Keohane, 1993), most experts agree it would have the effect of punishing 'late-developers'. As Aslam (2002, p. 176) explains, 'current emissions of developing countries ... are very low compared with those of industrialized countries, but are rising rapidly. This places developing countries at a severe disadvantage when it comes to negotiating emission control targets that are based on a grandfathering system'.

The extent of inequality in total emissions is startling to contemplate. With the latest figures at the time of writing, the United States emitted the largest proportion of carbon of any nation. Since the 1990 baseline, emissions have in fact increased in most nations, and in some nations substantially. Besides the ex-Soviet Union republics, whose economies largely collapsed after the transition to capitalism, only a few countries in the developed world are on track to meet even their modest Kyoto goals.

While many argue that the grandfathering approach is amoral and baldly based on political power in the international system, it does represent at least three understandings of justice. Entitlement theories of justice, both in their libertarian and Marxist forms, hold that individuals are entitled to what they have produced (Albin, 2003; Müller, 2001). As such, every nation possesses a common law (inherent) right to emit carbon dioxide. Grandfathering also exemplifies the justice principle of proportional equality—that nations are unequal and should therefore be treated unequally. While developing countries were not required to commit to scheduled reductions of emissions in the first round of negotiations, the decision to use 1990 as a baseline year is an implicit recognition of these two principles. Finally, grandfathering represents the pragmatic principle that if we can solve the problem we are closer to justice than if we insist upon a utopian plan which makes no progress. Cecilia Albin (2001, 2003) argues that in spite of the fact that international environmental agreements regularly institutionalize fairness norms—for example, the 'polluter pays', 'no harm', and 'shared, but differentiated responsibility' principles—their success is first and foremost dependent upon their ability to yield joint gains for all parties. She offers the example of Sweden and Finland, which, despite being victimized by the air pollution of neighboring Baltic countries, did not insist that the 'polluter pays' principle be strictly enforced. Quite the opposite. They financed a large foreign aid initiative to help the less developed countries responsible for the air pollution adopt more environmentally friendly technologies.

Carbon Intensity

Faced with pressure to sign the Kyoto treaty, President George W. Bush promised during his 2000 campaign to do so. However, after entering office, his position shifted and he withdrew the US from the treaty entirely. US National Security Advisor Condoleezza Rice told EU members in the spring of 2001 that the Kyoto Protocol was 'dead' without US participation, since the treaty requires that countries responsible for 55% of the total amount of emissions from the world's wealthy nations ratify it. A firestorm of reaction from Europe and environmentalists in the USA forced the Bush administration to provide an alternative plan to address the problem.

At the science center of the National Oceanic and Atmospheric Administration in Maryland, President G.W. Bush on 14 February 2002 announced that 'As president of the United States, charged with safeguarding the welfare of the American people and American workers, I will not commit our nation to an unsound international treaty that will throw millions of our citizens out of work'. Rather, he proposed a 'New Approach on Global Climate Change' plan in response to the treaty, and provided a new benchmark by which the US government would measure its own progress on the issue. He 'committed America to an aggressive new strategy to cut greenhouse gas intensity by 18% over the next 10 years' (White House, 2002a). The simple measure they proposed was emissions per dollar of GDP. The White House press releases argued that: 'The President's Yardstick—Greenhouse Gas Intensity—is a Better Way to Measure Progress Without Hurting Growth'. It continued, 'A goal expressed in terms of declining greenhouse gas intensity, measuring greenhouse gas emissions relative to economic activity, quantifies our effort to reduce emissions through conservation, adoption of cleaner, more efficient, and emission-reducing technologies, and sequestration. At the same time, an intensity goal accommodates economic growth' (White House, 2002b).

The carbon intensity approach is an outgrowth of Bentham's utilitarian theory of justice, which states that mutual advantageous and cost-effective solutions are also just solutions. Since everyone is worse off in the absence of aggregate net benefits, utilitarians argue that inefficient solutions are also unjust (Gauthier, 1986). The fair solution, with respect to greenhouse gas emission reductions, would therefore be to stabilize the climate as cost-effectively as possible, while maximizing global economic growth. Since developing nations currently offer the most cost-effective opportunities to reduce greenhouse gas emissions, the international effort to stabilize greenhouse gas emissions would predominantly focus on the developing world (Stavins, 2004, p. 8).

On the positive side, the carbon intensity approach forces the international community to think about designing solutions that will allow growth to occur while minimizing impact on the global climate. A number of analysts have also suggested that the carbon intensity approach creates greater opportunities for developing country buy-in, since it does not impose a 'hard cap' on their total emissions (Kim and Baumert, 2002).[11] An added advantage to this approach is that industrialized nations tend to do better in intensity terms, since their infrastructure is typically much better than that of poorer nations (Roberts and Grimes, 1997; Roberts et al., 2003). So, a carbon intensity approach could promote 'early action', which, according to Baumert et al. (2003, p. 6), is important because 'many developing countries believe that the industrialized countries lack credibility on the issue of international cooperation to curb greenhouse gas emissions, having done little to address a problem largely of their own making'.

On the downside, the proposals made by the Bush administration place no real restrictions on the future emissions of the US (since most analysts see the nation's efficiency as improving on its own by at least 18%) and are widely perceived as a repudiation of earlier commitments. The Bush administration's plan also does nothing about the existing stock of emissions and makes no effort to include 'exported emissions' caused by the offshoring of US industries to poorer nations. In addition, the carbon intensity approach has become a tool of political manipulation. The United States used this approach strategically at COP-8 and COP-9 in an effort to torpedo the Kyoto Protocol and delay post-2012 talks. US negotiator Harlan Watson urged Western nations at the New Delhi negotiations to 'recognize that it would be unfair—indeed, counterproductive— to condemn developing nations to slow growth or no growth by insisting that they take on impractical and unrealistic greenhouse gas targets'.[12] The following year at the Milan negotiations, US Undersecretary of State Paula Dobriansky tried to forge an unusual coalition with China and the G-77 by rejecting the need for developing countries to undertake scheduled commitments to reduce emissions (Dobriansky, 2003).

Per Capita

India, China, and the Group of 77 (actually a group of about 133 nations) have developed and advocated a series of proposals that account for carbon dioxide and other greenhouse gases on the basis of a simple, egalitarian principle. The idea is that every human on Earth has equal rights to the global atmosphere, and therefore allocations of how much each can pollute should be done on a per capita basis.[13] France, Switzerland, and the European Union have all endorsed this proposal.[14] Cambridge University economist Michael Grubb (1999, p. 270) calls it 'the most politically prominent contender for any specific global formula for long-term allocations with increasing numbers of adherents in both developed and developing countries'.[15]

Per capita proposals place rich nations at a sharp disadvantage, since most of them already far exceed the stabilization target (roughly 1 metric ton of carbon equivalent per capita). Poor nations, by comparison, stand to gain considerably from a per capita allocation of carbon entitlements because their existing levels of income and industrialization place them well below the 1 metric ton threshold.

Environmentally sustainable per capita proposals typically require that a global 'emissions budget' first be specified. The scientific consensus is that to avoid the worst effects of climate change, we need to stabilize the concentrations of carbon dioxide around or below 450 parts per million. However, others suggest that 350 and 550 parts per million are more appropriate targets. In any case, these proposals suggest drastic reductions for the world's richest nations, and commitments very soon for the poorer ones to reduce growth rates of their emissions and eventually stop and reverse them.

Under most per capita proposals, including the Contraction and Convergence model proposed by the Global Commons Institute, once the size of the emissions budget is specified, every global citizen is allocated an equal entitlement to the atmosphere. Rich countries, whose relatively small populations have already used a disproportionate amount of their atmospheric space, must 'contract' their annual carbon budget to a level of roughly 1 metric ton of carbon equivalent per person over the next century. Poor nations, whose citizens have thus far occupied very little atmospheric space, are allowed to increase their emissions for some time and eventually 'converge' with rich nations. Developing countries willing to restrict their emissions growth below their allowance have the opportunity to trade those allowances in exchange for funding or technical assistance through the Clean Development Mechanism, Joint Implementation, and other emissions trading mechanisms.

The key question surrounding the per capita approach is its political feasibility. Egalitarian principles played a prominent role in UN Convention on Law of the Sea negotiations (Baumert, 2002). However, many analysts consider the application of egalitarian principles to climate policy politically explosive and economically inefficient. Grubb and his colleagues (1999) describe one very telling interaction between rich and poor nations at the Kyoto negotiations that lasted late into the evening. At 3 o'clock in the morning, amidst heated debate over global emissions trading, China, India, and the Africa Group of Nations expressed their strong support for a per capita allocation of global atmospheric property rights. Chairman Raul Estrada and a representative of the US delegation responded that the 'Contraction and Convergence' proposal was a political non-starter and negotiations were immediately brought to a close.

It is important for readers to understand just how far apart the people of the world are in per capita terms. Twenty percent of the world's population in the high-income countries is responsible for 63% of the emissions, while the bottom 20% of the world's people is only releasing 3% (Roberts and Parks, 2007). According to our calculations, the average US citizen dumps as much greenhouse gas into the atmosphere as nine Chinese citizens, 18 citizens of India, and 90 Bangladeshis (from 2000 figures). Even more startling is that each US citizen on average pollutes as much as over 500 citizens of Ethiopia, Chad, Zaire, Afghanistan, Mali, Cambodia, and Burundi (Roberts and Parks, 2007). In 183 nations, people emit on average less than half as much as the Americans do. In 130 nations, it would take at least five citizens to generate as much carbon dioxide from burning fossil fuels as one US citizen does. In 90 nations, it would take over ten citizens to generate as much as one American. And in 30 of those nations, it would take over 100.[16]

Historical Responsibility

The polluter pays principle has been central to domestic and international environmental law for more than 30 years.[17] Brazilian scientists and government experts have developed a sophisticated proposal to address climate change based on this principle. They argue that a country's greenhouse gas reductions should depend on its relative contribution to the global temperature rise (La Rovere *et al.*, 2002, p. 158).[18] The reasoning behind the historical responsibility proposal is that carbon dioxide burned now stays in the atmosphere for 100–120 years. Therefore, it is important to account not only for future emissions, but all of the damage done in earlier years (Neumayer, 2000). The political implications are obvious: since virtually all the carbon emitted since 1945 is still in the atmosphere and 'early industrializers' are almost exclusively responsible for that damage, rich nations would be required to make deep and immediate cuts. Early estimates suggest that by 2010 Britain would have to reduce emissions by 66%, the United States by 23%, and Japan 8% (La Rovere *et al.*, 2002).

Given their tiny contribution to the existing stock of carbon emissions, it is not surprising that developing countries have been strong advocates of the historical responsibility approach. At their 2000 South Summit in Havana, the G-77 submitted the following statement as part of a larger manifesto:

> We believe that the prevailing modes of production and consumption in the industrialized world are unsustainable and should be changed for they threaten the very survival of the planet.... We advocate a solution for the serious global, regional, and local environmental problems facing humanity, *based on the recognition of the North's ecological debt* and the principle of common but differentiated responsibilities of the developed and developing countries. (G-77, 2000, emphasis added)

However, the historical responsibility proposal has failed to gain much traction in the policy community. To be broadly acceptable to people around the world, proposals for addressing climate change need to be relatively easy to understand, and making the historical responsibility principle operational requires fairly complex methods of calculation (Baumert, 2002). Nonetheless, the 2000 Special Report on Emissions Scenario' of the IPCC found that summed emissions 'supply a reasonable "proxy" for the relative contribution to global warming' of different nations, if 'limited to a few decades' (La Rovere et al., 2002, p. 168). The summed emissions from the high-income nations amount to nearly twice the tons of carbon of the middle income nations, and four times the cumulative emissions of the majority of the world, that live in the poorest nations. This is a highly contentious issue, but one which we believe must be considered if we are to address inequality and climate change. The polluter pays argument is that high-emitting nations, even if they did not know the danger of their behavior, still benefited from it and should be held responsible for its impacts. This logic holds in many national laws, including Superfund and other pollution laws in the United States.

A Way Forward: Hybrid Justice, Pathway Switching, and the Ecological Debt

Elsewhere, we have argued that poor nations and rich nations hold diametrically opposed views of 'climate justice' because of the highly asymmetric global distribution of environmental 'goods' and 'bads' (Parks and Roberts, 2005, 2006). Such inequality unfortunately makes it very unlikely that a North–South fairness consensus will spontaneously emerge on the basis of one of these four principles described above. The globalization of economic production and the transfer of industrial emissions to the global South has worsened this problem. Therefore, what is needed is moral compromise, or a negotiated 'justice settlement' (Aldy et al., 2003; Baumert et al., 2003; Blanchard et al., 2003; Stavins, 2004).

A number of proposals representing moral compromise have emerged in recent years. Bartsch and Müller (2000) propose a 'preference score' method, which combines the grandfathering and per capita approach through a voting system. Their proposal allows each nation, weighted by its population, to choose the methodology that it prefers. Each global citizen's 'vote' is then used to calculate national carbon emission allowances. Under this proposal, roughly three-quarters of the global emissions budget would be based on the per capita approach and one-quarter on grandfathering. Others have focused on more politically feasible per capita proposals that provide for 'national circumstances', or allowance factors, like geography, climate, energy supply, and domestic economic structure, as well as 'soft landing scenarios' (e.g. Baumert et al., 2003; Blanchard et al., 2003; Gupta and Bhandari, 1999; TERI, 1997; Torvanger et al., 2004).

The Pew Center for Global Climate Change has developed a hybrid proposal that assigns responsibility based on past and present emissions, carbon intensity, and countries' ability to pay (i.e. its per capita GDP). It separates the world into three groups: those that 'must act now', those that 'could act now', and those that 'should act now, but differently' (Claussen and McNeilly, 1998). The 'Triptych' proposal, designed by scholars at the University of Utrecht (and already used to differentiate commitments among EU countries), 'accounts for differences in national circumstances such as population size and growth, standard of living, economic structure and fuel mix in power generation' (Groenenberg et al., 2001). Its novel contribution is that it divides each country's economy into three sectors: energy-intensive industry, power generation, and the so-called domestic sector (transport, light industry, agriculture, and commercial sector) (Groenenberg et al., 2001; Evans, 2002). It applies the carbon intensity approach to the energy-intensive sector, 'decarbonization targets' to the power generation sector, and a per capita approach to the 'domestic' sectors. Similarly, the Multi-sector Convergence approach, developed by two research institutes in Northern Europe, treats sectors differentially and integrates per capita, carbon intensity, and 'ability to pay' (GDP per capita) approaches (Sijm et al., 2000; Ybema et al., 2000). Many other proposals exist.

We believe these hybrid proposals are among the most promising solutions to break the North–South stalemate. However, simply asserting that a 'negotiated justice' settlement is necessary avoids the more central question of whether and to what extent an agreement must favor rich or poor nations. As we have argued elsewhere, the greatest barriers to meaningful North–South cooperation are not differences in principled understandings of what is fair. Rather, divergent principled beliefs are a consequence of more fundamental root causes: incongruent worldviews and causal beliefs, persistent global inequality, and an enduring deficit in North–South trust (Roberts and Parks, 2007).[19] Therefore, along with developing a workable and fair 'hybrid justice' proposal, policy makers must redouble their efforts to allay the fears and suspicions of developing countries; rebuild conditions of generalized trust, forge long-term, constructive partnerships with developing countries across multiple issue areas; and create greater 'policy space' for governments to pursue their own development strategies (Roberts and Parks, 2007).

Attention is finally beginning to be paid to sectors and pathways of development. Several South Asian authors working on the Fourth Assessment Report of the IPCC have recently argued that 'development pathways ... societies choose today may be as important, possibly even more important, as the climate measures they take' (Najam et al., 2003). Initial discussions of this issue also began at the COP-10 in Buenos Aires in 2004. Our own research suggests that some development pathways insulate countries from economic volatility more than others, cause less local environmental damage, and give more options to planners; others are much more difficult to change (Roberts and Parks, 2007).

More in-depth analysis of development pathways under globalization is needed, but one can imagine a sophisticated hybrid proposal for assigning national carbon-dioxide emission quotas based initially on economic profiling of the consumption and production of nations. This would require that a future treaty be developed from the physical science of what the atmosphere can likely handle, principled decisions about which approach is fairest, and the practical social science of how different types of nations will meet their allowed emissions. This picture of national responsibilities for the world's emissions requires more than a static accounting of tons of carbon emitted in each nation. Rather, the rapid shifting of the energy- and natural resource-intensive stages of production to developing nations requires responsibility to be tied to the total carbon 'footprint' of products where they are consumed. Climate justice will require complex physical and social science calculations and many normative decisions about how to assess responsibility. 'Ecologically unequal exchange' must be considered in these calculations. Simply put, brute bargaining strength will never lead us to a workable climate treaty, in neither the sense of atmospheric stability nor the political or social sense.

Acknowledgments

The views expressed in this article are the authors' own and do not necessarily represent the views of the Millennium Challenge Corporation.

Notes

1. Wealthier nations that accepted Kyoto targets were listed in 'Annex I' of the treaty, and the rest, which were expected to take up limits only in future rounds of the treaty, were classified as 'non-Annex I'.
2. Rich nations indeed continue to consume more natural resources than ever before by almost any measure. In 1998, the richest 20% of the world's population consumed 46% of all meat and fish, 65% of all electricity, 58% of all

energy, 74% of all telephones, 84% of all paper and 87% of all cars. The poorest 20%, by contrast, consumed less than 10% of all these products (UNDP, 1998). There is a strong body of evidence that suggests that many of these resources originate in poor and middle-income nations. Arden-Clarke (1992) reports that two-thirds of all primary commodity exports come from the Third World. However, dollar-dependent export measures mask even deeper inequalities. Measuring national export–import ratios in terms of *physical weight*, the developed world becomes a much greater net importer of environmentally intensive products (Andersson and Lindroth, 2001; Fischer-Kowalski and Amman, 2001).

3   Arrighi *et al.* (1999) provide a damaging critique of these claims on development grounds, arguing that poorer nations receive sharply diminishing returns for industrialization.

4   Røpke (1999) argues that 'prices are distorted not only because of the present [environmental] externalities, but also because such externalities have existed for nearly two centuries and have been built into the social and physical structures of society as accumulated externalities'.

5   This coalition includes the New Economics Foundation, Jubilee Research, Oxfam, World Wildlife Fund, World Vision, Friends of the Earth, Greenpeace, Christian Aid, Action Aid, the Heinrich Böll Foundation, the International Institute for Environment and Development, Corporate Watch, Centre for Science and the Environment, and EcoEquity.

6   Bunker (1985) tried to extend thermodynamic law to global political economy. He argued that energy and matter are 'withdrawn from the natural environment of the extractive economies and flow toward and are concentrated in the social and physical environments of the productive economies, where they fuel the linked and mutually accelerating processes of production and consumption'. His argument, then, could be characterized as one of social entropy. Industrial capitalism, with all of its high energy outputs requires a constant flow of low-entropy inputs from other areas, in particular, the periphery and semi-periphery which houses the majority of low-entropy stocks.

7   Some would argue that this is nowhere more evident than in the climate change arena, where core nations undercompensate peripheral nations for their critical energy sources, and then, at the same time insist that they sequester their 'luxury emissions' by planting reforestation projects, potentially creating 'green deserts' which provide limited job creation and economic progress in the short-term.

8   Giljum and Eisenmenger (2004) rightly point out '[t]he implementation of a strategy of *absolute dematerialization* would lead to radical changes of economic structures in both North and South and to price changes on international commodity markets'.

9   1990 was chosen because climate science became well known then, with the first assessment report of the Intergovernmental Panel on Climate Change.

10 Because national emissions can vary greatly depending on economic conditions in any year, the target date of 2010 was expanded into a five year average of 2008–12.

11 Southern nations view pressure for scheduled emission reduction commitments as part of a larger Northern crusade to rein in their economic development. Former UNFCCC Secretariat staff member Joanna Depledge writes that '[a]bsolute caps on emissions are generally viewed, especially by developing countries themselves, as caps on development' (Depledge *et al.*, 2003, p. 56).

12 Harlan L. Watson, Senior Climate Negotiator and Special Representative and Head of the US Delegation Remarks to the Eighth Session of the Conference of Parties (COP-8) to the UN Framework Convention on Climate Change New Delhi, India, 25 October 2002.

13 Two groups have been promoting the idea of a per capita framework for years. The Global Commons Institute, led by Aubrey Meyer, has been promoting a 'contraction and convergence' approach which makes tough demands for reductions on the global North, but allows a transition period and lots of tradable permits to emit greenhouse gases in the short term transition period. The other group, with perhaps more clout because of its location in New Delhi, India, is the Centre for Science and the Environment, led by Anil Agarwal and Sunita Narain.

14 Other rich countries (e.g. Japan, Norway, Iceland, Poland) would reportedly accept the per capita principle if it were integrated into a larger approach (i.e. multi-sectoral, menu approach, etc.) (Baumert, 2002).

15 The European Parliament has advocated a 'progressive convergence towards an equitable distribution of emission rights on a per capita basis by an agreed date in the next century' (Cited in Baumert *et al.*, 2003, p. 182).

16 This article and nearly all the analysis and discussion of emissions inequality focuses on inequality *between* nations. However it is important to acknowledge and suggest future research on inequality of emissions *within* nations. We currently lack much data on intra-country variation in carbon emissions, especially in the poor nations, but Loren Lutzenheizer's 1996 analysis shows how US citizens with incomes over $75,000 emitted nearly four times the amount of carbon as those whose income is under $10,000 (Lutzenheizer, 1996).

17 The 'polluter pays' principle was endorsed by all OECD countries in 1974 (OECD, 1974).

18   Since the late 1990s, the Brazilian proposal has been significantly revised with improved understanding of how carbon is absorbed and released by the oceans, land and plants.
19   There are several widespread perceptions in the global South that reinforce a sense of mistrust of the North on climate change. First, there is a gaping divide between rich and poor nations in terms of how they define the issue of climate change. Rich nations tend to see climate instability as a 'global public bad' that affects all nations and requires the efforts of all nations. Poor nations tend to see climate change as a problem of Northern consumption. Second, poor nations typically prioritize developmental and local environmental issues over issues of international concern. Third, many Southern governments are deeply suspicious that 'Northern' environmental issues are but another way for the world's most powerful nations to limit their economic development. Fourth, there is a widely held perception among poor nations that their position in the world economy constrains their ability to make large strides in the area of environmental protection, particularly as exporters of commodities facing highly volatile prices and deteriorating terms-of-trade. Fifth, many developing countries believe that a distinction should be made between 'survival' and 'luxury' emissions. Parikh and Parikh (2002, p. 5), for example, argue that one might distinguish between the 'gas-guzzling, air-polluting automobiles in Europe and North America' and those emanating from the methane created by 'fermenting rice fields of subsistence farmers in West Bengal'. Finally, the North–South debate over how to account for carbon responsibility is plagued by conditions of *generalized* mistrust, due to the US repudiation of the Kyoto Treaty and industrialized countries overall not taking active enough steps to address the problem (Roberts and Parks, 2007).

References

Acción Ecológica (2003) Que es la Deuda Ecológica? Web document: http://www.accionecologica.org. Accessed 14 July 2003.
Adriaanse, A., Bringezu, S., Hamond, A., Moriguchi, Y., Rodenburg, E. & Rogich, D. *et al.* (1997) *Resource Flows: The Material Base of Industrial Economies* (Washington, DC: World Resource Institute).
Agarwal, A. & Narain, S. (1991) *Global Warming: A Case of Environmental Colonialism* (New Delhi: Centre for Science and Environment).
Albin, C. (2001) *Justice and Fairness in International Negotiation* (Cambridge: Cambridge University Press).
Albin, C. (2003) Negotiating international cooperation: global public goods and fairness, *Review of International Studies*, 29(3), pp. 365–385.
Aldy, J. E., Barrett, S. & Stavins, R. N. (2003) Thirteen plus one: a comparison of global climate policy architectures, *Climate Policy*, 3, pp. 373–397.
Andersson, J. O. & Lindroth, M. (2001) Ecologically unsustainable trade, *Ecological Economics*, 37, pp. 13–122.
Arden-Clarke, C. (1992) South–North terms of trade: environmental protection and sustainable development, *International Environmental Affairs*, 4(2), pp. 122–139.
Arrighi, G., Silver, B. J. & Brewer, B. D. (1999) Industrial convergence, globalization, and the persistence of the north–south divide. Reprinted in Roberts, J. T. & Hite, A. (eds) (2007) *The Globalization and Development Reader* (Oxford: Blackwell).
Aslam, M. A. (2002) Equal per capita entitlements: a key to global participation on climate change?, in Baumert, K. A. (ed.), *Building on the Kyoto Protocol: Options for Protecting the Climate* (Washington, DC: World Resources Institute), pp. 175–202.
Bartsch, U. & Müller, B. (2000) *Fossil Fuels in a Changing Climate: Impacts of the Kyoto Protocol and Developing Country Participation* (Oxford: Oxford University Press).
Baumert, K. A. (ed.) (2002) *Building on the Kyoto Protocol: Options for Protecting the Climate* (Washington, DC: World Resources Institute).
Baumert K. V. A., Perkaus, J. F. & Kete, N. (2003) Great expectations: can international emissions trading deliver an equitable climate regime? *Climate Policy*, 3(2), pp. 137–148.
Bhagwati, J. (2004) *In Defense of Globalization* (New York: Oxford University Press).
Blanchard, O., Criqui, P., Kitous, A. & Viguier, L. (2003) Combining efficiency with equity: a pragmatic approach, in Kaul, I., Conceicao, P., Le Goulven, K. and Mendoza, R. U. (eds) *Providing Global Public Goods: Managing Globalization* (New York: Oxford University Press).
Braudel, F. (1981) *The Structures of Everyday Life*. Vol. 1 of *Civilization and Capitalism, 15th–18th Century* (New York: Harper & Row).

Bringezu, S. & Schütz, H. (2001a) Material use indicators for the European Union, 1980–1997. Economy-wide material flow accounts and balances and derived indicators of resource use. EUROSTAT Working Paper, No. 2/2001/B/2, Wuppertal Institute, Wuppertal.

Bunker, S. (1985) *Underdeveloping the Amazon: Extraction, Unequal Exchange and the Failure of the Modern State* (Urbana, IL: University of Illinois Press).

Cabeza-Gutés, M. & Martinez-Alier, J. (2001) L'échange écologiquement inégal, in Damian, M. & Graz, J. C. (eds) *Commerce international et développement soutenable* (Paris: Economica).

Claussen, E. and McNeilly, L. (1998) *Equity and Global Climate Change: The Complex Elements of Fairness* (Arlington, VA: Pew Center on Climate Change).

Damian, M. & Graz, J. C. (eds) (2001) *Commerce international et développement soutenable* (Paris: Economica).

Depledge, J. 2002. Continuing Kyoto: extending absolute emission caps to developing countries, in Baumert, K. A. (ed.), *Building on the Kyoto Protocol: Options for Protecting the Climate* (Washington, DC: World Resources Institute), pp. 31–60.

Dobriansky, P. (2003) Only new technology can halt climate change, *Financial Times*, 1 December.

Evans, A. (2002) *Fresh Air? Options for the Future Architecture of International Climate Change Policy* (London: NEF).

Fischer-Kowalski, M. & Amman, C. (2001) Beyond IPAT and Kuznets Curves: globalization as a vital factor in analyzing the environmental impact of socio-economic metabolism, *Population and Environment*, 23(1), pp. 7–47.

Frank, A. G. (1969) *Latin America: Underdevelopment or Revolution* (New York: Monthly Review Press).

Gauthier, D. (1986) *Morals by Agreement* (Oxford: Clarendon Press).

Giljum, S. (2003) Biophysical dimensions of North–South trade: material flows and land use (Ph.D. thesis, University of Vienna).

Giljum, S. (2004) Trade, material flows and economic development in the South: the example of Chile, *Journal of Industrial Ecology*, 8(1–2), pp. 241–261.

Giljum, S. & Eisenmenger, N. (2004) North–South trade and the distribution of environmental goods and burdens. A biophysical perspective, *Journal of Environment and Development*, 13(1), pp. 73–100.

Giljum, S. & Hubacek, K. (2001) International trade, material flows and land use: developing a physical trade balance for the European Union, Interim Report, International Institute for Applied Systems Analysis (IIASA), Laxenburg, Austria.

Goldstein, J. & Keohane, R. (eds) (1993) *Ideas and Foreign Policy: Beliefs, Institutions, and Political Change* (Ithaca, NY: Cornell University Press).

Groenenberg, H., Phylipsen, D. & Blok, K. (2001) Differentiating commitments world wide: global differentiation of GHG emissions reductions based on the Triptych approach—a preliminary assessment, *Energy Policy*, 29, pp. 1007–1030.

Group of 77 (G-77). (2000) Declaration of the South Summit, Meeting held in Havana, Cuba, 10–14 April.

Grubb, M., Vrolijk, C. & Brack, D. (1999) *The Kyoto Protocol: A Guide and Assessment* (London: Royal Institute of International Affairs).

Gupta, S. & Bhandari, P. (1999) An effective allocation criterion for CO2 emissions, *Energy Policy*, 27, pp. 727–736.

Heil, M. T. & Selden, T. M. (2001) International trade intensity and carbon emissions: a cross-country econometric analysis, *Journal of Environment and Development*, 10, pp. 35–49.

Hornborg, A. (1998a) Towards an ecological theory of unequal exchange: articulating world system theory and ecological economics, *Ecological Economics*, 25, pp. 127–136.

Hornborg, A. (1998b) Ecosystems and world systems: accumulation as an ecological process, *Journal of World-Systems Research*, 4, pp.169–177.

Hornborg, A. (2001) *The Power of the Machine: Global Inequalities of Economy, Technology, and Environment* (Walnut Creek, CA: Alta Mira Press).

Inglehart, R. (1990) *Culture Shift in Advanced Industrial Society* (Princeton, NJ: Princeton University Press).

Kim, Y.-G. & Baumert, K. A. (2002) Reducing uncertainty through dual-intensity targets, in Baumert, K. A. (ed.), *Building on the Kyoto Protocol: Options for Protecting the Climate*, (Washington, DC: World Resources Institute), pp. 109–135.

La Rovere, E. L., Valente de Macedo, L. & Baumert, K. A. (2002) The Brazilian proposal on relative responsibility for global warming, in Baumert, K. A. (ed.), *Building on the Kyoto Protocol: Options for Protecting the Climate*, Washington, DC: World Resources Institute), pp. 157–173.

Lutzenheiser, L. (1996) Riding in style. Presentation at the American Sociological Association Annual Meeting, New York, 16 August.

Machado, G., Schaeffer, R. & Worrell, E. (2001) Energy and carbon embodied in the international trade of Brazil: an input-output approach, *Ecological Economics*, 39(3), pp. 409–424.

Martinez-Alier, J. (2003) *The Environmentalism of the Poor: A Study of Ecological Conflicts and Valuation* (Cheltenham: Edward Elgar).
Müller, B. (2001) Varieties of distributive justice in climate change: an editorial comment, *Climatic Change*, 48, pp. 273–288.
Muradian, R. & Martinez-Alier, J. (2001a) Trade and the environment: from a 'Southern' perspective, *Ecological Economics*, 36, pp. 281–297.
Muradian, R. & Martinez-Alier, J. (2001b) South–North materials flow: history and environmental repercussions, *Innovation: The European Journal of Social Science Research*, 14(2), pp. 171–187.
Muradian, R. & O'Connor, M. (2001) Inter-country environmental load displacement and adjusted national sustainability indicators: concepts and their policy applications, *International Journal of Sustainable Development*, 4(3), pp. 321–347.
Muradian, R., O'Connor, M. & Martinez-Alier, J. (2002) Embodied pollution in trade: estimating the 'environmental load displacement' of industrialized countries, *Ecological Economics*, 41, pp. 51–67.
Najam, A., Rahman, A., Huq, S. & Sokona, Y. (2003) Integrating sustainable development into the fourth assessment report of the Intergovernmental Panel on Climate Change, *Climate Policy*, 3(1)(Suppl.), pp. S9–S17.
Neumayer, E. (2000) In defence of historical accountability for greenhouse gas emissions, *Ecological Economics*, 33, pp. 185–192.
Organization for Economic Co-operation and Development (OECD) (1974) Recommendation on the Implementation of the Polluter Pays Principle, C(74)223 (Paris: OECD).
Parikh, J. (1992) *Consumption Patterns: the Driving Force of Environmental Stress* (New Delhi: Indira Gandhi Institute of Development Research).
Parikh, J. K. & Parikh, K. (2002) *Climate Change: India's Perceptions, Positions, Policies and Possibilities* (Paris: OECD).
Parks, B. C. & Roberts, J. T. (2005) *Environmental and Ecological Justice*, Palgrave Advances in International Environmental Politics (Basingstoke: Palgrave Macmillan).
Parks, B. C. & Roberts, J. T. (2006) Globalization, vulnerability to climate change, and perceived injustice, *Society and Natural Resources*, 19(4), pp. 337–355.
Princen, T., Maniates, M. & Conca, K. (eds) (2002) *Confronting Consumption* (Cambridge, MA: MIT Press).
Quiroga, R. (ed.) (1994) *El Tigre sin Selva. Consecuencias Ambientales de la Transformación Económica de Chile: 1974–93* (Santiago: Instituto de Ecología Política).
Roberts, J. T. & Grimes, P. E. (1997) Carbon intensity and economic development 1962–1991: a brief exploration of the environmental Kuznets Curve, *World Development*, 25(2), pp. 181–187.
Roberts, J. T. & Grimes, P. E. (2002) World-system theory and the environment: toward a new synthesis, in Dunlap, R. E., Buttel, F. H., Dickens, P. & Gijswijt, A. (eds) *Sociological Theory and the Environment: Classical Foundations, Contemporary Insights* (Lanham, MD: Roman and Littlefield Publishers).
Roberts, J. T. & Parks, B. C. (2007) *A Climate of Injustice: Global Inequality, North–South Politics, and Climate Change* (Cambridge, MA: MIT Press).
Roberts, J. T., Grimes, P. E. & Manale, J. (2003) Social roots of global environmental change: a world systems analysis of carbon dioxide emissions, *Journal of World-System Research*, IX(2).
Røpke, I. (1999) Prices are not worth that much, *Ecological Economics*, 29(1), pp. 45–46.
Russi, D. & Muradian, R. (2003) Gobernanza global y responsabilidad ambiental, *Ecología Política*, 24, pp. 95–105.
Ruth, M. (1998) Dematerialization in five US metals sectors: implications for energy use and CO2 emissions, *Resources Policy*, 24(1), pp. 1–18.
Sachs, W. (1999) *Planet Dialectics: Explorations in Environment and Development* (London: Zed Books).
Sijm, J. P. M., Jansen, J. C., Battjes, J. J., Volkers, C. H. & Ybema, J. R. (2000) *The Multi-Sector Convergence Approach of Burden Sharing: An Analysis of its Cost Implications* (Oslo: CICERO).
Simms, A., McGrath, J. & Reid, H. (2004) *Up in smoke? Threats from, and Response to, the Impact of Global Warming on Human Development* (London: NEF).
Stavins, R. (2004) Can an effective global climate treaty be based upon sound science, rational economics, and pragmatic politics? KSG Faculty Research Working Paper Series RWP04-020.
TERI (Tata Energy Research Institute) (1997) *Long Term Carbon Emission Targets Aiming Towards Convergence* (New Delhi: TERI).
Torvanger, A. & Godal, O. (2004) An evaluation of pre-Kyoto differentiation proposals for national greenhouse gas abatement targets, *International Environmental Agreements: Politics, Law and Economics*, 4, pp. 65–91.
United Nations Development Programme (UNDP) (1998) *Human Development Report 1998* (New York: United Nations).

Wallerstein, I. (1972) Three paths to national development in 16th century Europe, *Studies in Comparative International Development*, 8, pp. 95–101.
White House (2002a) Fact Sheet: President Bush announces clear skies & global climate change initiative. Available online at: http://www.whitehouse.gov/news/releases/2002/02/20020214.html (accessed 14 February 2002).
White House (2002b) Global Climate Change Policy Book. Available online at: http://www.whitehouse.gov/news/releases/2002/02/climatechange.html (accessed 14 February 2002).
Wiegandt, E. (2001) Climate change, equity, and international negotiations, in Luterbacher, U. & Sprinz, D. (eds) *International Relations and Global Climate Change* (Cambridge, MA: MIT Press), pp. 127–150.
World Bank (1992) *World Development Report 1992: Development and the Environment* (Washington, DC: World Bank).
Ybema, J., Battjes, J. J., Jansen, J. C. & Ormel, F. (2000) *Burden Differentiation: GHG Emissions, Undercurrents and Mitigation Costs* (Oslo, Norway: CICERO).

J. Timmons Roberts is Professor of Sociology at the College of William and Mary, Williamsburg, VA, USA and Fellow, Environmental Change Institute, University of Oxford.

Bradley C. Parks is Development Policy Officer in the Department of Policy and International Relations at the Millennium Challenge Corporation.

Index

Page numbers in **bold** represent figures. Page numbers in *italics* represent table.

Aall, C. 72
Aboriginal groups 96
activity; market 89
actors: interest groups 84; member states 87; policy 89
Affluent Society (Galbraith) 71
afforestation 63
Africa; urbanization *viii*
African National Congress (ANC): Green Scorpions 117–18; Mandela, N. 115, 116; Pan-Africanist Congress 111
African Wildlife Foundation (AWF) 99–100
agriculture: anthropogenic global warming 4; forestry 24
air: pollution 109–10; quality management 151
ambiguity: policy 63; resistance 59
American Democratic Party 71
An Environmental History of the World (Hughes) 11
Annex 1: countries 125; Parties 126
antipollution measures 16, *see also* pollution legislation
Apartheid: era 109–20; planning 112; zoning 112
Armitage, K.C. 135–45
Aswan High Dam 22
atmosphere; coal 21
Auld Reekie; Edinburgh 149

back to barriers 97
Bacon, F. 19
Bazilchuk, N. 165–8
behaviour; human 24
Big Smoke; London 149
Bill of Rights 116
biodiesel 148
biodiversity 20, 96; conservation 99; Convention on Biological Diversity (1992) 19; economic value 19; reduction 18; threats 17–20

biofuels 152
biosphere 1; holistic approach 44–5; model of systems 5
Biosphere Conference (UNESCO) 28–9
black people; status 113
Bonn Convention on Migratory Species 19
Brazil 126, 173
Brimblecombe, P. 147–59
Brown, L. 23–4
Brundtland Report; *Our Common Future* 111
bureaucracies 105
Bush administration 142, 144; global warming 144
Bush, President G.; climate change 166
business-as-usual approach 78

California; outdoor air 153
capital; population 71
capitalism 4
carbon: emissions *ix*; emissions market *ix*; intensity 175; responsibility 170; sequestration 63; tax revenue 35; taxes *xi*
carbon dioxide *viii–ix*; concentrations 33; inequality 171
Central Intelligence Bureau (CIA) 137
Challenge to Conservationists (Chapin) 97
Chernobyl plant (Soviet Union) 23
China: air pollution 6; fossil fuels 152; population growth 12
cities *viii*
Citizens' Submission Procedure; North American Agreement on Environmental Cooperation (NAAEC) 36
city states; land use 14
civilians; technological progress 78
Clean Air Act (1956) 156
Clean Development Mechanisms (CDM): Joint Implementation 130; two tier solution 126

climate change 2, 123; adaptation 28, 33–7, **34**; anthropogenic 3, 123; Bush, President G. 166; governance 27–40; international negotiations 130, 131; ozone depletion 42; responsibility 34, 37; United States of America (USA) 165–6; Villach workshop 123
closed forest: tropical forest 56; tropical forests 5, 55
coal 21, 150; atmosphere 21; reserves 21
collective action 63
colonialism; environmental damage 14
Commission 84, 85–6; Council of Ministers 82–3
Commission for Environmental Cooperation (CEC) 36
Commissioners; sectorialization 83
Common Agricultural Policy 83
communitarianism 30
community 86; environmental activity 85; indigenous 101; ocean's and seas 20; scientific 68
conditionality; indirect 59
conformism 67–80, 76; idealism 69; idealists 77
conformist strand; optimists 68
conservation 58, 96; biodiversity 99; energy 153; organizations 98, 100; transnational 103
conservation-preservation schism 44
conservationalists 95–6; nature 70
constructivism 30; world systems 29
Consultative National Environmental Policy Process (CONNEPP) 116
control; territory and land 101–2
Convention 35, 36
Convention on Biological Diversity (1992); biodiversity 19
Convention on International Trade in Endangered Species (CITES) 19, 85
cooling trend 137
Cooney, P.A. 143
Copernican Revolution 23
Copland, A. 11
core periphery relations; world systems and dependency (WSD) 122
core propositions; world systems and dependency (WSD) 122
corporations: environmental attitudes 4; green technology investment 6; impact on local populations 16
Council of Ministers; Commission 82–3
countries; upward mobility 122

culture: native peoples 72; relationship with nature 14
currency; foreign 115

Daly, H.E. 1, 4, 165–8; uneconomic growth 7
debt 60, 172; ecological 172; nature swaps 60
decision-making: process 34; rapid 156
Declaration on the Human Environment (Principle 1) 110
deforestation 55, 57, 71–2; rates 56; tropical 55, 58
degradation 55, 71; tropical forest 55
democratic regional system model; European Union (EU) 90
Democritus 18
Department of Defense; Office of Net Assessment 141–2
Department of Environmental Affairs and Tourism (1999); *State of the Environment Report* 109, 116, 118
destabilization; political 137–8
developed countries 62, 163
developing countries 36, 63, 125, 126, 128, 162, 167, 170
development 72; environment 58; geothermal 23; pathways 177
diesel engine 152
disasters 73; climate 169; weather related 3
discourse: definition 54; governance 47
distributive justice 31, 34; dilemmas 32; states 35
diversity: biological 72; cultural 72
Doha Declaration 62
donors; funding 100

Earth; temperature 123
Earth Day 137
EC policy: process 84; specialization 83
ecodevelopment 47
ecodomains; Nugent, S. 100
Ecologist 46
economic development 162–3
economic growth 67–80, 74; model 6; unlimited 7; World War Two 2
economy 20; environment 41; steady state 75
ecosystems; complex reality 99
ecosytemic rationales 43
Edinburgh; Auld Reekie 149
education; environmental 17
Egypt 22

emissions 28; greenhouse gases 35, 124–5, 127, 152, 162, 166; pollutants 124; private 154; reductions 125; trading 130
energy: alternative sources 23; conservation 153; environmental history 21; flows 173, 174; systems *viii–ix*
energy regime: less polluting *xi*; pollution intensive *viii*
energy-intensive economic activities *viii*
energy-intensive products; offshoring 171
engineers 154
environment: economy 41; globalizations 41–51
environmental activity; community 85
environmental concern; phases of 2–4
Environmental Conservation Act 112
environmental degradation; science and technology 3–4
environmental governance: constructivist understanding 30; insitutionalist understanding 30; realist understanding 29–30
environmental history 11–26
environmental regulations 15
environmental sector; institutional structure 84–7
environmental systems; human interference 4–5
environmentalism 136; global cooling 136–8
equality; Walzer, M. 31
equilibrium state 71
essentialism; strategic 101
Europe: ships 18; woodland 18
European Community (EC) 81
European Court of Justice (ECJ) 83
European environmental non-governmental organizations (ENGOS) 90
European Parliament (EP) 83
European Road Transport Agreement (ERTA) 85
European Union (EU) 61; democratic regional system model 90; environmental leader 81–93; institutional system 82; international leadership 81; law-making 86; two core tensions 88
European Union (UN): key international norms 87; negotiating stance 87
exhaustion; resource 70
exports 171, 173
extinction 19; rate 109

Fairclough, N.; institution 54–5
federal systems 83

fertility: decline *viii*; regime *ix*
fetishism; growth 75, 76
First Tropical Timber Agreement (ITTA1) 58
First World Climate Conference; World Meteorological Organization (WMO) 123
fishing stocks; depletion 14
flooding 138; Japan 142
food production: biotechnology 13; genetic technology 13
forcing mechanisms 137
forest: Indian policy 15; management 57, 60; preservation 19; tropical 53–66
Forest Convention 62
Forest Department; India 15
forestry: agriculture 24; scientific 57
fossil fuels 21; China 152; price 167
fourth policy; complexity 84
framing; policy 82
France; old people 154
French Forest Ordinance 21
Friend of the Earth 60
fuel: lead 150; wood 21
funding: donors 100; incentive structures 99
future: distrust 78; Jacoby, R. 78
Future of Life (Wilson) 24

G-77: formation 130; political entity 129
G8: 2005 meeting 2; countries 163; leaders 163; Summit 161–8
General Agreement on Tariffs and Trade (GATT) 15
General Electric 163; green technology investment 6
Germany 149
Gills, B.K. and Oosthoek, J. 1–9
Global Climate Coalition (GCC) 140
global cooling; environmentalism 136–8
global environmental organizations 44, 47
Global Environment Facility (GEF) 125
Global Indigenous Peoples' Movement 99
global institutions: ascendancy 15–16; environmental policy 16; local environments 16
global linkages; three kinds 54
global models 45
global system; fate of 4
global warming 124, 161; agriculture 4; anthropogenic 2; Bush administration 144; deniers 144; greenhouse gases 3; inequality 169; *New Scientist* 2; policy problems 81; political attitudes 3; politics 135–45; poorer

countries 124; science of 128; scientific consensus 2; Third World 127; United States Government position 2; winners and losers 126–7
globalism 54, 172
globalization: definition 54; distinguishing quality 42; environment 41–51; regulatory 149; understanding 42
globalization 28
Goodland, R. 70
governance: climate change 27–40; discourse 47; repressive 109–20
governments: member states 85; power 6
Grainger, A. 53–66
grandfathering 176; Kyoto Protocol 175
grassroots efforts; environmental education 17
Green Scorpions; African National Congress (ANC) 117–18
green technologies 5; corporate investment 6; General Electric 6
greenhouse gases: Annex 1 Parties 126; atmosphere 125; emissions 35, 124–5, 127, 152, 162, 166; fossil fuels 3
greenhouse warming 142
greening; nation state 29
Greenpeace 60
Greens 68
Gro Brundtland 76; poverty 76
growth 71; economic 74; fetishism 75, 76; money 76; qualitative 70–1; sustainability 74
Growth, Employment and Redistribution (GEAR) 115

Hanekamp, J.C.; and Verstegen, S.W. 67–80
Hansen, J. 139
hardwood; tropical 56
heat waves 33
Helvetius, C.A. 7
Hertsgaard, M. 5
historical responsibility 175
History of Marine Animal Populations 20
homelands 113; labour 113; land 113; urbanization 113
homogenization 128; ecosystem 18
How Many People Can the Earth Support? (Cohen) 13
Hughes, D.J. 11–26
humanity; pollution 139
humans 162; behaviour 24; danger and complexity 18; species 23
hunter-gatherers; land use 14

Hurricane Katrina 105; New Orleans 49
hurricanes 138
hybrid proposal 176, 177
hydropower 22
hyper-liberalism 4

ice age cycle 137
idealism 67–80; conformism 69, 77
idealization; native peoples 72
ideas; rules of the game 82
Igoe, J. 95–108
imports 174
income 77; per capita 71
India 44; National Biodiversity Strategy Action Plan 20; World Bank 17
Indian Environment Minister; Nath, K. 62
Indian forest policy 15; Forest Department 15; Joint Forest Management plan 15
indigenism 95–108
indigenous community 101, 104–5
indigenous leaders 98–9, 102, 104
indigenous peoples 96, 102–3, 104; conservation 96–7; state control 97
Industrial Revolution 21
industrial world; projects 44
industrialized countries 128, 163
inequality: apartheid system 115; biophysical 173; carbon dioxide 171; global warming 169; structure 172
Inhofe, Senator J. 135, 136
institution 82; complex 89; definition 54
institutional structure; environmental sector 84–7
institutional system; European Union (EU) 82
institutionalism 29; rational choice 29
institutionalization 55
interest groups; actors 84
Intergovernmental Panel on Climate Change (IPCC) 139
international governmental organizations (IGOs) 46
International Labour Organization; model 48
international leadership; European Union (EU) 81
International Monetary Fund (IMF) 15
International Union for the Conservation of Nature and Natural Resources (IUCN) 19
International Union for the Protection of Nature (1949) 19
internet 42–3
isolation; international 110

Jacob, M.: future 78; and Linnér, B-O. 121–33
Japan; flooding 142
Joint Forest Management plan 15
Joint Implementation; Clean Development Mechanisms (CDM) 130
jurisdiction; state 45–6
justice: distributive 31, 32, 34, 35; negotiated 176; procedural 31–2; settlement 176

Kakadu National Park 96
Kennedy, D. 136
Kissinger, H. 12
knowledge: disparities 127–8; production 99
Kyoto Protocol 126, 141, 165; grandfathering 175; history 87–8; tradable permits 89

labour; homelands 113
land: control 101–2; homelands 113
land use: ancient empires 14; city-states 14; hunter-gatherers 14
landscape 97; protection 72
Lash, J. 165–8; voluntary actions 166
law; international environmental 33
law-making; European Union (EU) 86
laws of nature; progress 7–8
lead; fuels 150
leadership; role 89
Limits of the Earth (Osborne) 71
Limits to Growth (Meadows and Meadows) 1, 69, 70
Linnér, B-O.; and Jacob, M. 121–33
living standards: behavioural change 6; Western society 77
Livingstone, Mayor K. 154
local environments; global institutions 16
logging 60; illegal 55; location 56; nongovernmental organizations (NGOs) 61
London 148, 154; pollution 150
Lonsdale, S. 18
Los Angeles: Mexico City 151; smog 149, 150
Luntz, F. 143

McClellan, White House Press Secretary S. 143
Malan, Doctor D.F.; National Party 110
Malthusian views 44
Man and the Biosphere Program (UNESCO) 17, 29
management: forest 60; tropical forests 55–7
Mandela, N.; African National Congress (ANC) 115, 116
Manners, I.; hybrid status 87

Marburger, J.H. 143
Marine Mammal Protection Act 15
market: activity 89; mechanisms 60; single 89–90
Martinez-Alier, J. 171–2
material flow 174; analysis 174
material progress; working class 71
materialism 172
Meadows, D.; scientific model 71
mechanisms; market 60
member states 83, 86; actors 87; EU Council President 88; governments 85; representatives 85
Mercier, L.S. 7
Mexico City; Los Angeles 151
middle ground 101
Mill, J.S; steady state economy 7
Minister of Environment Affairs 112
Mondon; Big Smoke 149
money; growth 76
Montreal Protocol on Substances That Deplete the Ozone Layer (1987) 3, 17
mortality: infant (Finland) *viii*; infant (Mali) *viii*; infant *viii*
Multilateral Agreement on Investment 48

Namibia 102
narrative; definition 54
Nath, K.; Indian Environment Minister 62
nation state 28; greening 29
National Adaptation Plans of Action (NAPAs) 32, 36
National Biodiversity Strategy Action Plan; India 20
National Party; Malan, Doctor D.F. 110
national regulation 43
nationalism; indigenous 101
nations 128; cold 170; core 173; goods exchange 173–4; poor 176; rich 176; rich and poor 170, 171; wealthier 170, 172
native peoples: culture 72; idealization 72
nature; relationship with culture 14
neo-liberalism; global hegemony 4
Neumann, R. 97
New Orleans; Hurricane Katrina 49
New Scientist; global warming 2
new technologies; resources 69
noble savages 103
non-Annex 1: countries 129; Parties 125
non-indigenous peoples 103
nongovernmental organizations (NGOs) 63; logging 61

North American Agreement on Environmental Cooperation (NAAEC); Citizens' Submission Procedure 36–7
North American Free Trade Agreement; Free Trade Area of the Americas 48
nuclear plants 22
nuclear power; United States of America (USA) 22
nuclear tests; impact 43–4
nuclear weapons 23
Nugent, S.; ecodomains 100

ocean's and seas; community 20
offshoring; energy-intensive products 171
old people; France 154
Oosthoek, J. 161–8; and Gills, B.K. 1–9
optimism: conformist strand 68; technology 74
Organization for Economic Co-operation and Development (OECD) 88
organizations 82, 87, 88; conservation 98, 100–1; global environmental 44, 48; landscapes 98; learning 89
Our Common Future 67, 70–1, 124; Brundtland Report 111
ozone depletion; climate change 42
ozone layer 43; protection 47; thinning 3

Paavola, J. 27–40
Pan-Africanist Congress; African National Congress 111
parks 97–8
participaon; recognition 32
Pessimism 68
petroleum 167, 168; resources 21
plants 22
plunder of the earth 69
pluralism 32
policy: actor 89; chain 84; conflicting frames 91; economic development 115; frame sustainability 85; framing; conceptualization 82; makers 156; space 176, 177
policy problems; global warming 81
policy-making: global scale 14–17; impact of globalization 15; local scale 14
political economy 122; economic growth model 4; environmental paradigm 3–4
political globalization 45; interpretations 28
pollutants: emission 124; secondary 151
pollution 20, 169–71; air 109–10, 155–6; control developments 117; fashion 154–5; global nature 157; indoor air 153; industrial 114; local air 147–59; London 150; problems 114; rights 89; understanding 158
pollution artisanale 148
pollution industrielle 148
pollution legislation 3; pollution tax 6
population: capital 71; crash 13–14; pressures 44
population growth: agriculture 12; China 12; environmental destruction 13; UN predictions 13
population growth *ix* 12–14
population *vii–viii*
poverty 103, 169–71; Gro Brundtland 76
power: distribution 32; hydrokinetic 22; nuclear 22, 23; relations 47; water 22
Prebisch, P. 172
preliminary model 176
primary smoke 152
primitive wilderness 103
pristine wilderness 97
proactive responses 33
procedural justice 31–2; recognition 32; social justice 30–1; Vienna Convention on the Law of Treaties 33
production; activity 172–3
progress: definitional crisis 7; European Enlightenment philosophers 7; idea of 6; laws of nature 7–8; redefinition of 6–7; rise of capitalism 7
Putin, V. 2

quality of life 70–1

radioactivity 22–3
rainforests 71
rational choice; institutionalism 29
reactive responses 33
Reason for Hope? (Goodall) 16
recognition: participation 32; procedural justice 32
Reconstruction and Development Policy (RDP) 115, 117
reforestation 63
renewable energy 5
renewable energy sector: Denmark 5; Germany 5; technologies 6; United States 5
representatives; member states 85
reserves; coal 21
resources: exhaustion 69, 70; new technologies 69; non-renewable 21; petroleum 21; renewable 21

Index   193

responsibility 35; carbon 170; climate change 34, 37
revolution 68
right-wing think tanks 140; media outlets 137
Rio Earth Summit 124
Robin, L.; science of empire 57
Ross, A. 138
rules of the game; ideas 82
rural populations *viii*
Russia 163

Saint Francis 76
science; technology 3, 73
science of empire; Robin, L. 57
Scientific American 1, 2
scientific forestry 57
scientific model; Meadows, D. 71
scientists; social 103
sectorialization; Commissioners 83
sequestration; carbon 63
settlement; justice 176
ships; Europe 18
Sierra Club 13, 73
Sierra Leone; UN Food and Agriculture Organization (FAO) 59
Silent Spring (Carson) 2
slaughter; wildlife 18–19
Smil, V. 22
smog: Los Angeles 149, 150; photochemical 157
smoke; sulphur dioxide 152
smoking guns 144
social justice 6, **31**; concerns 35; four issues 34
Socialists 43
society 71; behaviour 55; contemporary 154; sustainability 77; sustainable 70
Socolow, R. 135
sound science 105
South Africa 109–20; environment 110; households 116
South Asia; urbanization *viii*
sovereign state 1
space: convergence 95–108; making 96; sciences 46
Spaceship Earth 58, 95–108, 103
spatial uniformity 54
specialization; EC policy 83
specification; standards 86
standardization; process 90
standards; specification 86

state 29; jurisdiction 45–6
state control; indigenous peoples 97
State of the Environment Report; Department of Environmental Affairs and Tourism (1999) 109
steady state economy; Mill, J.S 7
Steel Valley; inhabitants 116–17
Study of Critical Environmental Problems (SCEP); Study on Man's Impact on Climate (SMIC) 136
sulphur dioxide 152
sustainability 73; debate 74, 78; growth 74; maintenance 75; policy frame 85; society 77; three definitions 68; three ideas 76–7
sustainable development 47; debates 47
sustainable forest management; definition 57

techno-environmentalism 43, 45
technological progress; civilians 78
technology: conformist worldview 73–4; criticism 73; green 6; operation 73; optimism 74; science 73
temperature 152; Earth 123
Tennessee Valley Authority 163
territory: concerns 83; control 101–2
terrorism 11–12
The Population Bomb (Ehrlich) 2
The Tragedy of the Commons (Hardin) 2
Third World: cities 16–17; countries 127; global warming 127; nations 171; role of states 129
Third Worlding; American poor 105
Three Mile Island plant (US) 23
Toynbee, A. 1
trade 177
Treaties; rules 85
tri-part international stratification system 122
tropical forest 53–66, 59, 63; closed forest 55; closed forests 56; countries 56; coverage 55; deforestation 55; degradation 55; management 55–7; open forests and woodlands 55
Tropical Forestry Action Plan (TFAP) 58

uneconomic growth 7
United Kingdom (UK); Clean Air Act (1956) 150
United Nations (UN): Conference on Environment and Development (UNCED) 17, 111, 121, 123; Conference on Science and Technology for Development (1979) 127; Environment Programme (UNEP) 17, 29, 88, 110–11; Food and Agriculture

Organization (FAO); Sierra Leone 59; Framework Convention on Climate Change (UNFCCC) 121; General Assembly 124; programs 17
United States of America (USA) 22; climate change 165–6; nuclear power 22
upward mobility; countries 122
urban black townships 102–3, 113–14; lack of electricity 114
urbanization: Africa *viii*; demand for resources 16; homelands 113; South Asia *viii*

Vaal Triangle 116–17
Verstegen, S.W.; and Hanekamp, J.C. 67–80
Vienna Convention on the Law of Treaties 33, 36
Villach 139; climate researchers 138

Wackernagel, ?.: ecological footprint 76; model society 76
Walzer, M.; notion of complex equality 31
water; power 22
wealth 169–71
Weart, S.R. 139
Wells, H. G. 1
Western society; living standards 77
White House; policy memo 139–40

wildlife; slaughter 18–19
Will, G. 137
Willoy, W.; Inuit Activist 95–108
Wilson, E. 24
Wirth, Senator T. 138–9
Wonderful Century (Wallace) 69
wood; fuel 21
woodland; Europe 18
working class; material progress 71
World Bank 15, 17; India 17
World Climate Programme (WCP) 138
World Conservation Strategy (WCS) 58
world economy 122
World Order Models Project (WOMP) 45
World Scientists Call for Action 141
World Summit on Sustainable Development (2002) 4, 62, 88, 116, 117
world systems and dependency (WSD): approach 122; coherent theoretical perspective 122; core periphery relations 122; core propositions 122
world systems theory 173
World Trade Organization (WTO) 15, 61
World War II 75
World Wildlife Fund (WWF) 61, 98

Zito, A.R. 81–93

Printed in the United Kingdom
by Lightning Source UK Ltd.
126649UK00001B/129-134/A